School Matters

The Junior Years

Peter Mortimore, Pamela Sammons, Louise Stoll,
David Lewis and Russell Ecob

Open Books

First published in 1988 by Open Books Publishing Ltd
Beaumont House, Wells BA5 2LD, Somerset, England

© Peter Mortimore, Pamela Sammons, Louise Stoll,
   David Lewis and Russell Ecob 1988

British Library Cataloguing in Publication Data

School matters : the junior years.
   1. Education, Elementary—1965-
   1. Mortimore, Peter
   372'.242   LB1555

   ISBN 0-7291-0194-0

Typeset by Character Graphics, Taunton
Printed and bound in Great Britain by
A. Wheaton & Co Ltd, Exeter

Cover photograph: Colin Alston

Contents

Chapter 1: The Search for Effectiveness 1

Chapter 2: The Schools 9

Chapter 3: The Headteachers and Deputies 40

Chapter 4: The Teachers in the Classroom 53

Chapter 5: The Curriculum 78

Chapter 6: Pupils' Progress 92

Chapter 7: Different Groups 117

Chapter 8: Teacher Expectations 163

Chapter 9: The Importance of School 176

Chapter 10: Differences in Effectiveness 206

Chapter 11: Understanding Effectiveness 218

Chapter 12: Towards More Effective Schooling 263

References 291

Appendix 1 302

Index 303

Acknowledgements

It would not have been possible to carry out this research without the continued support of the Authority, and of the headteachers, teachers, pupils and parents of the 50 Inner London schools involved in the study.

Our thanks are also due to the teachers who worked as field officers on the Project – Mary Hunt, Jennifer Runham, Dick Cooper, Pamela Glanville and Cathy Bunch. We are also grateful to past and present colleagues at Research & Statistics Branch, in particular, Andreas Varlaam, Brian Clover, Christine Mabey, Anne-Marie Hill, Colin Alston, Adrian Shaw, Veron Strachan and Adrian Walker. Pat Wood, Shirley McGillick and Barbara Andrews provided excellent support by their patient and efficient word processing. Audrey Hind and Kate Foot dedicated themselves to ensuring that our data were processed and stored throughout the duration of the study, and assisted with many of the analyses.

Helpful advice has been received from many sources, including the School Differences Study Group. Professor Harvey Goldstein (Institute of Education University of London) allowed the Project to make use of his multilevel program for the analysis of school effects. Dr. Tom Gorman and Mary Hargreaves of the Assessment of Performance Unit's Language Survey Team designed the oracy measures. The Leverhulme Foundation provided a grant for the Home Interviews with parents.

We are extremely grateful for all the help, co-operation and advice we have received.

1

The Search for Effectiveness

Does the particular school attended by a child make a difference? Will a child's progress in reading or writing be similar wherever she or he is taught? Are some schools more effective than others? These are just three of the questions, often posed by parents, which have recently stimulated researchers to investigate how much difference there is between the most and the least effective schools. Curiously, traditional educational research, carried out in Britain and in North America, has failed to address these important questions. This was probably because social scientists, such as Coleman et al (1966) and Jencks et al (1972), had argued that home background, including social class and economic status, were much more influential on a child's development. They reasoned that because the differences between families were much greater than those between schools, families were likely to exert the greater influence. Whilst it is undoubtedly true that an economically advantaged family – with comfortable housing, healthy diet, and time for stimulating educational experiences, contrasts starkly with an economically disadvantaged one – with inadequate, overcrowded or even a lack of permanent housing, poor diet and little time or money for educational experiences, it is also true that schools vary a great deal. The problem for researchers is how to tease out the effects of families from the effects of schools.

Two groups of research studies – one in the United States and one in Britain – have recently begun to address this issue. In the United States, a group of researchers including Weber (1971), Summers & Wolfe (1977), Brookover et al (1978, 1979), Edmonds (1979a, 1979b), Good (1979), and Goodlad (1979), have been active in challenging the view that the influence of school can only be trivial. In Britain a group of researchers (see Reynolds, 1985) concerned with school differences has carried out a number of pioneering studies designed to separate out the effects of home and school. Notable amongst the British group have been a study of Welsh secondary schools (Reynolds, 1982) and a study of 12 inner city secondary schools (Rutter et al, 1979). This latter study – written up in a book entitled *Fifteen Thousand*

Hours; Secondary Schools and their Effects on Children – was important because it developed a methodology to evaluate the effectiveness
of schools after having taken account of the characteristics of the pupils
entering those schools. The research team involved in *Fifteeen
Thousand Hours* included one of us.

Although these studies attracted methodological criticisms, their
impact was to encourage other researchers to develop suitable
techniques (see Aitkin et al, 1981a, 1981b; Gray, 1981a) and appropriate methods of analysis (Goldstein, 1980, 1984) to address this important question in a more sophisticated way. A recent American review
of the area of school effectiveness (Purkey & Smith, 1983) demonstrated that these studies have succeeded in identifying a number
of common factors. In other words, we researchers have managed to
clear the decks, and to develop generally accepted ways of answering
the questions with which we began this chapter.

Because most of the British research on school effectiveness has
been carried out in secondary schools, we decided to focus on primary
education. Somewhat surprisingly, this area of schooling had been
rather neglected. With the exception of Bennett's (1976) study of
teaching style, the 1978 survey by Her Majesty's Inspectors, the study
of teachers carried out by researchers from Leicester University (Galton et al, 1980; Galton & Simon, 1980; Simon, 1980) and a number
of smaller-scale projects (for example, Armstrong, 1980), education
for pupils below the age of 11 at the beginning of our study was
remarkably unresearched.

We decided, therefore, to fill this gap by mounting a study of the
junior years of primary schooling. In order to be able to examine the
progress of pupils, we knew the study would have to be longitudinal
and follow pupils through several years of school life. We also knew
that if we really wanted to discover whether individual schools made
a difference our work would have to be very detailed. Schools are
complicated places – as many parents have discovered. Finally, we
knew that if we wished our work to be taken seriously by parents,
practitioners and researchers it would have to be very rigorous,
demonstrate that the lessons of earlier work had been learned and
employ the appropriate methods of analysis, however sophisticated
these were.

What follows is our account of the study. The bare bones are that
we followed a group of 2,000 pupils through four years of classroom
life (from age 7 to age 11) in 50 schools selected randomly from the
636 schools in the Authority. In order to put flesh on these bones,
however, we spent the four years in close observation of the classrooms
and the schools through which our sample of pupils were passing. This
book is the outcome of the study: an account of the progress of the
pupils, and a description of their school days. We start with a formal
statement of our aims.

The aims of the study

We had four main aims: The first was to produce a detailed description of pupils and teachers, and of the organisation and curriculum of the schools. The second was to document the progress and development, over four years of schooling, of nearly 2000 pupils. Our third and key aim was to establish whether some schools were more effective than others in promoting pupils' learning and development, once account had been taken of variations in the characteristics of pupils in the intakes to schools. The fourth was to investigate differences in the progress of different groups of pupils. Special attention was paid to achievement related to the race, sex and social class backgrounds of pupils. In addition, we wanted to examine the effects of differences of age on children's achievement. In order to pursue these aims, we addressed the following questions: Are some schools or classes more effective than others, when variations in the intakes of pupils are taken into account? Are some schools or classes more effective for particular groups of children? If some schools or classes are more effective than others, what factors contribute to these positive effects?

METHODS USED IN THE STUDY

The data

Our data can be divided into three categories: measures of the pupil intakes to schools and classes; measures of pupils' educational outcomes; measures of the classroom and school environment.

1) Measures of the pupil intakes to schools and classes

We collected detailed information about pupils' characteristics in order to explore the effectiveness of schooling for different groups of children (according to age, social class, sex or race), and also to explore the impact of background factors upon educational outcomes.

Previous studies of school effects have been criticised on the grounds that their measures of intake were inadequate, and because they collected data at the level of the school, rather than the individual pupil (see, for example, work by Marks et al, 1983, which was criticised because of its failure to take proper account of differences in intakes, by Gray, 1983, and Gray and Jones, 1983). This sounds a technical and not very important point, but it is, in fact, crucial for all studies of school effectiveness. Whereas some researchers have related the average achievement of pupils in a particular school to the proportions of parents coming from particular social classes (this being better than ignoring social background altogether) we were able to relate the achievement of individual pupils to their own characteristics, including their particular social class background. Because of the use of individual data, it was possible for us to use more sophisticated techniques of analysis and, therefore, to take a fuller account of the impact of background factors than has been the case in many previous studies.

The background measures of pupils' characteristics used in our study covered two areas: the social, ethnic, language and family background of the children, and their initial attainment at entry to junior school. All information was obtained at the level of the individual child and, because of the longitudinal nature of the study, it has been possible for us to explore the cumulative effects of background factors over several years.

We also collected data about each child's attainments in assessments of reading, mathematics and visio-spatial skills, and obtained a class teacher's rating of behaviour at entry to junior school. This information enabled account to be taken of differences in the past achievements and development of pupils, which may have been influenced by their previous infant classes and nursery schools. It also provided the necessary baseline against which assessments of the later progress and development of individual children, during the junior school years, could be made.

2) Measures of educational outcomes

The results of studies of school effectiveness are dependent, to a large extent, on the choice of measures of educational outcomes. Most studies of secondary school effects have been criticised for concentrating on too few measures of educational outcomes (usually examination success and attendance), and studies of the junior age group have frequently focused only on children's attainments in the basic skills.

In our view the aims of primary education are, rightly, diverse. Basic skills are considered important by the vast majority of teachers and parents, but other areas – including aspects of development such as behaviour, attendance and attitude towards education – are also important. Studies which use only one or two measures of pupils' educational outcomes can give an unbalanced and simplistic view of class and school effects.

a) Cognitive outcomes We employed standardised tests of reading and mathematics. The tests used were: the Edinburgh Reading Test (ERT) and the National Foundation for Educational Research Basic Mathematics Test (BMT). These tests have been shown to be reliable and to be reasonable predictors of later academic success. Because of the considerable variations in children's attainments in these skill areas at entry to junior school, pupils were assessed regularly to enable us to investigate their progress over the junior years.

In addition to these tests we devised individually-based assessments of practical mathematics which were conducted in each school year. Also, to take account of the importance of writing in the junior curriculum, an assessment of creative writing was made on an annual basis. Furthermore, because of the acknowledged importance of pupil talk and interaction to their development in school, the oral skills of a sample of children were assessed in the fourth year, using exercises developed specifically for the study by the Language Survey Team of the Assessment of Performance Unit (APU) of the Department of Education and Science (see Gorman and Hargreaves, 1985).

Finally, during the fourth year we also collected information about each pupil's performance in the Authority-wide pre-secondary transfer tests of reading – the London Reading Test (LRT) – and verbal reasoning.

b) Non-cognitive outcomes We collected information about the children's behaviour in school (as assessed by their class teachers) using an instrument specially developed for the Project. This information was collected for each child in the autumn and summer terms of each school year. In this way it was possible for us to examine changes in behaviour over the years. In addition, a self-report measure of pupils' attitudes towards different types of school activities, curriculum areas and other aspects of school was used in each school year. Measures of each child's perception of how they were seen by the teacher and by their peer group, as well as their views of themselves, were obtained at the end of the third year, and full attendance data were collected about all children, individually, in each of the three terms of the first, second and third years.

3) Measures of the classroom and school environment
Our third group of data relate to the teachers, classrooms and schools involved in the study. Because of the interest in identifying which factors make some schools or classes more effective than others in promoting good educational outcomes, a wide variety of information about the teachers, classes and schools was collected.

a) School organisation and policies Information about school organisation and policies was obtained through interviews with heads, and deputy heads. Questions concerning their role, educational philosophy, qualifications and experience were included. Particular attention was paid to the way pupils were grouped into classes, the allocation of teachers to classes, the allocation of staff responsibilities, and teacher involvement in decision-making.

b) Class organisation and policies The class teachers of pupils in the sample were questioned about their qualifications, responsibilities, philosophy of education and involvement in decision-making. Information about their methods of assigning work to pupils, and their grouping strategies within the class, was also gathered. A plan of each classroom was obtained so that seating arrangements and layout could be examined. Detailed information about special needs teaching, the curriculum, and use of timetables was also collected.

c) Teacher strategies Classroom observations were undertaken in each of the three years. A systematic procedure was adopted because of the necessity for comparability over time and between classes. The instruments developed by the 'ORACLE' team from Leicester University were chosen because these had been used recently with a similar age group, and because they provided useful information about teachers' and pupils' activities (see Boydell, 1974, 1975; and Galton et al, 1980). In addition to the ORACLE system, an amended version of the 'SCOTS' schedule (Powell & Scrimgeour, 1977) was used to provide more subjective ratings of classroom behaviour and the activities of teachers and pupils. Extensive use was also made of qualitative data, including notes, case studies and verbatim descriptions provided by the field officers.

d) Views of parents Parents of all the sample pupils in eight of the schools were interviewed. These interviews, which took place in the child's home, were carried out by specially trained interviewers matched for ethnic background and speaking the appropriate home language. Parents provided validation of information obtained from schools about their child's background characteristics, and were asked about their views of their child's progress, and their own involvement with her or his learning.

e) School life We used a wide variety of methods to collect information about the pupils, classes, teaching staff and schools involved in the study. These included assessments of pupils (using written and practical tasks), self-report questionnaires and teachers' assessments of behaviour. The latter were used for the analysis of pupil progress and development. The use of questionnaires, interviews and observational data enabled a check on the validity of different measures to be made. This is important, for social psychology has shown that people are not always fully aware of their own behaviour. An interesting example of this occurred when the majority of teachers reported in interviews that they spent most of their time dealing with the class as a whole, rather than with individuals or groups. From systematic observations, however, it was clear that, in every year, teachers spent much more time communicating with individual children than with either the class as a whole or, even more extremely, with groups. These results, suggesting that peoples' perceptions of their own behaviour may not always correspond with what they actually do, point to the necessity of obtaining information from a variety of sources.

METHODS OF ANALYSIS

Analyses of our data were necessarily complex. Early research on school and teacher differences was criticised on methodological grounds (see for examples of the debate, Mortimore, 1979; Tizard et al, 1980; Goldstein, 1980; Rutter et al, 1980; Radical Statistics Education Group, 1982). The implications of such criticisms for analyses of school and teacher differences have been illustrated by re-analyses of the Bennett study which have resulted in substantial revisions to the original findings (see Bennett, 1978; Aitkin et al, 1981a; Prais, 1983; Chatfield, 1985).

As with all field work carried out in schools, the research design had to accommodate severe limitations. In order to overcome some of the methodological problems caused by these limitations, a variety of different statistical techniques were employed. The use of measures developed from quite different methodologies enabled checks on validity to be made. Whenever possible, test scores were adjusted for unreliability, and account was taken of the impact of clustering within the sample of pupils at the level of the school.

Three crucial aspects of the effects of junior schools on their pupils were investigated in detail.

The size of the effects, in terms of the proportion of the overall variation in pupils' progress or development which can be explained (in a statistical sense) by different schools, in comparison to that explained by the children's background characteristics.

The size of the effects of individual schools on their pupils' educational outcomes.
(For example, what difference in a pupil's reading progress over three years can be attributed to her or his membership of a particular school?)

The processes which relate to the effects of individual schools and classes on their pupils' educational outcomes.

In examining the overall impact of school membership during the junior school period, it was possible to draw on data collected over three full years. When the size of the effects of school and class membership were compared, however, it was necessary to examine the data for each year separately. This was because of the frequency of changes of teacher and pupil membership of classes between years. The use of a multilevel model for much of the analysis has enabled the separate effects of school and class, over the period of one school year, to be identified and studied (see Goldstein, 1986).

In addition to analyses of school and class effects, the attainments, progress and non-cognitive development of children were examined for all individuals and, separately, for different groups. When investigating differences in outcomes due to age, social class, sex or race, the analyses controlled simultaneously for all other background factors. This means that we could isolate the separate effects of any given factor, when the combined influences of all other background characteristics were taken into account. Thus, the effect of sex, for example, was identified net of the effects of age, social class, race and other background factors.

In addition to examining the overall relationships between progress and achievement in different cognitive and non-cognitive areas for all pupils, it was possible to examine the relationships for children with different characteristics (according to age, social class, sex and race). The relationships between attainment and progress and teachers' ratings of pupils' abilities were also investigated. Again, the analyses were conducted for all pupils and, separately, for children of different groups.

This was our research strategy in 1980. Seven years later, having collected an enormous amount of data about pupils, teachers and schools, subjected these data to rigorous statistical analysis, and attempted to interpret our findings in the light of the results of other research and our own knowledge of schools, we are ready to report our conclusions. The following 11 chapters represent our attempt to do this. We have tried to write in a non-technical way (and have published separately information on technical issues) but we hope we have included sufficient information about our data for readers to make their own judgements of the findings, and thus not to be restricted to our interpretations.

We have also included a considerable amount of description of the classes and schools which were observed in the course of the Project. Whilst not essential to our central argument about the impact of schools, we believe this material will be of considerable interest to both teachers and parents. In the light of the lack of detailed descriptions of what schooling is like during the years of childhood, we hope our contribution will prove useful.

In the following chapters we deal in turn with the schools; the teachers; the classroom; the curriculum; the pupils and their attainments, progress and development; and the expectations of the teachers, before turning to the results of analyses designed to test whether individual schools had differential impacts upon their pupils' educational outcomes. The final chapters examine the factors which contribute to effectiveness, and discuss some of the implications of our findings.

2

The Schools

Over the course of the Project, much information was collected about the 50 schools in the sample. This information covered both the givens, as we labelled them, and the policies. The givens covered all aspects of structure and organisation outside the direct control of the head-teacher and the rest of the staff. These include: the school building itself; resources dependant upon external funding; status, whether with (JMI) or without infant departments (JM); whether county or voluntary; and the size of the school, in terms of pupil roll. The policies incorporated any features over which the head and staff could exercise control. Policies comprised, amongst others: the curriculum; arrangements for allocation of pupils, and teachers, to classes; schools' promotion of equal opportunities policies; and the involvement of parents in the life of the schools.

SCHOOL 'GIVENS'

School buildings

Some schools were built in the latter half of the last century and have been partly or completely reconstructed. Others are housed in the original Victorian 'three-deckers' which have become the hallmark of the typical London school. These old buildings, however, have often been extended and adapted to accommodate more recent educational practices. The separate entrances for girls and boys, for example, are now merely a reminder of Victorian attitudes. Nearly half the schools were Victorian 'three-deckers'. The next largest group were buildings from the 1950's and 1960's. The rest had been built between 1970 and the present day.

A particular feature of schools in the inner city is that their space is limited. Few of the schools in the survey, for example, had playing fields. Most, however, had a small area set aside for plants, and a few also had a grassy play area. Nearly half the schools had two play-grounds, and these were sometimes brightened by murals.

Use of rooms within the buildings
Space was seldom so short that any class was without its own room.
In one school, however, two classes did have to share a room and
each class spent part of their day in a small open area in the corridor.
Six schools had some open plan classrooms though, in a few cases,
separate areas had been screened off or the entrance was bricked up.

All but seven of the schools had a library. Some had separate libraries
for infant and junior children; others for fiction and non-fiction books.
Libraries were also commonly used for other activities. Examples of
these included use as a pupils' resource section, storage for audio-visual
aids and space for watching television. Libraries were also often used
as a place for withdrawal of small groups who needed extra help.

Due to a shortage of space in many schools, accommodation used
for specialist purposes had to be shared. For example, sometimes
mathematics and language areas were combined. Similarly, in certain
schools, areas were set aside for music and art, or science and general
resources. The specialist area that most frequently had its own space,
however, was special needs teaching.

In 11 of the schools the importance of co-operation with parents
was emphasised by having a room specially designated for their use.
This gave parents the opportunity to meet informally, as well as providing them with a space within the school for classes in English or,
in some cases, handicrafts.

Accommodation difficulties
Inevitably, some buildings posed problems. When interviewed, the
majority of teachers cited difficulties, most of which were concerned
with the provision of facilities, space or layout. One example was the
inconvenience of teaching in a hall, when this also formed a
thoroughfare for teachers and pupils. Some teachers also complained
about difficulties of managing pupil movement and noise on the stairways in old buildings. Other problems arose from the necessity to
remove asbestos, lack of display or storage space, or were a result of
having to share facilities.

Resources

Resources for most curriculum areas, in the main, were available
within all schools. Provision of library books, on the whole, was good,
particularly non-fiction material. Art materials were usually plentiful,
and there was a variety of musical instruments in most schools. Drama
equipment, however, including stage boxes and lights, was much less
frequently seen. Practical mathematics resources, such as scales, blocks
and clocks, were in good supply in all but three schools. During the
course of the Project, the use of computers in schools became increasingly widespread; one school had eleven. There was also a fairly wide
selection of audio-visual equipment in most schools.

The visitor's view of the schools

Even before they meet any pupils or teachers, visitors can gain an impression of the school from walking in the corridors and open areas. Quite apart from the general state of repair, their feelings may be influenced by the nature and extent of displays of work, notices welcoming parents into the school, and even the presence of plants or flowers.

Schools were rated by us on their decorative order. Two thirds were in good condition, and most of the rest were rated as being fair. A very similar impression was gained of the condition of furniture. Graffiti on walls and tables was only noticed in seven schools, and even then it was not extensive. Decorators were seen in several schools and building work also took place in a few. This, however, sometimes caused considerable upheaval.

Just over half the schools had a noticeboard for parents and visitors. Generally, messages were written in English, but in three schools all notes were also translated. Many schools displayed a multi-lingual 'WELCOME' poster.

Schools also varied considerably in the amount and type of displays seen in corridors, on stairways and in the hall. Although some schools used all or nearly all available space for showing work, a few others made no use of it. In two schools, even the display boards were empty. Overall, in six schools, work demonstrating a wide selection of art and craft techniques was on show. However, in more than a third of schools, given the availability of resources, the range was surprisingly limited.

Photographs of school plays, journeys, clubs, teams or children at work were frequently mounted and displayed. Notices about school clubs and teams were also common. In a few schools interest tables, such as 'the seashore', were observed.

In most schools, pupil work reflected all ages and abilities. However, in a few it was clear that some teachers did not display the work of their pupils, and in some, only the best work was exhibited. In others, every pupil had an equal opportunity of seeing her or his work exhibited around the school.

Thus, although all of the 50 schools can be described as inner city schools, they displayed marked differences both in their physical structure and the uses to which rooms were put. They also varied considerably in the impression created by displays in open areas.

SCHOOL ORGANISATION

Schools with and without an infant department

In their interviews the heads of the 36 schools with infants described to us their advantages. The majority stressed continuity of the pupils' education. One head reported: 'The children know the staff and the building, so they only have to cope with junior life'.

Most headteachers also felt that the staff benefitted from the broader age range in the school. In this way they could get to know the pupils better, and make use of their knowledge, whilst broadening their teaching experience by working with both infant and junior classes.

A third of the heads also talked of the advantages of the combined system to themselves, and the broadening of their own experience. Closer involvement with parents was mentioned by several others.

One headteacher summed up all the positive comments when he said: 'I am convinced that the primary school as a totally embracing unit is the best possible arrangement for educating children'.

Two-thirds of these heads could see few disadvantages to their system. The small number of problems that were noted tended to relate to the headteacher's own lack of experience with either the infant or junior age range, or to extra organisational requirements.

For heads of those schools without infant departments, however, concern was expressed about the different ideas, philosophy and style of the junior and infant headteachers. As one head said: 'A child moving from one school to another, even in the same building, finds different patterns of organisation and outlook. Initially there are some problems connected with settling in. These would be obviated if they went to only one school'. Only one headteacher felt strongly that the separate system had considerable advantages, and that was only if a child had been labelled in her or his infant years and needed a fresh start.

Although headteachers were almost unanimous in favouring schools covering the primary age range, some class teachers of first year pupils nevertheless felt that there was a difference in teaching style and philosophy between the infant and junior departments of the same school.

County and voluntary-aided schools

Of the 50 schools initially involved in the Project, 35 were maintained fully by the Authority. Eight of the rest were voluntary Church of England schools, six were Roman Catholic schools, and one was managed in association with a non-denominational body. The ratio of the county to voluntary schools in the Project sample was similar to that in the Authority as a whole. All of the voluntary-aided schools covered the whole primary age range, whereas more than a third of the county schools only contained junior-age pupils.

Difference in the size of the sample schools

First year roll
The 50 schools differed markedly in the size of their first year junior intakes. The largest school received a total of 102 pupils at entry,

whereas only 16 entered the smallest school. This compares with an average first year roll of 36 pupils for the 50 schools as a whole. In all, ten schools had first year rolls of 45 or more pupils and ten had fewer than twenty-six.

Previous studies (Plowden, 1967; Barker Lunn, 1982) have suggested that schools with a small intake or overall roll may well be restricted to certain types of organisational strategies because of their size. Variations in strategy according to school size will be described later.

Overall junior pupil rolls
There were considerable differences between the schools in terms of overall junior rolls. Thus, at one extreme, 519 pupils were on roll at the beginning of the academic year 1980, compared with only 73 in the smallest school. The average junior roll for the 50 schools as a whole was 159 children. In all, ten schools had a roll in excess of 200, whilst at the other extreme, the smallest ten schools had rolls of fewer than 112 junior pupils. In the Authority as a whole at the same time (September 1980), a third of the JM and JMI schools had less than 112 junior pupils on roll. Conversely, 23 per cent had 200 or more junior pupils on roll. Such differences in overall school size have an impact on staffing levels and may influence organisational policy and the availability of posts of responsibility (see Luzio, 1983).

SCHOOL POLICIES

It has already been shown that schools varied considerably in their junior roll. We now turn to the policies affected by the size of the roll, both in terms of numbers of pupils and availability of staff.

Number of classes and class size

The average number of junior classes in both JM and JMI schools was eight, although there were five schools with less than five classes and five schools with 12 or more.

Although the planned pupil-staffing ratio of the schools was based on the roll, some schools had additional posts for special needs. Additionally, some heads had used their own resources (funded through a special Authority scheme) to pay for other posts. As a result of these factors, class sizes often differed considerably. The numbers of pupils in different years also often varied and a year group, in some schools, could be split into two unevenly sized classes. Sometimes this was because particular pupils were perceived as needing more teacher attention. In other cases, a particular teacher (often a new member of staff) was given a smaller class. In three schools teachers worked in teams. The mixing of pupils of different ages was also fairly common.

Some headteachers took the view that such a policy allowed greater flexibility of class size although, as is discussed later, others suggested that it could pose problems.

Over three years a total of 278 junior classes contained pupils in our sample. The average overall class size was 25. This figure was based on the actual numbers of pupils in each of the classes we surveyed in the Project. The average figure is somewhat higher than those calculated annually by the Inner London Education Authority (ILEA). This is because the latter take into account all teachers who are involved with class teaching. This includes nurture groups and those teaching staff (such as the head and deputy) who may teach a number of sessions, but are not actually responsible for a class. Thirty-three classes contained more than 30 pupils, though in nine of these team teaching was in operation. In 18 classes, there were 17 or fewer children. Within one school, the variation between two classes was 15 (one class contained 27 pupils; in another class there were only 12).

Criteria for allocation to class

In allocating pupils to a particular class the headteachers had to take two decisions: whether to keep children of the same age together in single-age classes or to mix age groups; and whether to take account of other factors relating to the pupils, such as their ability, behaviour or sex.

Single or mixed-age classes

In 22 of the schools, all pupils were allocated entirely on a year group basis. In the other schools, pupils either were organised into vertically grouped classes, or into a mixture of single and vertically grouped classes.

Headteachers were questioned about the reasons for adopting particular systems. In nearly all schools, falling rolls had influenced the decision to have mixed-age classes. A mixed-age system had been introduced, solely for educational reasons, in only two schools. These headteachers saw benefits such as security and continuity which, in their view, also allowed able pupils to be stretched.

Concern was expressed, however, by nine headteachers who thought that mixed-age teaching was more difficult for class teachers to organise. This was a view shared by Thomas (1985). Other disadvantages noted concerned the problem of coping with a two year age range, in addition to the wide ability range found within a single year group. Some heads also felt that more able children might not be sufficiently stretched if the work was geared towards the middle of the ability/age range.

Other criteria for the allocation of pupils to classes

Approximately nine per cent of heads grouped children according to their stage of learning. In almost all cases, in those schools where a mixed-age system was operated, it was also the aim to have a mix of ability in each class. In a few schools, there were some out-of-age children in otherwise single-age classes. These children were selected either because they were seen as very able or as slower learners. Occasionally, children were separated because of behaviour problems and, very rarely, because of a personality clash between a particular pupil and teacher. In most single-age classes, however, the pupils were allocated so that there was a mix of ability. This is in line with Barker Lunn's findings (1982). In classes containing first year children, five schools made a point of grouping siblings together. First year twins were grouped together or, in schools with mixed-age classes, a new first year child was often put in the same class as their second year sibling. When allocating classes containing first year children, six heads also took into account their previous grouping in infant schools.

The allocation of teachers to classes

The majority of class teachers did not always teach the same age range. A small number, however, preferred to specialise in teaching lower or upper junior children. The involvement of the headteacher in the allocation of teachers to classes will be discussed in a later chapter.

The school day

We examined the organisation of the school day in the 50 schools. In accordance with the results of other research (Hilsum and Cane, 1971), we found considerable variation between schools in the organisation of school times and breaks. Most of the schools divided the day into four teaching sessions separated by three breaks: mid-morning; a longer interval for lunch; and mid-afternoon. Nine schools, however, omitted the afternoon playtime, leaving one long session running from the end of the lunch break until hometime.

Schools also varied their starting times. These ranged from 8.50am to 9.30am, with almost half the schools beginning at 9.00am. The school day ended between 3.15pm and 4.00pm, with most schools finishing their day between 3.30pm and 3.45pm.

We calculated the total amount of time given to teaching in school. Table 2.1 shows the variations in the overall amount of daily teaching time in the 50 schools, once lunch and break periods have been deducted.

TABLE 2.1: Variations in overall teaching time per day

Length of teaching time (minus all breaks)	Number of schools
4 hrs 40	1
4 hrs 45	2
4 hrs 50	6
4 hrs 55	9
5 hrs	16
5 hrs 5	10
5 hrs 10	4
5 hrs 15	0
5 hrs 20	2

Overall average   4 hrs 59

Most schools operated a working day of approximately five hours, although several schools devoted considerably less or more of their day to teaching time. These calculations, of course, do not take into account time spent on organisational tasks or registration and assemblies. Neither do they apply to the time pupils actually spent on learning tasks.

The 40 minute difference in total teaching time between the schools operating the longest and shortest days means that the pupils in some schools received at least a half day's extra teaching per week (3 hours and 20 minutes). If this extra time is totalled over a whole year – say, 190 teaching days – this means that some children were receiving approximately 25 more days of schooling than others.

The average morning's teaching lasted two hours and 56 minutes; 53 minutes longer than the average afternoon session. The reason for this, according to many of the teachers, was that children are fresher in the morning and, therefore, more able to cope with a longer session – often of active learning. Our analysis of teachers' timetables indicated that many teachers devoted morning sessions to language and mathematics.

Schools varied in the way timetables were organised. In most schools, the first morning session was the longest of the day. The final session, after the break in the afternoon, was usually the shortest; in seven schools it only lasted for half an hour. In the schools where there was no afternoon break, pupils worked for two hours or longer after lunch. Classes in these schools, however, frequently switched activities halfway through the afternoon.

During the four years of the Project, the majority of schools made minor amendments to their school times. In most cases, this just involved bringing forward, or delaying, the start of morning or afternoon play. In ten schools, however, it was decided to have a longer lunch period and to work right through the afternoon.

CURRICULUM POLICIES

We asked headteachers which curriculum areas were given most emphasis in their school. The majority of heads stressed the value placed upon one or both of the basic skill subjects, mathematics and language.

All but three of the headteachers cited areas of the curriculum that they felt presently needed more attention. Science was the most frequently noted area, with nearly half the headteachers expressing a desire to give it more emphasis. Our field officers' ratings show that, over the period of the Project, science activities were seen rarely, if at all, in three quarters of the schools. The aesthetic curriculum (that is creative arts, music, art and craft, or drama) was also mentioned by a large minority of heads (40%) as needing more time.

The use of guidelines

Guidelines were available in all but two schools. Most schools had guidelines for all or most subjects. In the main, the guidelines in use had also been written fairly recently. Sixty-one per cent of schools were using guidelines prepared within the last five years, and another 12 per cent were currently reviewing or revising existing guidelines.

More than half the schools made use of both school and Authority guidelines, although some preferred to work only with the latter. These, however, were only used as a strict model in eight schools. Small subject-related groups of teachers were set up in some schools to produce guidelines. In eight schools, however, the choice of curriculum was left wholly to the individual class teachers.

The use of textbooks

Although there were textbooks in all schools, there was considerable variation in the range of subjects for which these were available. A third of the schools possessed books for five or more curriculum areas, whereas just under a quarter only had textbooks for one or two subjects, usually mathematics and language. Although all schools possessed some textbooks, there were differences in their use. In only four schools were textbooks closely followed. In a third of schools they were used selectively and, in five others, very little.

The aesthetic curriculum

Approaches to aesthetic areas of the curriculum varied between schools. As already noted, nearly half the headteachers expressed a desire to place more emphasis on various creative arts subjects. In half the schools, class teachers were responsible for taking their own music sessions. Sometimes, other teachers were involved, particularly with instrumental tuition, which was usually given by part-timers. Pupils in all but five schools had the opportunity to learn the recorder and, in more than a third, 50 or more children had recorder lessons. Guitar tuition was offered in nearly half the schools. Two schools ran steel bands, and more than 30 pupils in each learned percussion instruments.

A few other schools participated in music schemes set up by the Authority, such as The Tower Hamlets String Project. All children in certain year groups in these schools learnt the violin or 'cello. Our field officers observed singing activities fairly often in 18 schools, whereas instrumental work was only common in 14 schools. Sixteen schools held lunchtime clubs for music. Most schools, however, had musical entertainments, particularly at Christmas, and a few entered festivals or competitions.

Examples of drama and dance activities occurred much less frequently. In three-quarters of schools the field officers saw these activities either rarely or not at all. Where these did occur, class teachers tended to take their own dance and drama lessons, with post holders being involved in only two schools. Headteachers taught drama or dance in three other schools and one deputy head was responsible for drama. Twelve schools had lunchtime or after school drama or dance clubs. Plays were produced for parents and visitors in a minority of schools.

Use of tests

Some form of testing was used in all but three of the schools. For reading, schools relied almost completely upon published tests. Approximately half the schools used one reading test each year, and about 30 per cent gave pupils two tests. One fifth of schools, however, used no reading tests with any year groups. There were also minor variations within schools between years. Sometimes, for example, pupils would be tested in the first year, then not again until the third year.

In mathematics, the picture was very different. Schools not only made much less use of tests, but some also devised their own assessments. The variation in the number of published tests used was much smaller. Most schools made use of the Checkpoints scheme, and a couple employed the National Foundation for Educational Research (NFER) mathematics tests. Very little other testing was carried out in schools.

Setting

We explored the practice of setting children for different curriculum activities. Eleven headteachers reported that they used setting in some form for some age groups and some subject areas. Only three employed it for all four junior years: two for mathematics only, and one for language and mathematics. Mathematics was the subject most frequently cited as being set.

Special provision

The four areas for which there was special provision were English as a Second Language; learning difficulties; behaviour problems; and extension work for gifted pupils.

English as a Second Language (ESL)

Pupils received special help with English in half the schools. This usually took the form of group work taken by a part-time specialist teacher. Individual withdrawal of pupils was used in three schools.

In most schools, an unused classroom or extra room was designated for use by ESL teachers. Sometimes this had to be shared with another area of special provision. In two schools, the specialist teacher worked in the library.

By the third year of the Project, the number of schools providing second language help had risen to thirty-two. At this stage, in six schools, more than 50 pupils were in receipt of second language help. Provision was made for more than 80 children in four of these six schools.

Learning difficulties

Almost all schools had some form of provision for pupils with learning difficulties. This was usually devoted to children with reading and language difficulties although, in almost half the schools, help was also given for mathematics. Children received extra help in all curriculum areas in four schools.

Help was given by a variety of personnel, such as full-time and part-time specialist teachers, class teachers, deputy headteachers and headteachers. Sixty per cent of schools reserved a special room for withdrawal work. In three schools, however, all support for pupils with learning difficulties took place in their own classroom. The criteria for giving help were usually the general judgements of teachers, although diagnostic testing was used in a quarter of schools.

The amount of provision for learning difficulties declined slightly over the three years. In more than a third of the schools, between 21 and 50 pupils were having extra help and, in three schools, more than 50 pupils were given special support.

Behaviour problems

Just over half of the schools made some special provision for pupils with behaviour problems. Children were withdrawn for individual attention in nine schools, and group withdrawal took place in nine others. In a few schools, pupils were given support within the same sessions as those pupils with learning difficulties. Five schools made use of units outside the school premises. Sixteen headteachers reported that there were few pupils with behaviour difficulties in their schools.

Part-time teachers provided most of the help although, in a few schools, the head, deputy head or a full-time teacher without responsibility for a class, took special sessions with these children. In the third year of the Project, we asked headteachers how many pupils were receiving help for behaviour difficulties. In 20 schools, between one and ten pupils were given special support, and in two others 11 to 20 pupils received extra help. Only in two schools were more than 21 pupils given help for behaviour difficulties.

'Gifted'

Provision for 'gifted' pupils was less widely available. A fifth of heads felt that there were too few of these pupils in their schools to devote extra resources to them. In 14 other schools, heads reported that teachers made provision within their classrooms for pupils with particular talents. In those schools where specific provision was made, extension work in music was most commonly quoted. Four other heads catered for 'gifted' pupils by setting children for mathematics and one adopted the practice for English.

Homework

Just under a quarter of the schools had a policy that homework should be set, whereas in 17 per cent the idea was frowned upon. In the rest of the schools, there was no school policy on the issue. In these cases, it was left up to individual teachers to decide whether or not to set homework. In some of these schools homework was given 'if the pupils ask for it'.

Assemblies

Assemblies occurred in all schools. In addition to their function as a time for religious worship, they were often used for story-telling and discussions of current events and moral issues. Some schools arranged for individual classes to plan and conduct an assembly on a weekly rotational basis.

PARENTAL INVOLVEMENT IN THE JUNIOR SCHOOL

Many major research studies have shown that home background factors have a powerful influence on children's achievement, and that these factors are good predictors of later academic achievement for different groups (see Douglas, 1964; Davie et al, 1972, Hutchison et al 1979; or the review by Mortimore and Blackstone, 1982). The majority of such studies have treated home background factors as constant. However, some factors, such as parental involvement in their child's education, are susceptible to change. More recent research has shown that parental involvement in children's learning can promote achievement, even amongst otherwise disadvantaged groups. In particular, where schools encourage parental involvement through the institution of special schemes, marked improvements in children's reading attainments have been identified. (See for example, Rathbone and Graham, 1981; Tizard et al, 1982; and Mortimore and Mortimore, 1984.)

If the amount of parental involvement in children's learning and in school activities does have a positive effect upon childrens' progress and motivation, it may help to make some schools more successful. Because of the possible link between parental involvement and educational achievement, we felt it important to examine how varied the 50 sample schools were in their links with parents. It was also important to establish the extent of parental involvement in the learning activities of their children.

Accordingly, we collected information, from a variety of sources, about parents' links with schools. Questions about home-school links were included as part of interviews conducted with headteachers, deputy heads and class teachers. In a sub-sample of eight schools, we also conducted interviews with the parents of children in the sample, in the appropriate home language, during the summer term of the second year. Parents were asked about their involvement with the child's learning at home and their contacts with the child's school. This means that, for these schools, parents', teachers' and heads' views about the extent of parental involvement could be compared.

Parent-Teachers' Associations

Considerable variation between the 50 schools in the involvement of parents was identified. In the first year only half the schools had a Parent-Teachers' Association (PTA) and, three years later, only one additional school had instituted such a body. Moreover, of the schools that originally had a PTA, a few reported that it had ceased to exist or was dormant by the third year.

Amongst the 25 schools with a PTA, there were substantial differences in the frequency with which the Association met. In one school, the head reported weekly meetings, whereas in four schools the heads could not specify how often meetings were held, but acknowledged it was not often. The more usual pattern was for about three meetings each term.

Parent-Teachers' Associations most commonly discussed fund raising, followed by the organisation of social activities. Only 11 such Associations were reported to discuss educational issues.

In those schools which did not have a PTA (25), only six heads said that they would like one to be instituted. The reasons given by heads for not favouring an Association were various, including lack of support from parents, the formality of such organisations, the fear that such a body would be dominated by a small clique of parents, or that it would take too much time to organise.

Contacts between heads and parents

Heads were asked whether parents were able to call in at any time during school hours to talk. In the first year of the study, 19 reported that parents were free to call in at any time. However, half the sample said that, although parents were free to call in at any time, they did prefer them to make an appointment to discuss certain items. Only five heads said that they always expected parents to make an appointment. Seven heads set aside fixed times when they made themselves available to see parents. Others said that they were always available, if necessary.

By the third year some changes in the pattern of heads' contacts with parents had taken place. Thirty-six heads (almost twice as many as in the first year) said that parents were able to call in at any time, and more than three times as many made themselves available to see parents at fixed times.

Meetings arranged for parents

All but one of the schools organised meetings at which children's work could be discussed with parents. For the vast majority, these took the form of open evenings, although eight heads also arranged day-time meetings where parents could discuss children's work with the teachers. There was some variation in the number of meetings arranged. In four schools, more than three meetings were arranged, but, in most schools, the practice was to hold two meetings each year. In seven, however, only one meeting took place. Parental attendance at these meetings was reported to be very good in 11 schools and good in twenty-one. Only two heads stated that parental attendance at meetings was poor.

All but five heads arranged a variety of other meetings for parents. Most commonly these concerned educational matters and social events. Others included organisational meetings to explain the secondary transfer process and school journey plans. Meetings for parents of new entrants were mentioned by just under a fifth. Attendance at these meetings was good in the majority of schools, but nearly a fifth of the sample reported poor or very poor parental attendance.

Parental help in the classroom

In the first year, just over half the heads reported that some parents helped teachers in their classrooms. Parents worked with pupils of all ages in ten schools whereas, in 11 others, parents helped only in lower school classes (those for infants or first and second year junior pupils). Only two heads said that parents helped only in classes with older age pupils (third and or fourth years).

On the whole, with only two exceptions, heads felt that such parental help was successful. Some problems were reported, the most common being difficulty in finding the 'right' kinds of parents. Despite these problems, views were generally favourable. As one head commented: 'The more parents come in, the more they understand what we are trying to do in the school'.

Of heads who did not have any parents involved in classroom work only four reported that they would like to encourage parents to help in classes. Various reasons were quoted by the remainder for being against the idea. Some explained that class teachers did not favour the practice; others felt that parents were not professionals; and a few felt that it was better for parents not to be too involved: 'It would be a lovely idea, but if you open it, it is invidious to select some and not others ... you know immediately who are going to be the 'problem' parents'.

The number of parents helping in classrooms varied. In the third year of the Project, only five schools had more than ten helpers currently working in the school. In the majority of the schools there was no parental help in classrooms. However, where parent helpers were used, the help was spread more evenly throughout the school. It is possible that the small numbers of parents helping in the third year may be the result of many single parents finding it necessary to get employment. Over the three years, the number of single-parent families rose from 17 to 25 per cent. Alternatively, it may be that many schools preferred not to have parents working in classrooms, for the reasons quoted above.

In the majority of schools, parental help consisted of hearing pupils read (19 schools) and assisting with art, craft, cooking and sewing activities (mentioned by 22 heads). In ten schools, heads stated that parental help in classes was confined only to non-academic areas such as art, craft, sewing, cooking, games or general help.

Other types of parental help

In the vast majority of the sample schools, some parents helped with school visits. In nine schools, parents also helped with school journeys.

Assistance with general fund raising was mentioned by the heads of 21 schools. Eight heads reported that parents also helped with the production of school plays.

When asked in the third year whether any changes in the school's relationships with parents had occurred over the previous three years, thirteen heads felt that the relationships had improved and ten commented that parents were now more involved and aware. Only one head thought that relationships were poorer than was formerly the case.

Deputy headteachers' views on contacts with parents

We conducted interviews with deputy headteachers in 48 schools during the third year of the study. The majority stated that their role involved particular contacts with parents. For 13 of the deputies these special contacts only arose when they covered for the headteacher, but in 12 schools (a quarter of the sample) the deputies stated that parents would approach them rather than the headteacher and, in two cases, the deputies saw their role as mediating between the head and parents.

Despite a generally favourable view, deputy heads were more likely than headteachers to comment on problems involved in using parent helpers in the classroom. This could be because many were class teachers and had immediate experience of parents working in their classes. Only seven deputies (compared with 13 heads), thought there were no problems. The most commonly reported problems were the unsuitability of parents (mentioned by 8) and that parents' objectives differed from those of class teachers (cited by 9). The deputies' views thus corresponded fairly closely to those of the heads, who reported that finding the 'right' kind of parent helpers was the main problem area.

Class teachers' views on contacts with parents

Some teachers mentioned difficult relationships with parents and parents' negative attitudes to education when talking about the families of their pupils. More than one in ten mentioned a problem which they perceived to be due to lack of parental interest in children. A very similar proportion mentioned problems due to children from disadvantaged families amongst their intakes: 'They do not always get the attention they need.', and 'Poor housing and social conditions ... Children arrive without breakfast'. A few teachers (less than 2%) mentioned, specifically, problems due to aggressive and difficult parents.

Overall, however, 88 of the 233 class teachers interviewed reported no problems with the intakes to their schools and 41 teachers mentioned the helpfulness and interest of parents in their children's education as one of the advantages of their intakes. One teacher commented: 'Some are very interested in their children's progress and will ask to hear them read at home', and a teacher in the East End of London said: 'It's a privilege to work in this area. I don't know if I could work elsewhere. The parents are very supportive. I value these children and parents'. Overall, more than three times as many class teachers made favourable comments than made unfavourable comments on parental interest in their children's schooling.

Informing parents about children's progress

Parents' evenings, where parents could talk individually to their child's teacher, were cited most frequently as the means of informing parents of the child's progress. A minority of teachers reported that, although there were parents' evenings, they did not have the opportunity to talk privately with parents. More than a third of the teachers sent out a written report to parents. Teachers also had the option of asking parents to come in to see them. It must be remembered, however, that our field work was completed in 1984. Within a few months the number of parents' evenings and reports had been drastically curtailed by the action taken by teachers in support of their 1985 and 1986 pay claims.

Parents' views of their children's schools and their contacts with staff

We interviewed the parents of 222 children attending eight schools. A detailed discussion of the interviews is given in Varlaam et al (1985). Here, however, the main findings from the parental interviews are noted.

Parents' satisfaction with school

Over half of parents were very satisfied with their child's school and a further quarter were generally satisfied. Less than ten per cent of parents were seriously dissatisfied. When asked if there were any things that they particularly liked about their child's school, 80 per cent of parents named one or more aspects. The most commonly cited reason for liking the school was its 'good atmosphere', but a fifth said that they liked the staff of the school and a number liked the school because the teachers were 'accessible'. Examples of comments were: 'The teachers' attitudes. They seem willing to talk to you ... you feel comfortable when you go there'. '... The teachers are nice and helpful. They care'. 'The teachers are very involved, not just in their academic work, their personalities – they try to bring them out. All the children seem very outgoing and unshy'.

A substantial minority of parents had no particular dislikes about their child's school. The most common cause of complaint, however, was bad discipline in the school, followed by a worry that their child was not stretched sufficiently by the school work. Problems or difficulties with staff at the school were mentioned by one in ten parents, though lack of staff contact was only mentioned by five parents in all. One parent responded: 'The teachers are not strict enough ... the school does not do much itself ... the boys run riot ... children are not taught enough'.

The vast majority of parents felt that their child's school tried to involve parents and only a very small minority felt that parents were kept at a distance by the school. Parents gave various reasons for feeling that the school involved them. By far the most common reason was that they felt welcome in the school, followed by involvement through social functions and, for a minority, through Parent-Teachers' Associations.

One parent, when asked what made her feel that the school tried to involve parents, responded: 'Everything's run by the parents ... the social functions'. Another said: 'They are always eager for you to go in – there's a lot of open evenings'. A third parent commented: 'The PTA association is constantly meeting, trying to get people involved in what they are doing, what's going on at the school'.

Of those parents who felt that the school kept them at a distance, some cited the lack of a PTA as a problem, whereas others felt that parents were 'only used for fund raising'. Some said that they would like to be invited to give more help. A few parents said that, although the school tried to involve them, they were not particularly interested or did not have time to become involved.

Parents' contacts with staff

Nearly all families had experienced some contact with the headteacher of their child's school. In over half the cases, both the mother and the father had met the head, although for 38 per cent of pupils, the mother was the only parent involved. The parents varied considerably in the number of times they had met the headteacher. One in ten parents had only met the head on one occasion, whilst nearly a quarter had met the head between two and four times. For a third of parents, meetings with the headteacher took place very frequently.

Contact with the class teacher was more common. Only a small minority of parents had never met their child's class teacher (seven per cent), whereas 42 per cent had met the teacher fairly frequently.

Parents' attendance at school meetings

Only eight per cent of parents reported that they had not attended a parents' evening during the school year. For nearly half, both the father and the mother went to the parents' evening(s) although for 39 per cent of pupils only the mother had attended. Over a quarter of parents reported that only one parents' evening had been held during the year at their child's school, and 37 per cent stated that two meetings had been held. Just under a fifth of parents mentioned three or more meetings in the year.

The most common reason given by parents for not attending school meetings was work commitments (during the day) or late arrival home from work (in the evenings). This was mentioned by over a fifth of parents. Only six per cent said that baby-sitting problems prevented their attendance. Five parents reported that they did not speak English and another five complained that they did not know any one else who would be attending and had not wanted to go by themselves.

Parental help in the class room and on outings
Only just over ten per cent of parents had helped in the classrooms of their child's school, although not necessarily in their child's class. Sixty-five per cent of parents had never been on school or class outings. In contrast, 12 per cent had been on three or more outings over the year.

Differences between schools in parental contacts and views
It was possible to compare parents' responses in each of the eight schools to see whether parental satisfaction, views and involvement varied. In four schools no parents, or the parents of only one pupil, expressed dissatisfaction with their child's school. Amongst the other schools, however, the parents of a minority of pupils were not satisfied with the school.

Differences were also found in the proportions of parents who cited things they specifically liked or specially disliked about their child's school. Thus, in two schools the parents of more than a third of pupils did not name anything they specially liked about the school, whereas only one pupil's parents in another school did not name anything they specially liked. In two of the smaller schools, for example, parents commented on the advantages of the size: 'Being small, they've got more time to see the kids. I've always liked it.' and ' ... Not big classes nor overcrowded. The teachers can teach all the children'.

In four schools, at least half the pupils' parents did not name anything they disliked about their child's school. In contrast, in another two schools only a few parents had no special dislikes. In one school, for example, several parents expressed concern at the high turnover of staff, expecially when this occurred during the school year: 'We want longer term teaching staff'.

The sample schools also differed in the extent to which the pupils' parents felt the school wanted to involve them. Thus, in one school all the parents felt the school liked them to be involved and, in another, all but one parent held this view. In a third school, however, only just over a half of the parents felt the school wanted them to be involved.

In one school, none of the parents had ever helped in any classrooms whereas, in another, nearly a third of parents had been involved. In the majority of sample schools, only one or two parents had helped in a classroom. In most of the schools, similar proportions of parents had helped on school outings and journeys, usually around a third.

EQUAL OPPORTUNITIES

In the third year, we asked all the headteachers if sex-stereotyping was a problem in their schools, and two-fifths reported that it was. Six identified problems as existing within the curriculum itself, though only two felt it was an area for concern in games and physical education. A further seven headteachers felt that problems sometimes arose in social situations, both inside and outside the classroom.

Two thirds of the headteachers reported that the promotion of anti-sexist activity and the development of equal opportunities for girls and boys were discussed at staff meetings, though only four heads said that such discussions occurred frequently. Two schools had members of staff with special responsibilities for this area, though in only one did the teacher receive a salary scale point. At one school, it was the subject of discussion at a governors' meeting, where it was decided to have a meeting for parents with an invited speaker: ' ... the children get their attitudes heavily influenced by the home. Therefore, if one can talk to the parents about it, it's a good place to start ... In school, we must be aware of it all the time'.

Forty per cent of the headteachers felt that racism was a problem within their schools. Eight said that it tended to be expressed in the form of name calling. A similar number noted it as a problem in the playground. A further ten felt it was largely brought in from outside the school. Only two heads considered it was a major problem within the classroom.

Nearly three-quarters of the headteachers reported that the promotion of anti-racist activity was a subject of staff meeting discussions, and one third said it was discussed frequently. Four schools had members of staff with responsibility for this area, and three had members of staff responsible for combined gender and ethnic issues. In only two schools, however, did these positions carry a salary scale point. One head felt that promotion of equal opportunities should be 'a joint responsibility amongst the staff'.

STAFF MEETINGS

We considered it important to examine the nature of staff meetings in the schools because they often provide a forum for policy discussions. In all but seven of the survey schools, there were regular staff meetings. Most often, these took place during the lunch hour, but meetings were also frequently held after school and, occasionally, during playtimes or before school.

Staffs varied in the topics they reported as being discussed at their meetings. The curriculum and general administration were most frequently on the agenda. Individual children, matters of discipline, contact with parents and in-service training, however, also featured in some discussions.

Teachers were asked whether there was adequate discussion about the curriculum at staff meetings. Nearly half felt that there was too little attention given to this matter, although almost as many were satisfied with the amount. On the subject of teaching techniques – that is not what was taught, but how it was taught – a similar picture emerged. Forty-four per cent of teachers thought that more time could be devoted to such discussion, whereas 42 per cent felt that the present amount was adequate.

Teachers in schools where staff meetings were not regular occurrences, were unanimous in their opinion that they would like to attend regular meetings. Although, as with parents' evenings, the ensuing teachers' action meant that, in reality, very few meetings were likely to have been held over the the next couple of years.

OUTSIDE INFLUENCES

Any description of schools must take into account those areas where the institutions interact with, and are influenced by, outside agencies. Some of these agencies constrain the work of the schools, whilst others aim to support them.

Other institutions

The headteachers of six of the 14 schools without infant departments felt that relations with their feeder infant schools were good, but the rest felt there was room for improvement. A few reported a lack of contact between teachers in their own schools and the teachers from the infant schools, but the most commonly cited reasons for poor relations had to do with differences in philosophy and teaching methods.

All of the schools had some contact with the secondary schools to which their children transferred. In the vast majority of cases this involved visits by members of staff and children, most often in the year prior to transfer. A number of headteachers mentioned the problems involved in making and maintaining links with all the secondaries involved. One commented: 'We send children to a variety of schools, so we can't have in-depth contact'. and another, 'The biggest difficulty is that we transfer pupils to between ten and twelve schools. Having links with all is impossible'.

A few schools were involved in liaison projects, working upon areas such as curriculum continuity with several other primaries and secondaries. Many headteachers described informal links that had developed between their own schools and the local secondaries. One pointed out: '... we exchange equipment, make use of their technicians'. and another, 'Their children come to us on child development courses'. One school had access to a minibus belonging to a nearby secondary school, another had visits from physical education and dance specialists, and a third had an hour's 'cello tuition per week provided by a local secondary school. Further information on secondary transfer procedures, and the liaison between the primaries and the secondaries to which the pupils transferred, are described in a series of bulletins reporting the results of the Secondary Transfer Project (see Appendix 1 for details).

Shared buildings

Only five of the 50 schools were sole occupants and users of their premises. The remainder shared their buildings, for at least some of the time, with other organisations and institutions. A number of buildings contained separate infant and junior schools and some had floors given over to adult education institutes. In nearly two-thirds of such schools the headteachers felt that this presented no problems at all and a similar proportion of class teachers felt the same way. However, headteachers from half of the remaining schools mentioned a certain degree of inconvenience caused by their not being sole occupants. A similar number reported problems with maintenance and cleaning, and a few had problems with security.

Parents and the community

Heads must bear in mind the feelings and opinions of parents and their aspirations for their children. Parent representatives on the schools' governing body are frequently involved in school policy decisions. The school may also be influenced by the views of the local community. In many areas, schools need to cater for children of many religions and diverse cultures in their assemblies. Extra teachers may also be required for the teaching of English as a Second Language, or for mother-tongue teaching in specific languages.

Governing bodies

School governing bodies play an important part in determining the overall policy of a school and in appointing new staff. In recent years, the composition of governing bodies has broadened and now consists of representatives of the Local Education Authority (who form a majority for county schools), parents, teachers and teaching-support staff. In the case of voluntary schools, there are also representatives from the appropriate Diocese or other body (who form a majority). Inevitably, the influence of the governing body will vary from school to school. In general, however, with the widening of representation, the trend has been for governing bodies to take a greater interest and to become more involved in discussing with the headteacher the general direction and aims of the school.

Local authority policies

Schools are also answerable to inspectors or advisors within the local education authority. Mention has already been made of the growing influence of the Authority curriculum guidelines. In addition, the Authority can influence the resourcing of schools through the differential allocation of funding according to indices of need, particularly through the positive discrimination resources scheme.

Government policies

Central government can also influence schools, as the Secretary of State has considerable powers under the 1944 Education Act for instituting particular educational policies for the local authority and school to follow (and is now seeking to increase these powers through the Education Reform Bill). In addition to national policies, enshrined in Acts of Parliament, the government has scope for influencing schools through the drafting of regulations and through the publication of reports by Her Majesty's Inspectorate.

Divisional Offices

The vast majority of headteachers were, on the whole, satisfied with the support they received from their local divisional offices. However, a large minority, approximately two-fifths, felt there were some problems in obtaining supply teachers. For seven headteachers the problems were quite pronounced, though it was acknowledged that supply teachers were often simply not available. As one headteacher put it: 'If they haven't got one, they can't send one. They do their best'.

Inspectorate support

Most headteachers were satisfied with inspectorate support, though several felt that individual inspectors visited their schools too infrequently. Again there was awareness of the problems of insufficient staff and too many schools to visit. One headteacher remarked: 'They're so widespread that unless there is a crisis they can't give the time needed'. A number of headteachers pointed out that though informal visits were rare, requests for assistance were almost always responded to promptly. As one headteacher said: 'If I phone, she'll be in. Very supportive'.

Other ILEA services

Slightly more than half of the headteachers reported problems with other Authority services. These ranged from minor irritations, such as workmen arriving unexpectedly, to chronic problems such as a persistent lack of response on the part of some agencies to requests for assistance, or frequent changes of personnel making the building of relationships particularly difficult. One headteacher, for example, complained at having had seven education welfare officers in ten years. Another said: 'We fill in lots of forms and then perhaps we don't see our welfare officer for two to three weeks. If someone could go round the next day, the problems might not develop'.

The two agencies most commonly criticised were the Schools' Psychological Service (SPS), and the Education Welfare Service (EWS), though there was some awareness that such services were often: ' ... overworked and understaffed'. On the other hand, a number of headteachers clearly had good working relationships with these, and other agencies. One headteacher said of the SPS 'The educational psychologist is very supportive, will come, will advise and see children ... talk to parents'. And another commented: 'The primary support team, the remedial reading team, and psychological service – Excellent!'

Problems tended to be highly specific and usually focused upon one, or maybe two of the Authority's services. Very rarely did headteachers feel discontented with all, or even the majority of support services, and there was a substantial minority for whom there were no problems at all. One headteacher summed up her feelings as follows: 'At the moment, I'm quite happy with the Authority'.

CHANGE IN THE JUNIOR SCHOOL

Schools are not static institutions. Teachers join and leave. The pupil population changes regularly through the annual transfer of fourth year pupils to secondary schools and the arrival of new first years, as well as in less planned ways. Schools, particularly in urban areas, are also subject to many less predictable changes. These include: staff turnover through job changes, maternity leave, long-term sickness or, in exceptional cases, death; the arrival and departure of large numbers of individual pupils; changes in school rolls due to demographic fluctuations; building problems such as the discovery of flaking asbestos or lead; and unexpected events, such as fires. We were continually surprised by just how much change of varying kinds was experienced by the sample schools during the four years of the study.

Some of the areas in which change was experienced amongst the sample schools will now be outlined. In order to maintain confidentiality, however, many of the most unusual events cannot be described. Nonetheless, it is hoped that some indication will be given of the amount of change that took place.

Pupil mobility

Pupil mobility during the junior years is relatively high compared with that at secondary level (see Sammons et al, 1983). Of the 1,826 pupils in the original sample, only 1,411 (77%) remained in the same school during the first three years of their junior education. Overall, 415 children from the original sample left the schools. A further 505 children, of the relevant age group, joined the schools during the same period. Of these newcomers, 227 (45%) moved again during this three year period. These 227 children, therefore, attended at least three different junior schools in less than three years. Taking these children into account, over three years a total of 547 children of the same age group left the 50 schools.

There were marked differences between schools in the extent of pupil mobility. For example, during the first year of junior education, seven schools lost more than 15 per cent of their original first year intake. In contrast, four schools had not lost any of their original first years and, in a further nine schools, only one first year pupil had left during the year. This compares with a figure of eight per cent for the pupil sample as a whole.

Similarly, there were marked differences between schools in the numbers of newcomers entering first year classes during the year. Six schools received more than 15 per cent of new pupils. In four schools, however, no new pupils joined and in 15 schools only one new pupil joined during the first year. Over three years, differences in pupil mobility between the schools became very marked. Thus, in six schools a third or more of the original sample of pupils had left. In contrast, in four schools less than ten per cent of the original sample had left during the same period. At one extreme, one school lost 61 per cent of pupils of the sample's age (expressed as a percentage of the original first year intake to the school) – a total of 22 pupils. During the same period this school gained 21 pupils (representing 58% of the original first year roll). Thus, the membership of the year group changed dramatically, even though, in terms of numbers of pupils in the sample's age group, the school had only one fewer pupil at the end of the summer term 1983 than in September 1980.

In contrast, at the other extreme, one school lost only two pupils of this age group and gained only one newcomer during the equivalent period. In this school, therefore, the membership of children in this year group had remained virtually unchanged over the three years.

In schools where the membership of classes changes considerably over one year, the class teacher(s) will have to cope with the task of integrating these new pupils and of fostering a feeling of class identity in a fast changing environment. Difficulties may be experienced by new pupils if they have not covered the same curriculum as the rest of the class they have joined. New entrants also have to develop new friendships and break into established groupings.

Changes in overall junior pupil rolls

Over the late 1970's and early 1980's, inner London experienced a dramatic fall in primary pupil rolls. Although this fall has been experienced in nearly all parts of the Authority, the problem of falling rolls has been more acute in some divisions than in others. Declining rolls have resulted in a number of school closures and in the amalgamation of schools in some areas.

Resource allocations and the numbers of staff employed have also been affected. A rapid fall in roll may place a great strain on the organisation of schools when difficult decisions about which staff may be lost and how to group pupils into classes have to be made. Additional problems can occur if year groups are of very different sizes (see Barker Lunn, 1982).

However, in recent years, one or two parts of the city have experienced increases in junior and infant rolls. If roll increases are rapid, problems of adjustment may also be experienced by schools. Staff shortages and insufficient resources may result where there is a rapid or unexpected rise in roll. Time is required to adjust resources and staff allocations to take account of the increase in pupil numbers.

Of the 50 schools, the majority experienced a fall in their junior roll over the three years of the study. Only a minority of schools – seven in all – had an increase in roll over the equivalent period.

The effects of declining numbers were not evenly distributed. At one extreme, one of the schools experienced a reduction in the junior roll of 50 per cent between September 1980 and September 1983. In contrast, another school increased its roll by 38 per cent in the same time span. The more common experience, however, was a decline. In all, ten schools had a fall in roll of 30 per cent or more, but only six schools had an increase of ten per cent or more.

The average change was a fall in roll of nearly 15 per cent and, only a minority of schools (nine in all) had a change of less than a ten per cent roll increase or decrease over the three years.

Changes in class teachers during the year

Changes of class teachers during the academic year may well have an effect upon the pupils' progress. Such changes can be due to long-term sickness, maternity leave or to change of job. If classes are disrupted on several occasions during the year, or in several consecutive years, this factor may well affect the behaviour and attainment of children over the year. Because of this, we felt it was necessary to establish the extent to which children in the sample experienced such changes of teacher.

A number of sample classes experienced a change of class teacher during the school year and, in a small minority of cases, two or more changes of class teacher within a year. In year one, for example, out of a total of 98 classes in the 50 schools, 16 classes experienced at least one change of class teacher over the year. Of those, three classes had been taught by three teachers. The percentage of classes that had not experienced any change of class teacher remained very stable in all three years, at around 86 per cent.

There were also differences between the schools in the extent to which classes experienced a change in class teacher during any one year, over the course of the Project. Thus, in 18 schools none of the classes experienced a change of class teacher during the academic year in any of the three years. In contrast, 22 schools which contained pupils in the sample, had at least one change of class teacher in one or more of the classes, during the three years. Furthermore, in six schools, one or more changes of class teacher had occurred during the school year in each of two years.

Changes of class teacher during the year may have a disruptive effect on children's behaviour or learning. The new teacher may have different expectations of her or his class, different methods of teaching, or a different approach to the curriculum compared with her or his predecessor.

Change in class teachers between years

In addition to change of class teacher during the school year many, if not most, children experienced a change of teacher between years. We investigated the extent to which schools operated a system whereby the same teacher was involved with the same pupils in two or more years. In many of the schools, it was common for at least one class teacher who had taught pupils in their first year to be involved with the same children in the second year. Continuity of class teacher between first and second years occurred for at least one of the teachers in 26 of the 50 schools.

Such continuity may prove to be advantageous for children who have a good relationship with their class teacher. For the children who do not get on with a particular teacher, however, such continuity denies them an opportunity for a fresh start.

It should be borne in mind, however, that, in schools where a year group was split into several classes or where pupil mobility was high, the membership of a class may vary considerably between years, even though the class teacher remained the same across years. Clearly, in the schools which experienced high pupil mobility and changes of staff during the year, pupils' learning environments will have been very unstable. Thus, for example, three of the schools in which more than one change of class teacher took place during one or more years of the Project, also had high rates of pupil mobility (above 40% leavers or newcomers in the age group over three years).

Change in headteacher and in deputy headteacher

The role of the headteacher has an impact on the organisation of a school, on the relationships between staff, on levels of staff satisfaction, and on policies affecting the curriculum. The actions and personality of the deputy head may also have an effect on staff morale, the curriculum, and school organisation.

A change in the headteacher or the deputy headteacher, therefore, may cause upheaval in the school. Some new heads like to be 'new brooms'. They may have very different views from the previous head about school organisation, pastoral care, curriculum policies and class teacher autonomy. The appointment of a new deputy may also result in a change in the deputy's role. The head may place more confidence in a new deputy and treat the change as the opportunity to delegate more of her or his own duties. Alternatively, heads may be more cautious in the amount of responsibility given to a new deputy, until they see how she or he copes in the new position.

In five of the 50 schools, a change of headteacher occurred at the start of the Project and, in a further 11 schools, a new head was appointed during the study. In seven cases, schools that had a change of head during the Project also had, for a time, an acting head. This was usually the deputy, who occasionally had to continue with her or his existing duties in addition to those of acting headteacher. In three schools, the acting head became the new head at a later date.

Headteachers of nine schools were either absent for a lengthy period, or were frequently absent for short periods during the four years. In four schools this was due to serious or recurring illness; in three to attendance on a course and, in two cases, for legal commitments.

Two schools had a new deputy head at the start of the study and a further 11 experienced a change during the four years of the Project. There were also acting deputy heads, for a period, in five other schools. This means that, overall, 18 schools had either a new deputy or acting deputy during the course of the Project.

A lengthy period of absence or illness of deputy heads occurred in ten schools. In four schools deputy heads took maternity leave, and three went on secondment. In other situations, an acting deputy replaced the deputy head when she or he took on the role of acting headteacher. The extent of change which can take place in the leadership of a school may be seen in the following example. In one of the schools the deputy head went on maternity leave and an acting deputy was appointed during the first year of the study. In the second year, in this school, the headteacher left and was replaced, in an acting capacity, by the original deputy, who later became headteacher. An acting deputy head was appointed during this period but was replaced in the third year by a permanent deputy. Therefore, two heads and three deputies or acting deputies were in place over two-and-a-half years! Such dramatic changes in personnel are rare but, where they occur, it is difficult to establish and maintain consistent policies and practices.

Changes in organisational and curriculum policies

With the arrival of new headteachers, deputy heads and other teachers, changes can be seen within schools. Falling rolls affect resources, which in turn influence organisational decisions. Even within schools where pupil and staff mobility is low, reorganisation sometimes take place. Teaching arrangements, for instance, changed in several schools, such that some schools adopted mixed-age teaching, whereas others reverted back to year-based classes. One school used team-teaching for the first time and discovered that they were: '... working in a more co-operative and open way. The atmosphere of the school is more positive'.

New headteachers sometimes redesignated their school's posts of responsibility, although they stressed that they tried not to make too many changes too quickly. In several schools, as a result of falling rolls, scale points were lost when the holder left the school. This, one head reported, adversely affected staff morale.

Inevitably, over the course of a four year survey, schools will make amendments to their curriculum. Sometimes, this is due to the arrival of a new headteacher or postholder. The publication of Authority guidelines or other schemes of work may also be an incentive for change. Some schools, however, will constantly assess and revise the curriculum, as a matter of policy.

Fourteen headteachers described specific curriculum changes that had taken place over the previous three years when they were interviewed during the third year of the Project. These included the introduction of specific teaching schemes for use throughout the school, development of a particular curriculum area, structured parental help with reading at home, a greater emphasis on anti-racist and multi-ethnic education, and a more unified approach amongst the staff towards the curriculum.

The increase of in-service training within school was also mentioned. One head reported on its value to the school: 'The willingness of teachers to discuss openly – even criticise openly – to make statements confidently in an open situation, has been a considerable development.

We've got people thinking far more about what they're doing and why they're doing it, and specifying their aims in greater detail. It's good for the class teachers' personal development, but mainly it has made teaching more effective'.

Disruptive Events in the Lives of Sample Schools

Building works and decorations

The most common disruption to schools during the Project years was caused by building work and decorations. Many of the primary school buildings within the Authority are old, often dating back to Victorian times. These buildings require frequent maintenance and decoration. In addition, the discovery of hazards caused by particular substances – especially asbestos – in older buildings necessitated major building work in some schools. Attention has also been paid to potential hazards of flaking lead paint in recent years.

In 11 schools, teaching was interrupted by decorating or building work which lasted for at least several weeks and, sometimes, for a term or more. In eight of these schools, major building or conversion work was involved (including rewiring, plumbing or the removal of asbestos). For four of these schools, the work was of such a substantial nature that the school buildings had to be closed during term time.

Even where buildings were not forced to close, classes were often disrupted by the general dirt and noise occasioned by the work, or were required to move location. These difficulties may have had an adverse effect on staff and pupil morale, and may also have reduced the amount of work class teachers could cover during a given year. The detrimental effect of building work was noted by one head: 'The school went through a bad patch. The work was done at short notice. The standard of work and behaviour went down ... '

School amalgamations

A number of ILEA schools have been amalgamated during the 1980's as a result of falling rolls. Four of the sample schools experienced an amalgamation during the period of the Project. A further two had been amalgamated just before the Project commenced, and another school was due to be amalgamated at the end of the survey. In all cases, the amalgamation consisted of the joining of a separate junior school with an infant school to create a JMI. Such amalgamations can involve a change of head or possibly other members of teaching and support staff, a restructuring of posts of responsibility, and can affect staff relationships and morale. As one headteacher described the experience: 'The effect is on the staff as a whole. Instead of two separate staffs, we have to come together and work together. We must try to see ourselves as primary teachers, not just junior and infant teachers – looking at the continuity of policy and attitudes through the school'.

Inspections

Four schools were inspected during the course of the study, either by HMI or by the Authority's own Inspectorate. An inspection usually causes additional work for members of staff in a school, especially for the head and the deputy. Changes in organisational practices, the curriculum or deployment of staff may be recommended as a result of the inspection. Tensions may be caused amongst staff during the inspection, or afterwards, if they consider the report is critical, unfair or incorrect. If an inspection report is favourable, however, staff morale is improved by the process.

Thus, overall, during the survey years the sample of schools was by no means static. Changes in pupils and staff, school size and organisation, and the characteristics of intakes, had an impact on many of them. In some cases, declining pupil numbers led to further change through amalgamations or staff redeployment. However, it is apparent that there were marked differences, between the 50 schools, in the extent of change they experienced during this period.

SUMMARY

In this chapter, many variations between the 50 schools have been described. In some cases, these differences were striking. Schools varied both in terms of aspects not under their direct control, the 'givens' (for example, their rolls or buildings) and, perhaps more importantly, in terms of policies, over which they generally had complete control. The impact of these differences on pupils' educational outcomes will be analysed in a later chapter. Next, however, we will report on the headteachers and their deputies in the 50 schools, and how their roles and responsibilities varied.

3

The Headteachers and Deputies

The previous chapter detailed how the schools in the study differed in terms of their organisation and resources, as well as in terms of overall policies. We now turn to an examination of the ways in which the headteachers and their deputies differed, looking in particular at their characteristics, roles and responsibilities as well as at their activities in and around the school.

THE HEADTEACHERS

Just under half of the headships were held by women at the end of the project, though four years before, the picture had been rather different with two thirds of the heads being men. Similarly when we began the research the greatest number of heads were over 55 years old. By the end of the Project, nine of these had retired. Only two headteachers were not from English, Scottish, Welsh or Irish backgrounds. Although 16 had some secondary training, the majority (62%) had been trained exclusively to teach the primary age range. More than half of these had only been trained to teach junior pupils.

Not all headteachers had entered teacher-training colleges straight from school. Almost half of them had either done national service, or some other work before starting their teacher training. Once they were teaching, only 23 heads had experienced no interruptions to their career. Of the rest, most had spent some time on further academic studies. Four had taken up advisory posts, and four others had taken time out to have children. In most cases, they had only spent one year away from school though, interestingly, two had been out of teaching for periods of more than five years.

For some, headship was a new experience. Of 12 heads who had been appointed to their present post within the previous two years, seven were in their first headship. In contrast, more than a fifth of heads had been in post for more than 11 years.

A substantial minority of about 40 per cent also had outside responsibilities – for example, some form of committee work or as local councillors – and a few of these had a number of other such involvements.

Their role

A newly appointed primary school headteacher is faced with a variety of responsibilities, many of which are quite different to her or his main qualification for the job: that of having been a successful classroom teacher and, usually, a deputy head.

A number of research studies have identified a wide variety of duties for which headteachers are responsible (see, for example, the Plowden Report 1967; Cook and Mack, 1971; O'Shea, 1984). These responsibilities include: management and organisation; curriculum innovations; staff development and teacher training; team-building; and parental involvement.

In many urban areas, headteachers are faced with the added task of dealing with problems related to inner city life. This, in itself, can provide a lot of additional work and cause considerable extra stress.

Headteachers' aims for their pupils

One headteacher, in attempting to describe those attitudes he hoped his pupils would have developed by the time they left the school wrote: 'I would hope that the child has a marked sense of moral responsiblity, is socially aware and has confidence in her/his own identity and abilities. That through a broad experience of varied activities she/he will emerge with a 'light in the eye' and a flexible approach to learning, appreciating that educative discovery is pleasurable and that effort and industry are rewarding'. The response of another was: 'Enquiring mind. The ability to find and use information from various sources. An understanding of the application of the basic skills. Tolerance and consideration of others. Confidence to face new experiences'. Forty-eight of the headteachers gave similar accounts of their aims, which could be grouped into personal, social, cultural, intellectual and religious/ spiritual. Intellectual aims were further sub-divided into: autonomy, basic skills, and general intellectual competence.

Personal, intellectual and social qualities were mentioned most frequently by headteachers. The heads differed, however, in the emphasis they gave to the different types of intellectual aims. Just over half stressed the acquisition of basic skills, whereas this was not mentioned by the rest. Surprisingly, five headteachers did not refer to any intellectual qualities. In order to understand further how headteachers attempt to realise these aims, we need to look at their role within the school.

Headteachers' views of their role

We asked headteachers what aspects of their job they saw as most important. The majority of responses noted fulfilling the needs of staff in terms of their cohesion, development and loyalty. One headteacher summed this up when he stated: 'It is always important for the head to work closely with the staff and to encourage the positive aspects that can be drawn out of teachers'.

An understanding of the teachers and children was also a high priority, as was leadership through maintaining standards and setting goals both for staff and pupils. As another head commented: 'As a headteacher, leadership matters greatly. You must be the one to put in the 'nth' bit. You must make sure that the educational aim is high enough, so that children are reaching where you want them to go. That's always your long-term goal'.

More than half of the heads talked about the importance of developing new curriculum initiatives and objectives. Finally, a minority also mentioned the importance of understanding parents' problems and developing links with the local community. Over the course of the Project, there was a considerable increase in the number of heads who emphasised the value of pastoral work and involvement with parents as part of their role.

The curriculum

Headteachers were asked about their involvement in curriculum policy. They varied in the amount of freedom they allowed teachers with regard to the curriculum. Although only five heads stated that they had total control, a large minority drew up guidelines or made policy suggestions, and three others took part in discussions in which they attempted to influence curriculum policy. Other heads preferred not to be involved in the development of curriculum policy and left this to individual teachers to decide.

Although many headteachers did not normally intervene with individual teachers' approach to the curriculum, some heads stated that they gave more guidance to inexperienced teachers and others reported that certain teachers needed particular help.

Influencing teaching strategies

Headteachers did not confine themselves to influencing curriculum development. When they were asked about their involvement in the mechanics of teaching, only five headteachers stated that they never attempted to influence teaching strategies, although half of the rest only intervened selectively, when they considered it necessary. This level of involvement was far greater than that reported by heads in an earlier research study (Hilsum and Cane, 1971), where half of the headteachers indicated that they gave teachers a completely free hand.

Decision-making

The situations in which headteachers can exercise varying degrees of authority are plentiful. They can, for instance, use staff meetings for this process. Staff meetings were chaired most frequently by headteachers and, in almost all the schools, heads were involved in drawing up the agenda for meetings.

When allocating the school's budget, there was variation in the amount heads involved staff in consultation and in deciding upon priorities for expenditure. Just under half took complete responsibility for decisions. Consultation with individual members of staff on the budget took place in a quarter of schools. In a third of schools, there were also group consultations between headteachers and staff.

In the annual allocation of teachers to classes, headteachers varied in the amount of choice they gave the teachers. In over a third of cases, teachers expressed their preference for a certain age group to the headteacher, who then made the final decision. However, twelve heads took full responsibility for assigning classes to teachers. Slightly more intervened only if teachers came to no agreement amongst themselves.

Teaching

The majority of heads had some form of weekly teaching timetable. Most frequently this involved class and group teaching. However, the proportion of headteachers working with individual pupils had increased to almost two thirds over the course of the Project, as had their involvement in group work. Headteachers who taught classes generally worked with pupils of all ages, although a minority only taught the upper junior years and a couple worked mainly in infant and first year junior classes.

Headteachers devoted different amounts of time to teaching. A fifth taught for half a day each week, whereas a third spent one whole day teaching. Five heads devoted at least two days per week to class, group or individual teaching.

There were also other occasions when headteachers were called on to take classes. More than three-quarters were available to cover classes in the event of short-term staff absences. However, of these, only 13 put themselves forward as the first option. The others made use initially of supply teachers, floating teachers, part-time teachers or their deputy heads.

Other contact with children

Apart from their contact through teaching or at assemblies, all but two headteachers mentioned other links with pupils. Almost half stated that they saw children regularly whilst doing lunch duties, and eight also came into close contact with pupils through lunchtime clubs or activities. After school activities, playground duties and school journeys were also occasions when headteachers had a chance to mix with pupils. However, the most frequent form of contact was meeting children around the school during the day. About half the heads had an 'open door' policy for pupils. This also included occasions when pupils were sent to them for praise or admonition. Comments such as, 'I see them all day long' and, 'they're in and out of my room' were frequently made by heads.

Pastoral care of pupils

Children were sometimes sent to headteachers to be praised for good work or good behaviour, or to be disciplined for poor effort or bad behaviour. Most of the heads had their own system of rewarding pupils. Most commonly, rewards took the form of praise given privately in the headteacher's room, although almost half the heads made use of assemblies or public displays around the school to show off good work. An award system was operated by more than half of the headteachers, and five heads reported that they informed parents when they were pleased with a child's work or behaviour.

For poor work or behaviour, all but four headteachers operated their own punishment system. Children most frequently were sent to headteachers for a private telling off, and faced the loss of privileges or being kept in during playtime in almost half the schools. Parents were involved more frequently than in situations concerning good work or behaviour. Although the possibility of suspension was mentioned by several heads, only one quoted this as the first option open to them. A minority of heads were unspecific in giving details about a punishment system, believing that the punishment should always be designed to fit the particular crime.

Involvement with staff

Headteachers' relationships with staff encompass a number of different roles and duties. They are legally responsible for the well-being of the pupils and the management of the staff. They are expected to strive for high standards and to satisfy the expectations of parents, governors and the community. They are required to respond to policy directives issued by government or by the local education authority. They must allow access to inspectors from the LEA or HMI. Their style and personality frequently influences the climate of the school.

At a more mundane level, they have to keep the school running as smoothly as possible and do their best to ensure that when conflicts arise – between teachers or between a parent or a pupil and a teacher

– these are settled as quickly as possible. It is when facing these difficulties that the headteachers talked of their isolation, and many reported that they used the deputy head as a link between themselves and the staff.

Staff appraisal and development

When questioned about staff appraisal, all but two headteachers stated that they had some means for assessing, informally, the performance of their staff. Frequently, this involved an intuitive assessment of classroom atmosphere when visiting the room. Some headteachers made use of the opportunity of teaching classes to gauge pupils' reactions to school and classroom activities. The appearance of classrooms, and display on the walls, provided another focus for assessment. Monitoring children's work and behaviour was also a commonly cited form of teacher appraisal.

The teachers' actions outside the classroom were not excluded from the attention of heads. Almost a third of heads felt that teachers' attitudes and statements were a useful pointer to successful or unsuccessful classroom activity, and teachers' records of work and children's progress offered a similar source of information to some heads.

A large majority of heads reported that they observed teachers in the classroom, although many did this only on a casual basis. A smaller proportion stated that they observed all teachers, though their classroom visits generally lasted no longer than a few minutes.

Some headteachers told us that they monitored the progress of pupils through a system of record keeping. Nearly half saw the records regularly. Of the others, some said they looked at records occasionally and others only saw them 'when necessary'. Nearly a fifth of heads, however, did not see the records at all.

We asked the headteachers whether they encouraged their staff to go on in-service education courses. Half of the heads were keen for staff to attend any courses, whereas 13 – without raising any objections if teachers requested to go – did not necessarily encourage them to do so. Nine others stated that teachers were encouraged to attend courses if the subject of the course was related to the school's needs. Only two headteachers stated they were not keen for staff to attend courses in school time.

The headteachers' own attendance on courses was also varied. Apart from school based in-service courses, seven, for example, attended a course on a regular basis. These courses included the Broader Perspectives course designed by the Authority to show heads the best practice in a number of other Authorities in the country and, in our third year, courses for multi-ethnic education, and computing.

Other contacts with staff

Many headteachers felt that their pastoral role extended further than just dealing with pupils' problems. Counselling, not only of parents, but also of staff, including support staff, was very much part of their role. One head said: 'Relationships with staff are so important. That's why I put so much into it. Unless relationships with staff are good, you cannot get anywhere. This includes the ancillary and cleaning staff'. Of course, many of the links between headteachers and staff that we have discussed are formal. On their visits to primary schools, field officers frequently saw headteachers in informal discussion with individual teachers or with the whole staff. A minority of heads also sat in the staffroom at playtimes, while many who did not, came in at various times to chat to teachers.

Not all information coming to heads about pupils was passed on to teachers. The main concern for holding back certain details was the protection of the child and parents' confidentiality.

Contacts with parents and outside agencies

Headteachers stressed the pastoral side of their role in connection with parents. This aspect of their role will be discussed in more detail later. A large minority of heads also saw it as their responsibility to establish links with the local community. As one reported: 'I work in the local community. I see my role as not only being in the school. I'm involved at all sorts of levels. It is important to me that the school is seen as part of the local situation'. The attendance of heads at local meetings outside the school was also reported by several as an important means of contact with the community. Headteachers, then, have a key role to play in the life of the school. The importance of this role will be examined in a later chapter. What is already perfectly clear, however, is that the role of head is complex and demanding: they have to be manager and supervisor, mentor and supporter, model and friend.

THE DEPUTIES

In contrast to the headteachers, the majority of deputy heads were women. Three were still under thirty. Most were of English, Scottish, Welsh or Irish origin. As with headteachers, training had largely been for the primary range and the most common qualification was the teaching certificate. However, a quarter had gained further qualifications since their original training. Their length of teaching experience ranged from five to 40 years. Nearly a third of the deputy heads had spent between 11 and 15 years in teaching. Most had been in their present job for between three and ten years.

Their role

The role of the deputy head falls between two more easily defined roles: that of the headteacher, who has oversight of the whole school; and the class teacher, who is responsible for what goes on in her or his own classroom and, in some cases, a particular area of the curriculum. Of the many other tasks to be completed by heads in primary schools, responsibility for some may fall to the deputy head. Across schools, the role of the deputy head can also vary considerably, depending upon the needs of the particular school and the philosophy of the headteacher.

Other studies have generally paid little attention to the deputy head's role within the management structure of primary schools. Plowden (1967), however, suggested that headteachers should delegate more of their duties 'than is commonly done'. Coulson and Cox (1975) also pointed out that heads who do not give their deputy the opportunity to take decisions are placing them at a disadvantage in the future: ' ... the many deputies who eventually become heads do so having had very little experience of facing the problems and making the decisions which constantly confront them after promotion' (p. 102).

Management courses are run at the Authority's teachers' centres for those interested in deputy headship. However, many deputies have reported that even though they have attended these, they feel unprepared for the demands of their new job, mainly because of the very different roles that heads expect deputies to fulfil. Many of the personal qualities and skills required of a deputy head are no different from those essential to all experienced teachers. A Primary Management Studies Report (1978) offered the following advice to new deputy heads: 'Fundamentally this post is of major importance in the primary school. It is a working relationship with the headteacher and the other staff in the school. It is especially important because of the high expectations of everyone involved and of the need to be able to care for the school in the absence of the head' (p. 1).

Class teaching deputy heads

Three-quarters of the deputy heads were also class teachers. The majority felt that having a class had distinct advantages. Most commonly cited were the extra contact with pupils and the belief that they were not losing touch with teaching. Other responses include a greater appreciation and understanding of staff feelings and attitudes. Nearly a quarter said that it gave them the opportunity to set an example of good teaching practice to their colleagues, and this point was reiterated by many deputy heads when asked about the most important aspect of their role. There were some disadvantages, however, and two-thirds described the difficulties associated with their dual role. Of these, more than a third talked about its limiting effect on support to other teachers, not getting to know all the children, lack of contact with parents, and a general loss of familiarity with what was going on in the school. The remainder spoke of a conflict between administration and classwork, in that they either could not attend sufficiently to their class teaching, or that there was insufficient time for the many administrative tasks.

Non class-teaching deputy heads

All of the deputy heads who were not responsible for one class had some sort of teaching commitment. Half of them were involved in individual and group withdrawal teaching, and most of the others had a regular teaching timetable releasing other class teachers throughout the school. In addition they usually covered the classes of teachers who were absent. However, half of them shared this duty with other, part-time staff, and, sometimes, with the headteacher.

All the deputies felt that not having their own class could cause certain problems. The majority were concerned about losing contact with teaching, other members of staff and pupils, and this caused difficulties in responding to them. However, all but one also felt that there were advantages in not being a class teacher. Nearly half thought that they were able to get a clearer picture of the school by being one step removed from the classroom and coming into contact with a cross section of pupils. A third mentioned better links with parents and pupils. A couple felt that the absence of class responsibilities enabled them to deputise more efficiently when the headteacher was not at school.

Administrative responsibilities

Where the deputy heads' roles differed most markedly from those of other teachers was in the day-to-day organisation of the school, for which they were often responsible. Their administrative tasks often included arrangements for staff cover during the day and also on those occasions when members of staff were absent. One reported: 'I am responsible for the day-to-day running of the school; to see that everything goes smoothly'. Nearly three-quarters of the deputy headteachers reported that taking over the headteacher's role, if they were not in school, was one of their responsibilities. This included taking assemblies and dealing with parents' queries.

Involvement in policy decisions

There was some variation in the extent to which deputy headteachers perceived that headteachers involved them in matters of school policy.

Several said that they worked closely with the headteacher, and felt that this was the most important aspect of their role. One deputy emphasised the feeling of many when she said: 'I am aware of the loneliness of headteachers. They do need a shoulder to lean on, and they need to discuss things ... '. When asked specifically if they were involved in policy decisions, the majority reported that they were, and three-quarters of these claimed they were very involved. All of those with limited or no participation were keen for more responsibility and the opportunity to share their own experience.

The majority of deputy heads were included in the informal appraisal of their colleagues. In most cases, this took the form of discussions with the headteacher about staff and school development. More than half of the deputy heads interviewed participated in the process of allocating pupils to classes and classes to teachers, although most of these emphasised that staff preference was also an important consideration.

Pastoral care – pupils

Several deputy heads said that it was part of their job specification to be involved in upholding school discipline. Just under half stated that they had their own system of rewarding good work or behaviour, whereas slightly more had their own punishment system as a deterrent to bad work and behaviour. On the whole, deputy heads felt that it was an important part of their role to have contact with as many children as possible, and that they should be a person to whom a pupil could turn in times of trouble or pleasure: '... that I should be available to the children, if they want to search me out or show me something ... willingness to sit down and listen'.

Pastoral care – staff

It was apparent that deputy heads did not only see themselves as someone to whom the children could turn. Their desire to be approachable to other teachers and ancillary staff was a theme that recurred throughout the interviews. Just over half mentioned that they saw themselves as a link between the headteacher and the staff; a sounding board for headteachers and a mediator for teachers' suggestions: '... I act as a sort of buffer between staff and head ... there are still some teachers who won't approach a headteacher'.

A small number also had particular responsibility for the welfare of ancillary staff, whose views also needed to be represented, and a further minority were also responsible for probationary teachers in their capacity as 'designated teachers'.

Advisory role – curriculum

Along with all their other duties, several deputy heads retained responsibility for an area of the curriculum. Others said that it was one of their duties to have an overview of the curriculum throughout the school. Some deputy heads gave a lead in the curriculum through their own class teaching. More than two-thirds of deputy headteachers saw it as part of their role to try to influence the teaching strategies of their colleagues, most frequently in the areas of organisation and technique.

Desire for a change of responsibility

Just under half of the deputy heads reported that they would like to change their responsibilities given the opportunity. Most of the comments emphasised the dual role of teaching and administration and its inherent problems. Nine teachers wanted more involvement in administrative tasks, whereas three felt that they would be happier with less.

The other area mentioned was the curriculum. Four people were keen to be more involved in curriculum development, and another wanted to spend more time on advisory teaching. A general dilemma for class-teaching deputies was expressed by one deputy: 'I'd like to see more of the school but, on the other hand, I don't want to see less of my class'.

Responsibility for change within the school

More than half the deputy heads stated that they had been, wholly or partly, responsible for some of the major changes in their schools. They had been involved with a range of initiatives concerning the curriculum, teaching style and use of resources, and reorganisation of staff policies concerning equal opportunities for pupils.

Job satisfaction and career development

Nearly two-thirds of the deputy heads were satisfied or very satisfied with their job. A minority expressed a mixture of satisfaction and dissatisfaction. Most of the remainder cited excess pressure as a reason for discontentment, although other reasons included a feeling that their skills were not being fully used and that they were not being given enough responsibility.

The majority of deputy headteachers felt encouraged to attend in-service training courses, although nearly half of them reported that the initiative was principally their own. Eighty per cent had attended at least one course in the previous two years.

The deputy heads were also asked how they saw their career developing. Almost a third said that they were interested in becoming a headteacher at some stage in the future. A minority thought that they would stay in their present job until they retired. The idea of a sideways move to another deputy headship, or perhaps into advisory work, appealed to five deputy heads.

The most important aspects of the deputy's role

For most deputies the most important aspect of their role was connected in some way with interpersonal relationships between the headteachers, teachers, parents and pupils. A few deputies stressed that their own relationship with the headteacher had to be strong in order to create a good atmosphere in the school. The confidence of staff and parents was mentioned as important in order to gain the confidence of the children. Also, their availability to staff and pupils was considered vital. Taking the middle position between headteacher and staff was reiterated, as was the need to keep everything running smoothly and trying to take the pressure off the headteacher and teachers. The other main aim, quoted by one-fifth of deputy headteachers, concerned the creation of good standards within the school, through the curriculum, continuity of approach and the staff getting together as often as possible. Several deputies also emphasised the need to be able to: '... take over and fill in for anybody, be it headteacher or dinner helper, so that the school can tick over without others noticing or suffering ... being able to cope!'

The headteacher's view of the deputy's role

Just over a third of heads wanted to change the responsibilities of their deputies. Reasons tended to be similar to those expressed by deputy heads seeking change, with a emphasis on less class teaching commitments and developing their administrative functions. Two-thirds of heads, however, were very satisfied with the responsibilities undertaken by their deputy heads and had no desire to make any amendments.

SUMMARY

In this chapter the characteristics and roles of heads and deputies have been described. The question of their influence will be addressed in a later chapter, but it is already clear that they play a vital role in the life of the school. Implications for the selection of headteachers and for the training of heads and deputies will also be addressed later.

4

The Teachers in the Classroom

This chapter is concerned with the work of teachers in the classroom. This includes: their characteristics; the aims teachers have for their pupils and the planning that takes place before the pupils arrive in the classroom; the class atmosphere; details of classroom management; constraints and influences upon the teacher in the classroom; and assessment of pupils and record keeping.

CHARACTERISTICS

Of the 221 teachers who worked with the children over the three years, three-quarters were women, although the proportion of men was larger amongst the group who taught older pupils. The age range of teachers was fairly wide. There was a tendency for the younger and older teachers to work with younger children, and those in the middle age bracket to teach older children. Only eight per cent of the teachers were from ethnic minority backgrounds.

There were more Scale 2 teachers working with the sample children than Scale 1, Scale 3, or deputy headteachers. Those teachers on the highest scales, however, tended to work with the older children. More than half the teachers had spent between five and 14 years in teaching, although just over one-quarter had taught for less than five years.

Many of the sample had experienced junior training, although one-third had been trained to teach infants as well, and another third had included secondary work within their training. There was a tendency for teachers of first year pupils to have trained for the infant or even nursery and infant age range.

TEACHERS' AIMS

We asked each class teacher to say what qualities they hoped a child would have developed by the time she or he had left their class. From their responses it was possible to identify a range of different aims. We sorted these into seven broad categories which we had adapted from those identified in a study of teachers' aims carried out by the Schools' Council (see Ashton et al, 1975). These are described next.

Personal development

Aims clearly directed towards the development of the child as an individual were placed in this first category. Self-respect, self-confidence, reliability, and a healthy self-image were frequently occurring aims of this type. For example, one teacher hoped the children in her class would develop '... self-confidence and self-discipline'. Another stated he wished his children to be '... self-critical, accepting criticism as well as praise. Above all I think a sense of humour is essential'. Personal qualities were also often expressed in the form of short phrases or single abstract nouns, such as 'happiness' and 'honesty'.

Social and moral aims

These focused upon the child's attitudes towards, and interactions with, other people. Sometimes the context would be the relatively narrow one of the school, class, or peer group; at other times, the wider social world would be invoked, and sometimes teachers referred to more abstract qualities of 'caring and sharing'. For example, one teacher hoped her children would develop '... a caring attitude to others less able than themselves'. Another hoped for '... an interest in, and thought for others', and another wished to '... develop an increased sensitivity to the needs of others in the school community'.

Cultural aims

This is the most general of the seven categories. Aims of this kind tended to be expressed in forms which put the child in relation to the 'world at large', or 'the environment'. They also frequently involved qualities of awareness or sensitivity. For example, one teacher wished '... to develop an appreciation of the natural world and a wish to conserve what we have'. Another teacher wanted to encourage a general '... awareness of surroundings ...'. Cultural aims are well summed up in one teacher's wish that her children should have some '... understanding of their place in the world'.

Aims related to basic skills and subject areas

This fourth category is the first of three that can be broadly described as intellectual aims. Aims placed in this category make explicit reference to skills or competences in particular curriculum areas, most often language and mathematics. Some teachers simply wished to promote 'basic literacy and numeracy', but some others were more detailed and specific. For example, one teacher wished his children to develop '... a basic knowledge of maths, the four rules especially reached to a good standard. Basic grammar rules understood and put into practice'. Another teacher wished to encourage 'Basic music skills, rhythm and pitch discrimination etc...', in addition to literacy and numeracy.

Autonomy

Autonomy is another highly specific intellectual aim concerned with critical thinking, curiosity, independence and the ability to work alone. Some teachers used the term 'autonomy' itself in their statements, whilst others spelled out the ability to work on one's own apart from the teacher. Some teachers wanted the children in their classes to be 'inquisitive', whilst others wished to foster 'constructive curiosity'.

General intellectual competence

This is the most general of the three intellectual aims. It includes those aims which express relations between the children and their work in looser, and more all-encompassing, terms than those which fall into the two previous categories. Instead of specifying particular skills or abilities, teachers often wrote that they wished children to develop '... general communication skills ...' or the ' ... ability to learn by observing and listening'. A number of teachers stated that they wanted their children to have '... the ability to express themselves clearly'. Another wished her children '... to be able to discuss with peers and teachers in a sensible and thoughtful manner' and another urged '... the ability to find out information and use it correctly'.

Religious and spiritual aims

Only three teachers specifically expressed aims of this kind. In each of the three cases, these aims were clearly of great importance to the teachers concerned, as can be seen from the one example below. 'But most of all I hope to develop in each pupil true and deep spiritual values and convictions based on Christianity'. One or two teachers added comments to the effect that their statements were to some extent idealised, there being little time in three short terms to influence, significantly, the behaviour of a class of children. Another teacher commented: 'Often, the qualities to be fostered depend on the individual, plus the cohesive nature of the class'.

Once the aims had been subdivided into the categories listed above, it was possible to examine the frequencies with which different types of aims, and combinations of aims, occurred. Over the three years, the aims most frequently mentioned were intellectual, personal and social. Aims of these three types were included by 78, 76 and 77 per cent of all teachers respectively. Fifty four per cent of all teachers made some mention of autonomy, and 45 per cent included general intellectual competence among their aims.

Very few teachers restricted themselves to just one type of aim. The vast majority of teachers were concerned with a range. Overall, slightly more than a third of all teachers included in their statement a combination of personal, social and intellectual aims. Other teachers sought to balance their aims in different ways, and some included aims of a social, personal or even intellectual nature under the more general cultural category.

PLANNING

Planning issues involve long-term organisational choices, usually resolved before the term begins, such as: whether the work should be timetabled or not; whether forecasts of work need to be submitted to the headteacher; how the classroom should be arranged; and how it should be decided where the children sit. In addition, the length of time teachers spent in day-to-day preparation and planning, and the amount of contact they had with the pupils' previous teachers are examined.

How was it decided where the children sat?

Very few teachers in the sample permitted their children total freedom of choice. Overall, only ten per cent always allowed the children to choose where they sat. Nearly a quarter said that they determined where the children sat without taking into consideration the children's wishes. Almost a third of teachers, however, shared the responsibility with the children: some would modify their plans to allow friends to sit together; some would allow children an initial choice but would keep apart badly behaved children.

Over all three years a quarter of the teachers interviewed reported that, for some of the time at least, they not only took sole responsibility for determining where their children sat, but they did so by grouping together children of similar abilities. Nineteen per cent said they relied upon judgements of behaviour when working out who should sit where. These two factors – ability and behaviour – were the two most frequently mentioned by those teachers who organised the seating entirely on their own.

Classroom layout

In order to describe systematically the ways in which teachers arranged their classrooms, a distinction has been made between groups and rows of children's tables. Tables or desks were considered to be in groups whenever the seated children tended to face in towards one another, facilitating conversation, co-operation and collaboration (see Plan 1).

Figure 4.1: Classroom Plan 1

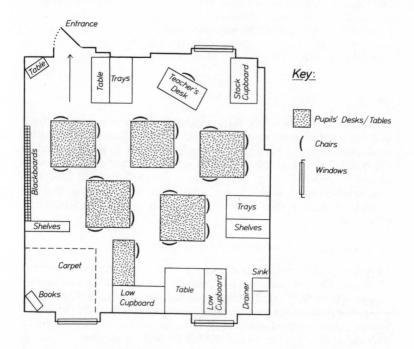

Tables or desks were considered to be in rows whenever they were placed end to end such that the children seated in the rows tended to face the same way. In contrast to groups, rows of tables tended to restrict forms of interaction and collaboration. Teachers had a preference in all three years for grouping tables rather than having them in rows, and whenever they grouped them they tended to prefer groups of four or six. Similarly, they showed a preference for short rows of two or four whenever they arranged tables in this manner.

Most teachers also preferred arrangements of varying sizes in their classrooms. There were very few classrooms with only one kind and size of arrangement. Over half the teachers in each year kept the children's tables or desks separate from the rest of the furniture, placing the latter round the walls and grouping the former roughly in the middle of the room, either in groups or in twos (see Plan 1). A minority of teachers tried to integrate the classroom furniture in order to create distinct work areas (see Plan 2).

Figure 4.2: Classroom Plan 2

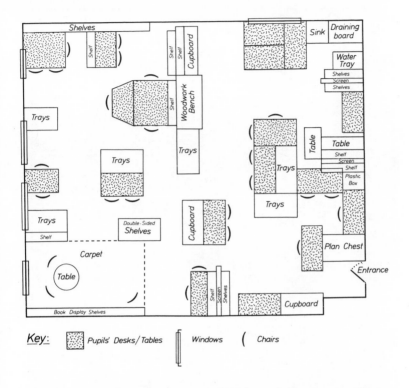

The remainder preferred a combination of these two patterns, perhaps creating one special corner for work in a particular curriculum area whilst keeping the rest of the tables and chairs grouped together. The most commonly occurring special areas were reading and book corners and art and craft corners. Only ten per cent of the classrooms had the tables and desks all facing the same way in rows, and these were usually arranged predominantly in rows of two (see Plan 3).

Most teachers preferred to position their own desk – if they had one – in such a way that it faced the children's tables directly and, in 85 per cent of cases, the teacher's desk was in a position which permitted an uninterrupted view of the entire classroom.

Discussion with previous teacher

The vast majority of teachers who were in a position to discuss their children with the teacher who had taken them in the previous year

Figure 4.3: Classroom Plan 3

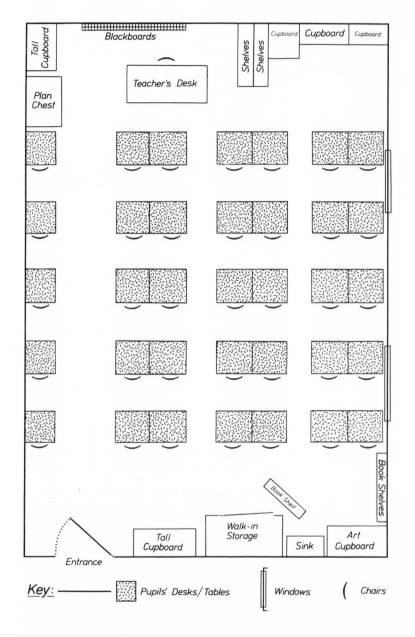

reported that they had in fact done so – only seven per cent said they had not. Approximately half of the teachers reported that they discussed their children both before and after transfer of classes.

Preparation of forecasts

In the first year, 38 per cent of teachers said they were asked by their headteachers to provide some kind of forecast of the work they intended to do. In years two and three the numbers rose to over 50 per cent. Only a minority of teachers, however, said that they were required to discuss their forecasts with their headteachers.

Timetables

Between two-thirds and three-quarters of teachers used a timetable. The majority of those teachers who did not use a timetable tended to make plans weekly. A large minority, however, planned on a daily basis, the proportion increasing from 14 per cent in the first year to 30 per cent in year three. A similar trend towards an increase in control of the children's activities was also discernible amongst those teachers who reported that they used timetables. The proportion of teachers who followed detailed timetables rose from 41 per cent in year one to 54 per cent in year three. There was also an increase over the three years in the proportion of teachers following timetables closely from 17 to 39 per cent.

Preparation time

During the second year of the Project, we asked teachers how much time they spent preparing work each week. The responses of those teachers who were able to offer a figure are shown in Table 4.1.

TABLE 4.1: Time teachers reported they spent preparing work

Hours per week	% of teachers
	(N = 80)
Less than 1	2
1 – 5	25
6 – 10	59
11 – 15	10
More than 15	4

There was a tendency for those who adhered to a more detailed daily timetable to spend more time preparing work each week than those following a rough timetable, or none at all.

Various studies have discussed the potential importance of school climate or ethos (see Findlayson, 1973; Rutter et al, 1979; and the reviews by Anderson, 1982; and Strivens, 1985). In addition to school climate, the ethos or atmosphere of the classroom is also important (see Moos, 1978). Thus, the atmosphere of a classroom may permeate all the activities which take place within it. Here we explore some of the ways teachers can influence the mood of the classroom.

Display in classrooms

The display in a classroom may considerably enhance classroom atmosphere and provide a stimulating environment for the children. The wall space in more than half the classrooms we observed over the three years was covered either completely, or for the most part, with a wide variety of materials. Only partial use of display space was made in most of the other classrooms.

In general, children's pictures were more likely to be displayed in the classroom than were examples of their written work, teacher-produced materials or printed materials. Although there was some drawing or painting work in virtually all classrooms, a number of teachers, especially in the third year, displayed nothing else.

There were displays of craft work, such as three-dimensional models, pottery or needlework in approximately half of the rooms in all years. There were also tables devoted to areas of interest, such as growing, shore life, or the seasons. Such interest tables were found in just over a third of the classes.

The quality of classroom displays was also assessed by our trained field officers. The arrangement, layout and overall aesthetic impression were rated on a five-point scale from very good to very poor. Forty-one per cent of displays were considered to be very or quite well planned. In contrast, just over a quarter were rated as not particularly pleasing.

How teachers start the school day

The first session in the morning is regarded by many teachers as the most important time of the day, when the mood and pace of teaching and learning can be set. Most pupils arrived at their classrooms at the start of the school day although, in a few schools, some children were found there for up to a half an hour beforehand. These early pupils often chatted to their teachers or helped them to set up the room.

When school officially started, most classrooms were already open and pupils could just wander in. However, some teachers collected their pupils from the playground or made them wait at the classroom door to be let in. This tended to happen more frequently with older children.

Overall, more than two-thirds of classrooms had a carpeted area, though it appeared that teachers, on the whole, preferred not to make use of it early in the day. Children usually went straight to their tables.

In just under half the classes, teachers and pupils chatted for a few minutes before settling down to work. More usually it was the pupils who initiated the conversations. Some teachers did not encourage discussions at the beginning of the day, appearing to be keen to get the day started. However, some of these teachers did take time to discuss non-school topics later on in the day. In the majority of classes, work commenced soon after the children's arrival. In a few, however, children were still wandering around and talking to friends ten minutes after arrival.

Teachers varied greatly in their registration practice. Overall, a similar number of teachers called out the register before work started as those who waited until the children were settled with work. As the children got older, teachers tended to mark the register silently, perhaps in order to minimise distraction.

Although few classes started their day with an assembly, quiet reading and 'early work' were often followed by assembly. In first-year classes, teachers more frequently gave children work to do on arrival, either in the form of blackboard early work or by instructing them about work to be undertaken. In all years, sessions involving the whole class were rare first thing in the morning.

Quiet reading occurred in a third of classes and tended to be more common in the later years. Sometimes it was combined with other activities, such as handicraft or finishing off other work. In a small minority of classes children came in and started work without being told what to do.

Organisation of work

In each of the three years, the majority of teaching sessions were considered by our field officers to be, on the whole, well organised in the sense that there was plenty of work for the children to do. In contrast, a small proportion of lessons were rated as poorly organised. This group of sessions was largest in year two and considerably smaller in year three.

In sessions where the teacher ensured there was plenty of work for pupils to do, the children were observed to be more involved in their work. Although there was ample work for pupils to do in most lessons, fewer sessions were considered to be especially bright or interesting.

Lessons, on the whole, evoked fairly consistent interest in most pupils, particularly in the third year, when the proportion of lessons rated as unstimulating fell to only three per cent (compared with seven per cent and six per cent in years one and two, respectively). Sessions where sufficient work was organised for pupils tended to be rated as more interesting. Pupils were also seen to be more industrious during stimulating sessions and were more able to manage their own work without constant direction from the teacher.

Teachers' involvement with pupils

In all years, the teachers spent the vast majority of the time in the classrooms actively involved in some way with their pupils. The total proportion of time spent not interacting, however, rose from 15 per cent in the first year to just over 21 per cent in the third year. Some of this time, of course, was spent dealing with outside interruptions, such as pupils delivering messages or requesting help. Intentional non-interaction, however, increased over the three years (from 8% to 10%). This included the kind of classroom 'housekeeping' that involves getting equipment out of cupboards, preparing materials or tidying up.

Small talk

We considered any classroom conversation that was unrelated to class or school activities to be a component of classroom atmosphere, but only a very small amount of classroom time was devoted to such small talk in all years (0.8%) and this decreased after the first year. In year three, none was heard during the observation periods in 60 per cent of the classrooms. In all years, though, there were extreme cases where greater amounts of chatting occurred, taking up as much as five per cent of observed time. Apart from this, some teachers, particularly those of first year classes, devoted a period of time at the start of the week to children's news. This usually took place either at the beginning or end of the day and pupils were commonly gathered around the teacher on the classroom carpet, or at the teacher's desk.

How the teachers ended the day

The end of the day is also considered by many teachers to be a valuable time for going over the main features of the day or for settling the pupils with a story. Some teachers preferred to draw the children together for such an activity, whereas others continued with normal work until hometime.

As the children moved up the school, teachers more frequently continued with work started earlier in the afternoon. The use of a story declined as the children got older, although storytelling remained a common classroom activity at other times in the day. In addition to carrying on with work or telling a story, some teachers used a quiz or led a discussion at this time. A few schools held an assembly and in five per cent of classes the opportunity was taken for some clearing up.

Teacher enthusiasm

In describing classroom atmosphere an important component is the degree of enthusiasm shown by the teacher. About half the teachers showed neither overt pleasure nor signs of boredom when they were teaching. Most of the others (37% in year 2 and 42% in year 3) appeared to enjoy teaching the class, demonstrating enthusiasm in their work and interest in their pupils. However, a minority appeared to dislike their class or to be unenthusiastic about the teaching undertaken. This was true of slightly more teachers in year two (19%) than in year three (13%). It was noted by a field officer that in one class: 'The atmosphere in the room is great! The teacher is totally involved with the children and is concerned that they should be happy and interested in their work. The teacher is gentle, amusing, quiet, unruffled, and keen on work'. Of another a field officer reported: 'The teacher was very much in control, quiet and businesslike, and concentrated very much on the task'. But of a third it was said: 'In general, this teacher gave the impression of weariness and a lack of interest'. On the whole the majority of teachers gave the impression of a positive or at least neutral attitude, but a few did not appear to enjoy their work.

There were strong positive relationships between teachers' attitudes to their classes and the amount and interest level of the work they provided. Thus, teachers who showed obvious enjoyment for teaching, also provided ample work for pupils and work was also usually more interesting. In classes where teachers displayed a positive attitude, pupils also appeared to be more involved and interested, and were able to work without constant supervision.

Relationships in the classroom

Another indicator of classroom atmosphere is the relationship that exists between the teacher and the pupils. Assessments were made of teachers' attitudes towards personal relationships with pupils, whether they saw their role as educator only or were also involved with the children as people. In both the second and third years, more than a third of teachers appeared to have a friendly relationship with their pupils.

It seemed that first year teachers were most neutral in their relationship with children and third year teachers, as a group, most informal. Second year teachers tended to vary more in terms of their social relationship with their pupils. It was observed of one teacher that there was, 'No sign of a warm relationship with the children beyond bounds of the classroom. The teacher ignored all small talk initiated by the children. Good manners, behaviour and hard work were all that was important'. Another third year teacher was seen to be, 'Pleasant to the children but not over friendly. She did not communicate very much with them. She was generally rather deadpan'. But one first year teacher was described as: 'A very cheerful person, smiling a lot and chatting with interest and animation to the children. The teacher is obviously interested in them and cares about them. The teacher teased them and allowed them to tease her'. Not surprisingly, a strong relationship was found between the ratings given for the teacher-pupil relationships and the positive attitude of the teacher. Overall the picture that emerged was of a relatively pleasant and supportive atmosphere, with many teachers showing an interest in the children above and beyond the bounds of the classroom. Small talk, however, was fairly limited. The learning environment as represented in classroom displays emphasised children's pictorial work. Considerable variation was recorded, however, between classrooms in the general climate offered to pupils.

MANAGEMENT OF CHILDREN'S ACTIVITIES DURING THE DAY

Once the pupils are working, teachers employ various strategies to ensure continuity of classroom activity and maximum attention to the task at hand. For example, routine details need to be attended to. Materials and equipment often have to be distributed, and groupings of children arranged. At the end of sessions it may be necessary to organise pupils to tidy the classroom or prepare themselves for a different activity. Teachers may also be concerned about the amount of pupil movement and talk in class. Furthermore, monitoring of pupil activity may occur, with special attention given to their behaviour. The teachers, themselves, may vary their own voice level and amount of movement in the classroom. They may also have the help of other adults in the room.

Information and directions

Overall, teachers occupied themselves with managerial details for approximately one-tenth of the time they were observed. However, the proportion of time spent on this activity varied over the three years, with routine matters taking up less time in the third (8.2%) than first and second years (10% and 10.1% respectively). This change in the level of activity was in contrast with the Oracle survey findings, where the percentage of such interactions rose as the children moved up the school (Galton et al, 1980). There was also considerable variation between teachers in time spent on routine management; a few teachers devoting more than a quarter of their time to giving information and directions, whereas others spent virtually no time on such matters.

Amount of pupil mobility and level of noise permitted

Some teachers allow more pupil movement in the classroom than others. Teachers may even have different preferences for different activities so that, for example, all children may be required to stay in their places for mathematics but are allowed to move around and collaborate during project or topic sessions.

In all years, pupils in approximately half of the sessions were allowed movement with certain restrictions. Thus, they were free to move to the teacher and to collect materials, but prevented from working in areas other than those specified by the teacher. In only a very small minority of sessions (less than five per cent in each year) were children free to leave the classroom in connection with their work.

Within the classroom, each teacher responded differently to how much pupil talk they would permit. The level of talk, however, often varied from one activity to the next. The number of sessions where talking occurred almost all of the time decreased over the three years. Over the same period of time, there was an increase in the imposition of silence when the teacher was talking to the class.

Examination of the ratings made at different times during the day revealed interesting variations. In all years there was an increase in the amount of noise throughout the day, with the exception of the final sessions, of which a sizeable minority were quiet. This was related to the amount of movement allowed during the time when the teacher was telling a story. The penultimate observation session of the afternoon, however, tended to be noisier than most other sessions. Classes were often clearing up at this time, before settling down for the story. Some classes, however, did their clearing up at the end of the day and this would probably account for the high level of noise in nearly 40 per cent of classes at this time.

Pupil noise was found to be significantly negatively related to the amount of work organised by teachers and the level of pupil involvement with their work. Thus, children talked more when there was less work for them to do and also when they did not appear actively to be interested in the task at hand. Noise was also related to the amount of movement, such that in sessions where pupils talked more, the extent of pupil mobility around the classroom was greater.

Teacher mobility around the classroom

The degree to which teachers move around the classroom varies considerably. Some ask the children to come to them for help or feedback, whereas others prefer to monitor activity by moving around the children while they work. We were unable to collect systematically information about teacher movement in all classes. However, in a sub-sample of eight classes, observed for extra days in the second year, the location of teachers when they were talking to pupils was monitored. There were four places where teachers and pupils could interact: at the teachers' desk or base; at the pupils' workplace; with teachers and pupils together, but not at either of their bases; or with either teachers or pupils calling to the other across the classroom. Overall, just under half of the interactions took place across the room. The remainder were almost equally spread between the three other possible locations. One-quarter of contacts started by the teacher, however, took place at the pupil's base. There were noticeable differences between the eight teachers in their amount of classroom movement (see Table 4.2).

TABLE 4.2: Location of teacher-pupil interactions in eight classes

% of interactions:

	At teacher's base	At pupil's base	Together elsewhere in the room	Called out across room	Total N of interactions
Teacher 1	17	14	16	53	539
Teacher 2	9	21	19	51	372
Teacher 3	25	18	13	44	295
Teacher 4	27	12	11	50	405
Teacher 5	15	25	20	40	204
Teacher 6	11	25	21	43	220
Teacher 7	5	36	37	22	279
Teacher 8	35	15	6	44	318

Teacher 7, for example, spent very little time at his own base and twice the average time with the pupils at their own base or elsewhere in the room. Conversely, teacher 8 sat at her desk for over a third of the time and moved to other areas to talk with children much less frequently.

Observations show that, during sessions when children were working individually or in groups, 38 per cent of teachers tended to move around the classroom a lot. However, a further third remained at their desks most of the time.

Teachers' use of voice

The use of voice as a practical tool by the teacher is not always consciously planned. However, children respond differently to quiet and noisy teachers. More than half the teachers spoke at a level whereby they could only be heard by the children they were addressing at the time. Several others, particularly in the first two years, were audible to other members of the class when they talked to individuals. The number of extremely quiet teachers was small, although it increased as the children moved up the school (from 4% in year 1 to 9% in year 3). Although teachers did differ in the level of voice employed in the classroom, it was clear that the variation between them was not as wide as it was in other areas of pupil management.

Use of other adults in the classroom

During observation days, helpers were seen in many classes, particularly during art, craft and cookery sessions and, occasionally, listening to children read. Sometimes they withdrew groups of children from the class for cookery or craft work, and helped with aspects of classroom 'housekeeping'.

Monitoring of pupils

We observed systematically the amount of time the teacher spent monitoring pupils at various times throughout the day. This included instances when teachers were silently observing classroom events to see that everything was running smoothly. From the first to the third year, teachers' silent observation of classroom activity almost doubled. Over the same period of time, observation also showed that there was an increase in the proportion of sessions in which pupils appeared able to sustain their work even in the absence of the teacher. In general, there was a drop in teachers' intervention in classroom activity over this period, which was reflected in a fall in the amount of verbal interactions from 68 to 60 per cent. Although the majority of teachers spent a limited amount of time monitoring, there were variations between them. In the third year, in particular, a sizeable minority of teachers (15%) monitored the class for more than a tenth of the time.

Control of pupils' behaviour

Some previous research has treated control as a separate area of the teachers' role (see Hilsum and Cane, 1971). From observations made during this Project, however, it appeared to be part of the teacher's general classroom management. Teachers not only display reaction to children's behaviour by verbal responses, but also by indicating approval or disapproval with tone of voice and their non-verbal behaviour.

The teachers' methods of control were rated by field officers in two different ways. All interactions concerning pupils' behaviour whether neutral, positive (praise) or negative (criticism), were recorded systematically at the time they occurred. For example, Teacher: 'You've tidied away very quickly. Well done!' (smiling) (PRAISE) Teacher: 'Be very sensible in the playground, won't you?' (NEUTRAL) Teacher: 'Stop this messing around at once!' (angry) (NEGATIVE) The teachers' general approach to discipline was also rated on a five-point scale at the end of each observation day.

The incidence of teachers' negative comments to pupils about behaviour decreased over the three years. By the third year, nearly half of the teachers were not heard to make any such remarks. Neutral comments, however, though slightly fewer in number in the first year, increased in the second year before decreasing slightly in the third year.

When considering the decline in critical control statements over the three years, it is interesting to note that the percentage of pupils with learning behaviour problems, as rated by teachers, also decreased over this period (from 14% to 11%). If teachers saw an improvement in pupils' ability to concentrate and their perseverance in learning as pupils became older, it is perhaps not surprising that they were able to devote less time to behaviour control.

Most teachers in each year tended to adopt a variety of control techniques, although this number decreased after the first year. Few teachers in any year were extreme in their manner of control either in terms of deterring poor behaviour through coercion (7% to 9%) or always encouraging pupil self-control (5% to 6%). However, there was a trend for some teachers in the second year to employ coercive means more frequently, whereas teachers in the first year tended to opt for more persuasive techniques. This may reflect a slight increase, in the second year, in the percentage of pupils identified as having aggressive behaviour problems (from 4% to 6%).

Teachers in all years were asked about their methods of dealing with good and bad behaviour. Response to good behaviour was largely confined to individual verbal praise (75% mentioned this), although a fifth of all teachers also stated that they indicated approval by means of facial expressions. Other less frequently mentioned techniques included: praising a pupil in front of the class (11%); giving stars or team points (17%); and sending the pupil to see the head or another teacher (8%).

Teachers were questioned at the same time about methods of praising good work or effort. Overall, there were almost four times as many mentions of work praise than praise for good behaviour though it was found from observations that teachers in fact praised pupils' work very infrequently. On average, less than one per cent of their time was spent in praising pupils. However, several teachers did report that they just 'expected good behaviour', and expressed some surprise at being asked how it was rewarded.

Poor behaviour elicited a variety of reactions from teachers. Most frequently cited sanctions for poor behaviour were verbal admonitions (61%) or keeping pupils in at playtime (60%). Sending pupils to the headteacher and withdrawal of privileges (which meant pupils missed educational visits or games sessions) were mentioned by around half of the teachers. There was some change in the way teachers dealt with poor behaviour over the three years. Reporting a strategy of discussing poor behaviour privately with the particular pupil increased substantially, from 18 per cent in the first year to 41 per cent in the third. Parents were also more likely to be informed about incidents in year three than in the first and second years.

The pattern of relationships between the frequency of reward and punishment techniques cited by teachers was remarkably consistent. For work, teachers were more likely to name a greater variety of rewards than punishments, whereas, in connection with behaviour the reverse was true; many more punishments than rewards were cited.

There was considerable variation in all years between teachers in their approach to classroom control. This variation was borne out by field officers in their case notes. Of one first year teacher, the field officer wrote: 'She definitely tried to praise rather than blame and if she had to criticise (always constructively) either an individual or the whole class, she always ended on a positive note'. Another field officer wrote about a first year teacher who had an extremely demanding child in her class: 'The teacher managed almost always to get to him before he did anything .... when he crawled past her feet to put away his milk bottle while she was telling the class a story, she ignored him and he crawled back past her again without a noise, then listened to the story'. But for one of the third year teachers the comments were very different: 'There was no perceptible system of discipline. The teacher turned a blind eye to flagrant breaches of normal classroom standards until the desk had to be banged or a child bellowed at'. Finally, of one teacher the field officer commented: 'He is rarely ruffled, mainly matter-of-fact, and uses reasoning, although this was hardly necessary today (and I've seen this class causing several problems in the past). He said of one of the most difficult children, he's OK, as long as you allow him to be a little bit naughty each day'.

TEACHERS BEYOND THE CLASSROOM

The class teacher's role, in so far as it is centred upon activity within the classroom, was discussed in the previous section. Further aspects of that role are considered here: the responsibilities of postholders; the extent to which teachers were encouraged to attend in-service training courses; the amount of non-teaching time that was available; the extent to which informal discussion of curriculum matters was possible, and the degree of job satisfaction felt by the teachers in the sample. In addition, the position of probationers, and the role of teachers with no class responsibility is examined. The problem of staff absence is also considered. Finally, the role of those teachers who had responsibility for special needs is described in detail.

Postholders

Altogether there were 279 teachers holding posts of responsibility, and these were spread out very unevenly amongst the schools, the largest one possessing 13 posts, the smallest ones only three. Nearly 90 per cent of postholders had responsibility for one area only. Most of these posts were for distinct areas of the curriculum. A sizeable minority of postholders, however, were responsible for more than one area. Most commonly this was a combination of two, or occasionally more, curriculum areas (such as mathematics and environmental studies, or art and drama).

When describing the duties of their postholders, most headteachers reported that they expected them to have a general oversight of a particular area. Apart from keeping an eye on things, however, a number of more specific duties and responsibilities were mentioned. The two most commonly cited were, first, that postholders should be responsible for maintaining and/or ordering resources, books, materials etc. Second, that postholders should be able, and prepared, to advise colleagues. Of the 279 posts described by headteachers, 44 per cent were held by teachers whose duties included the former, and 57 per cent were held by teachers whose duties included the latter. A substantial minority (22%) worked for some or, in a few cases, all of their time with children in their particular area. Thus, three quarters of all music postholders taught music to children other then those in their own classes. A few such postholders had no class teaching responsibilities at all. Similarly, 57 per cent of physical education and games postholders, and 19 per cent of art and craft postholders also spent at least some of their time working with children from other groups and classes.

Over the three years, 135 postholders were interviewed. Just over half reported that they had a number of duties and responsibilities including any, and in some cases all, of the ones noted above, plus the preparation of school guidelines, and the holding of workshops. Twenty-two per cent of teachers reported that their sole responsibility was the care and maintenance of equipment, whilst six per cent said their role was primarily that of adviser. The responses of a further six per cent were divided equally between teaching and the preparation of guidelines as major or sole duties. Four per cent reported that they had no particular duties or responsibilities.

More than half of the postholders had decided all, or most, of their responsibilities and priorities themselves. Only 36 per cent overall felt they had received adequate direction by the headteacher. It is perhaps a cause for concern that almost two-thirds felt they were under-used and would have liked to do more. Very few teachers reported that they wished for a change of post and only two per cent expressed a desire to do something completely different.

Headteachers were concerned with the nature of the posts, sometimes suggesting amalgamations, changes in their nature, or even their complete removal. Often this was because headteachers had inherited scale post structures when they were appointed, and were in the process of trying to effect change. As one head put it: 'Our thinking has moved on. Areas of responsibility ... need to be more curriculum-based'.

All of the postholders interviewed were also class teachers, for the most part with full responsibility for teaching their classes. Forty-two per cent of them felt that there were major disadvantages to combining these two roles, one third reporting the problem of too much work and not enough time. This particular problem was reported with increasing frequency in each of the three years. Very few teachers felt there were any clear advantages to their position, two per cent citing the opportunity to see other classes and other teachers at work, and a further five per cent reporting their appreciation of the chance to try out new ideas, and work with other teachers.

Attending courses

Teachers were asked whether they were encouraged to attend in-service training courses, and the vast majority reported that they were. Over two-thirds, at some time, had asked their headteachers if they could go on courses and in only two per cent of cases were such requests turned down. Some headteachers needed persuading but, on the whole, most were happy for their staff to go on courses. Headteachers and their deputies sometimes drew the attention of members of staff to particular courses. Nearly two-thirds of teachers reported that their headteachers had either suggested that they go, or had been willing to let them go. There were considerable differences between schools on this issue. Some heads clearly took into consideration the needs of the school before making a decision about allowing, or encouraging, teachers to attend courses.

Non-teaching time

In each of the three years, a substantial minority of teachers (44% overall) had either no non-teaching time or less than one period per week. Thirty-five per cent had more than one period, though the proportion fell from 45 per cent in year one to 25 per cent in year three.

Informal discussion

The vast majority of teachers had opportunities for discussing the curriculum informally with other members of staff and approximately two-thirds felt that the amount of discussion they had was about right. A further 25 per cent, however, felt they had too little discussion, and this proportion rose from 17 per cent in year one to 35 per cent in year three.

Teacher satisfaction

All the teachers in the sample were asked how satisfying they found their jobs as teachers and, when appropriate, how satisfying they found working in their present schools in comparison to schools they had taught in previously. Eighty-five per cent were either satisfied or very satisfied with their jobs, though a smaller proportion (62% overall) reported finding their present jobs just as satisfying as previous posts, or even more so. (These responses were elicited in the period prior to the 1985 teachers' pay claim and the ensuing industrial action.)

Probationary teachers

Sixteen probationers were involved at various times in teaching the sample: six in the first year, six in the second and four in the third year. The majority said that they were quite satisfied with the support they had received from their teacher tutors, though the amount of contact probationers had with their tutors varied, from once a fortnight to 'as often as required'. The majority also reported that they had been released, as part of divisional induction schemes, for all, or nearly all of the half days allocated for that purpose.

Staff absences

Almost half of the headteachers reported some problems with staff absence. Short-term absences were reported more commonly than long-term absences. In both cases, heads were concerned about very few teachers. Schools varied in the amount of teacher absence. For example, during the spring term 1983 in three schools there had been no absences noted, whereas in one school ten per cent of total teacher days were lost through absence.

Teachers with no class responsibility, specialist teachers and part-timers

In the third year almost two-thirds of the headteachers reported that they had members of staff who were not currently responsible for classes. The most common reason for deploying staff in this way was for special needs work. Other reasons included the need for floating teachers and the creation of supernumeraries through falling rolls.

Two hundred and forty one teachers from the sample schools who did not work with Project children completed questionnaires about their backgrounds, careers and (where appropriate) their posts of responsibility. Twenty-one per cent of the responses were from part-time teachers. The largest single group of part-timers were music teachers (35%). A further 18 per cent worked wholly, or for most of their time, in special needs teaching. Sixteen per cent covered all subjects, and another 20 per cent taught 'basic' subjects, and were expected to cover for absent colleagues.

Thirteen per cent of the teachers who completed the questionnaire made their contribution to the school through teaching particular subjects or skills. Again, the largest group were music teachers, comprising over two-thirds of specialist staff. Most of which were employed as general music teachers, less than half taught a particular instrument.

Special needs teachers

All except two of these teachers, known at the time of the study as remedial teachers, were women. With only one exception, all at some time had taken a class. More than half had spent five years or less in special needs work. Training for these teachers differed slightly from that of ordinary teachers with more people entering as graduates. A higher proportion of these teachers also had a least an element of secondary training (28%) in comparison with class teachers. Quite apart from their initial qualifications, 78 per cent had taken courses related to their present job.

A higher proportion of special needs teachers than of class teachers had taken breaks in their career to have children. A large minority had left teaching for a period of years for this purpose. A few had taken time out to further their academic qualifications.

At the time of interview, just over half were employed full-time by the school. Of these, all but four had posts of responsibility. In the main, the posts were related to language or special needs work.

The vast majority of special needs work in the schools was carried out in the area of language and reading. All of the teachers interviewed spent some time on reading and over three-quarters included work on written language. The majority of teachers (56%) also contributed to second language teaching, though for only three was it the major or sole responsibility. One quarter had separate ESL groups. Over three-quarters of the teachers were also responsible for dealing with children who had behaviour difficulties.

Almost all of the teachers interviewed kept records of their work. These ranged from the behaviour and attendance of the children to detailed comments on their progress in reading and writing. Most of the records kept were in these latter areas. Just over half of the teachers were prepared to show their records to others, either headteachers, class teachers or parents.

Discussion with other members of staff and parents
All of the special needs teachers said they were able to discuss the children they taught with at least some of the teachers from whose classes the children were drawn. At the time of interview, the vast majority had taken part in such a discussion during the previous week. Although many were satisfied with the nature of the contacts they had with teachers, just over a third expressed a wish for more formal discussions in staff meetings.

In contrast, far fewer special needs teachers felt able to discuss their work with language postholders. Of course not every school had such a postholder but, in those schools which did, almost a half of the special needs teachers felt either unwilling or unable to enter into discussion with the teacher responsible. Three-quarters of those who were unable to discuss their work said that they did not particularly want to, or that they did not feel it would be helpful. This is perhaps a reflection of the fact that language postholders and special needs teachers often have different attitudes towards, and approaches to, language teaching. The situation was reversed with mathematics in that almost 80 per cent of teachers interviewed reported no problems in discussing their work with the postholder though, of course, not many of the special needs teachers worked in this area. Approximately three-quarters of the special needs teachers made themselves available to talk to parents during parents' evenings, and two-thirds of this group reported that at least half of the parents invited would attend.

Conditions and constraints
Only half the teachers responsible for special needs teaching had their own room in which to work. A few worked in the school library and a few worked with the pupils in the classroom but, for a quarter, their workplace within the school varied according to the demands and pressures of school life. A similarly large minority reported that they were sometimes moved out, from wherever they were working and, for most of those who were moved out there was no particular alternative site, such as the library, to which they could retire. Three-quarters of the teachers said that they were sometimes interrupted.

Only 50 per cent of the special needs teachers were involved in deciding which children they should teach, though rather more helped in deciding when children should no longer attend. In both cases, the decisions tended to be taken on the basis of the experience and knowledge of those involved, though slightly more than half the teachers reported that some form of testing was used as an aid to deciding which children required special needs help.

The special needs teachers' views of their role
Sixty per cent of the special needs teachers interviewed found their job satisfying. The remainder expressed mixed views or were generally

dissatisfied. A number felt it was good to see the children progress. One teacher said: 'It's satisfying to be able to show children there are things they can do'. Another commented: 'I enjoy it very much, but I'm looking forward to getting back into the classroom'. A number of teachers remarked upon the differences between their current responsibilities, and those of the class teacher. One commented: 'It's vastly different from class teaching. I would like to work more closely with what children do in class'. When asked about their career development, about a fifth of the teachers felt they had gone as far as they could. A similar proportion expressed the desire to return to normal classroom teaching. In fact, three-quarters said that they did not see their careers developing in the special needs field.

ASSESSMENT AND RECORD KEEPING

Over and above the necessarily informal, though essential, assessments that teachers carry out from day to day, there are other types of assessments undertaken for specific school or class purposes. These include the allocation of children to teaching groups, and the monitoring of progress. Such assessments tend to be pursued in rather more formal ways and sometimes involve the use of tests.

Record keeping tends to be allied closely to the kinds of judgements that teachers make of their pupils. Sometimes records are kept simply in the form of samples of the children's work. More often, however, they are written by the teacher and involve notes on work successfully completed, and details of strengths and weaknesses. Some teachers also include items such as reading ages, acquired through a formal testing procedure.

In each year we asked class teachers of our pupil sample what forms their record keeping and assessments took, whether and in which areas they employed tests and kept records, and how they allocated children to groups. In addition, they were asked to rate the ability of the children in their classes at the beginning and end of each school year.

Tests used by teachers

Seventy-two per cent of teachers said they made some use of commercially produced tests to assess their pupils' reading. The proportion decreased from year one (77%) to year three (64%). Of the teachers who did use tests, the vast majority (68%) used only one. The most popular was the Schonell Graded Word Test. Half of the teachers who used reading tests made some use of this particular one. The next most popular were the Neale Analysis, and GAP tests.

In mathematics the situation was different. Far fewer teachers made use of commercially produced tests, and a much smaller range of tests was employed. Approximately two-thirds of the teachers made no use of tests at all. The most popular means of assessment in mathematics proved to be the Authority's own Checkpoints system. Almost half the teachers who said they used commercially produced tests, stated that they made use of this method of assessment. In addition, 29 per cent of teachers used National Foundation for Educational Research tests and 11 per cent drew upon the School Mathematics Project scheme.

The teachers were asked how frequently they used tests. For reading, the vast majority of those who used tests (87%) employed them either once or twice a year. For mathematics, however, almost a quarter used tests three times a year, and a similar proportion reported that they used them 'as necessary'.

In all curriculum areas the majority of teachers allocated children to groups on the basis of their knowledge of the children. For language and mathematics groups a minority of teachers used tests, and one teacher reported using tests for grouping children for history.

Class teachers' assessments of the ability of individual pupils

Information about class teachers' assessments of pupil ability was collected for individual children on a regular basis. Teachers were asked to rate each child in the class in terms of a five point scale. This ranged from very high ability to very low ability. The information was collected in the autumn and summer terms of the second and third years, to enable relationships between teachers' perceptions and children's attainment in cognitive assessments to be explored. It was also collected in order to establish whether pupils' background characteristics (specifically, age, sex, ethnic group and social class) were related to teachers' judgements. We report in detail on the findings of these analyses in Chapter Seven. Overall, there was good agreement between different teachers in their perceptions of the abilities of individual pupils. Only a tiny minority (2%) of children were assessed very differently in ratings made at different times. Furthermore, teachers' judgements of pupil ability were found to be strongly positively correlated with children's performance in each of the reading, writing and mathematics assessments made in the second and third years. The correlation between teachers' judgements of ability and children's skills in oral communication was slightly less strong. This suggests that performance in reading, writing and mathematics may be given greater weight than oral skills by teachers when they judge pupil ability.

Teachers' records

Each year, the class teachers were asked if they kept any records over and above the annual record sheet. Ninety-five per cent reported that they did so. The most frequently occurring type of record was a reading record in which details were kept of books and/or pages read by the children (71%). Sixty-one per cent kept records of areas covered in mathematics, but only 28 per cent did the same for language work. Very few teachers kept records of any kind in curriculum areas other than language and mathematics. The results of spelling tests were recorded more frequently than those of tables tests or reading tests (by 19% of teachers, 8% and 7% respectively). Twelve per cent made a record of the work covered by the whole class, and a tiny minority kept samples of the children's work.

SUMMARY

In this chapter we have concentrated upon variations between teachers in the ways they organised the pupils and work within the classroom. We have presented data on how teachers' time is spent. We have also reported on the sorts of interactions that occur between teachers and pupils. Finally, we have commented upon the records kept of pupils' work and behaviour.

5

The Curriculum

In Chapter 4 we described the teacher in the classroom. A major facet of life in a junior classroom must be the curriculum and in this chapter we will attempt to describe how it was delivered in our sample schools.

In studying the school curriculum, it is important to keep in mind that what teachers plan for their pupils to learn, only has effect when it is enacted or realised by the pupils themselves. Barnes (1976) points out that, 'a curriculum made only of teachers' intentions would be an insubstantial thing' (p. 14). In addition it is just as important to look at the way particular curriculum areas are taught, as it is to examine the subject matter itself. As HMI (1985) have stressed: 'Teaching and learning styles strongly influence the curriculum and in practice cannot be separated from it' (p. 7). They warn that, 'it is too easy to define the content of each subject with no reference whatever to the learning processes to be used' (p. 9).

Here we shall examine not only aspects of teachers' intentions but how those intentions were worked out in the classroom. In particular, we shall report how teachers divided up the subject matter of the curriculum; the strategies teachers employed when teaching in their chosen curriculum areas; the interactions that took place between pupils and teachers concerning classroom work, and the guidelines, books and other resources used to give substance to curriculum plans.

DIVIDING THE CURRICULUM

Unlike their counterparts in secondary schools, who are bound by fairly rigid subject divisions, primary teachers enjoy considerable freedom to determine how the subject matter appropriate to their age group should be divided. The teachers in the sample detailed the areas in which they worked with their children and these included language, mathematics, history, geography, science, project/topic work, environmental studies, biology, social studies, physical education, music, drama, religious education, and art. Not every area was named by each teacher. Some areas, such as geography or history, were mentioned by very few. The variation was very largely the result of the degree to which individual teachers chose to replace smaller subject divisions by broader areas such as project work or environmental studies. Some teachers chose to maintain the traditional boundaries, keeping each subject area separate, whereas at the opposite extreme, a few teachers attempted to organise almost the entire curriculum around a particular project theme.

It would be a mistake, however, to consider teachers as varying in this respect along a simple sliding scale with maximum subject separation at one pole, and minimum separation at the opposite pole. The poles are not necessarily mutually exclusive; it is quite feasible to teach both separate subjects and integrated projects, and we observed many teachers who adopted both these practices. Nevertheless we found it was possible to indicate roughly the extent to which teachers in the sample were prepared to integrate different areas.

Distinct or integrated subjects

The five categories described below were based upon the accounts given by teachers of the curricular areas they taught, and the extent to which they used project work (or an equivalent) to cover broad areas of the curriculum. Their attitudes towards subject areas and their combination and/or separation had also to be considered. The information was obtained for all class teachers of the pupil sample during the second year. The teachers could be allocated roughly into the following groups.

Group 1. Six teachers (7%) who divided the curriculum into distinct subjects, with no project work, and no attempt at integration.

Group 2. Twelve teachers (14%) who taught all, or nearly all, subjects separately, but made some attempt at integration, e.g. , they might have one project lesson each week.

Group 3. Twenty-six teachers (31%) who taught mathematics and language separately (as well as physical education, music, games etc.), but integrated other curricular areas such as history, geography, and science into project work.

Group 4. Thirty-three teachers (39%) who taught mathematics and language separately, (along with P.E., games, music etc.), but also integrated them into project work whenever they felt it was appropriate. For these teachers, however, the emphasis was upon mathematics and language being taught separately, even though they might be integrated too.

Group 5. Seven teachers (8%) who taught all, or nearly all, subjects (excepting PE, games, music etc.) in an integrated way within projects. Mathematics and language were sometimes taught separately, but the emphasis was upon as near complete integration as possible.

All the teachers in the sample taught at least some mathematics as a distinct subject, and almost all taught language in the same way.

There were four (three from group 5, and one from group 4) who integrated all their language work into projects. Overall, the teachers were more likely as a group to avoid integrating mathematics into project work, and conversely more likely to adopt such integration for language.

Thus although it is difficult to give a simple account of how the teachers divided up the curriculum, there was clearly a tendency to favour some, but not full, subject integration. Most teachers preferred to unify as much of the curriculum as possible through project or topic themes, whilst retaining the distinct character of subjects such as mathematics, and to some extent, language work.

STRATEGIES EMPLOYED BY TEACHERS

Moving from organisation of the subject matter to the organisation of the teachers' time, we can now consider three broad inter-connecting issues. First, how the curriculum, as outlined above, was divided up during the individual teaching sessions; second, the issue of classroom groupings (i.e. how the classes, rather than the subject areas, were divided up); and third, the amount of freedom children were given by their teachers to organise and direct their own work.

The distribution of subjects in teaching sessions

Teachers tended to prefer teaching in one curriculum area at a time. Almost three-quarters of the observations took place during single subject lessons, the remainder occurring when the children were working in more than one curriculum area. Interestingly this is in strong contrast to the amount of time teachers reported (in interview) that they spent on teaching single subjects. During these sessions classes worked in up to five different areas but, in just under a half, they were divided into only two. Some subjects were observed more often as distinct separate lessons than in combination with other subjects. This happened, for example, in history, drama, and project work. Other subjects, such as art and craft, were observed far more frequently in combination (78% of all art and craft observations in one year showed the subject in combination with other curricular areas). Mathematics and language were observed far more frequently than any other subject areas. Eighteen per cent of all observations occurred when the classes were working solely on mathematics and 15 per cent when they worked solely on language.

Classroom groupings

The traditional approach to the study of classroom groupings has been to consider three levels: the individual pupil, the group, and the class. Classroom groups, however, can take a number of forms and have a variety of functions. Galton et al (1980) identify three types: the 'base' group; the 'curriculum' group; and the more ad hoc kind of group which they describe as being 'evanescent' or 'ephemeral'. Particular children within a class may belong to any or all of the three types of groups. The possibilities, however, are not exhausted with these three, and as Galton et al point out: 'Many junior school classrooms develop a complex internal structure, the dynamics of which are difficult to comprehend by a visitor'. (p.68)

In addition to considerations of how pupils are grouped in classrooms, there are the parallel issues of how much of the teacher's time is spent interacting with classes, groups and individuals, and the extent to which teachers organise work at these levels. When all these factors are considered, the possible variations in teacher behaviour become so complex that they are not readily describable in terms of simple teaching styles or approaches, a strategy that has been adopted in previous studies (see Bennett, 1976; Galton et al, 1980). In fact, our analyses of observational data (using the technique of probabalistic clustering) indicated that teachers could not validly be divided into a number of categories on the basis of differences in teaching style. Teaching strategies were much more complex than the notion of teaching style implies.

Criteria for group membership

Of those teachers who did make some use of groups, (70% of the total), the vast majority based at least some, if not all, groups on the ability of the children. For approximately half (49%) this was the sole criterion employed. Only one-third made use of more than one set of criteria for determining group membership. These teachers reported that they would group children of similar ability together for those subjects they considered to be basic (usually language and mathematics) but use other criteria, such as mixed ability, friendship or a random selection for groups in other curriculum areas and for other functions.

Time spent on classes, groups and individuals

We have seen, in the section on planning, that there was a decided preference amongst teachers for grouping tables together, rather than positioning them in rows. Despite this, only 13 per cent said they spent more time on groups than on individuals or on the class as a whole.

The percentage of teachers who reported that they spent more time on individuals than on either groups or the class increased from 21 per cent in year one to 34 per cent in the third year. There was a similar increase in the percentages who said they spent more time on groups and on the class. In contrast, there was a decrease over the three years in the proportion of teachers who said they spent most of their time on a mixture of audiences: class, group or individual. This fell from more than a half to under a quarter.

A very different perspective, however, is provided by the records, made during classroom observation, of the kinds of audience with which teachers interacted. In the second year, for example, 23 per cent of all teachers' communications were with the whole class, nine per cent were with groups, and 67 per cent were with individuals. In the third year the comparable figures were: 24 per cent class, 11 per cent group and 63 per cent individual. In fact, teachers spent most of their time talking to individuals and the pupils most usually worked alone (68% of observed time).

Interestingly, the relative amounts of teacher time on these interactions remain broadly similar, irrespective of the stated preferences of teachers. Thus, for example, it made little difference whether teachers reported spending more time on groups or on classes: in both cases they actually spent much more time in each of the three years communicating with individuals. It is clear that, although teachers were asked whether they spent more time on the class as a whole, or with groups or with individuals, their replies were influenced by their perceptions of their work organisation rather than by their classroom acts.

Although collaborative and co-operative group work was observed far less frequently than other forms of activity, a number of teachers did encourage inter-pupil co-operation within their classrooms. The proportion of lessons where co-operation and collaboration were encouraged increased over the three years.

In conclusion, most teachers made use of groups when organising their classrooms and many grouped children of similar ability together, particularly in basic subject areas. However, teachers tended to communicate more frequently with individual pupils than with groups of children or with the class as a whole, though there were clear differences in the perceptions of teachers when they were asked to consider how much time they spent on the three different levels. Not a great deal of collaborative work was observed.

Work direction

Although teachers ultimately must take responsibility for the organisation and direction of the curriculum within the classroom, they often vary in the degree to which they permit or encourage children to direct the course of their own work. The extent to which the sample children were free in this respect has been examined from three distinct, but related, points of view. First, the extent to which the children were able to manage their work once it had been allocated to them. Second, the extent to which children were given responsibility for organising a programme of work for a whole day, or a part of a day. Third, the extent to which the children were encouraged to make choices relating to the content of the work they did. Some children demonstrated competence in work management in the majority of sessions observed over three years (64%), and in a large minority of sessions (25%), there were few signs of teacher control once tasks had been allocated.

In all three years it was found that the vast majority of teachers preferred to instruct tasks singly, and to retain almost complete control over the amount of time spent on the work, and the way in which the work was undertaken, except in areas that the teacher considered peripheral. Pupils were able to exercise control over an extended programme of work only in a small minority of lessons (under 15%). Similarly, in the majority of sessions observed in each of the three years, the work to be undertaken was determined largely by the teachers alone, with the children, at most, having a limited degree of choice in a restricted range of contexts.

TEACHERS' AND PUPILS' WORK CONTACTS

The main purpose of the classroom observation was to record the contacts that took place between teachers and pupils. The interactions described here are those that derive from situations where the children were work-oriented and are grouped into: communication of factual information (extending knowledge); higher-order contacts (encouraging problem-solving); task supervision; and feedback on work.

Communication of factual information

In contacts of this type the teacher, 'either by means of questioning or providing statements refers to the substantive content of the topic under study or investigation ... be it practical or theoretical' (Boydell, 1974a). The aim is to build upon the children's repertoire of information. For example:
Statement: 'Like many other animals, hedgehogs hibernate in the winter'.
Question: 'How wide is the playground?'
The use of questioning, aimed at building upon the children's learning, tended to be less frequent than the straightforward statement of facts.

For both the use of questions and of statements there were considerable variations among teachers. In each year, some teachers were never observed asking factual questions whilst, for others, ten per cent of observed time was taken up in this way. The range between teachers was even wider for factual statements, particularly in the third year when some teachers were not heard to make any.

Higher-order contacts

Questions and statements by the teacher which are classified as higher-order encourage pupils to make more reasoned or imaginative responses to their work. For example:

Teacher: 'To find the price of the pair you have to multiply by two because the price is only given for one.'

Teacher: 'What different ways can you think of to measure the length of the classroom?'

Teacher: 'How do you think the story will end?'

Teachers were seen to spend a much smaller amount of their time using statements or questions of this kind than those which require factual answers. The figures were even smaller for open questions, where the teacher was prepared to accept more than one answer, than for closed questions where a particular response was expected. Over two-thirds of the teachers were observed to make no use of open-ended questions. Over the three years only one per cent of observed time was devoted to questions requiring problem-solving. Teachers made a similar number of statements offering reasoned or imaginative statements. Once again, approximately one per cent of observed classroom time was taken up in this way. Individual teachers, however, showed considerable differences in the use of higher-order questions and statements.

Approximately one-tenth of all teachers' time was concerned with the detailed content of children's work. There was, however, substantial variation between teachers in the amount of time they spent communicating about 'task' matters. For example, the second year, one in ten of class teachers devoted less than six per cent of their time to this kind of work contact. In contrast, at the other extreme one in ten spent over 17 per cent of their time communicating in this way.

Questions and statements concerned with task supervision

Contacts of this type are concerned with telling children what to do or how to do it, and with ascertaining whether instructions have been understood. For example:

Teacher: 'Draw a picture at the end of your story.'

Teacher: 'Drop the penny into the water like this.'

Teacher: 'Can you remember how to use this apparatus?'

The amount of time teachers devoted to task supervision varied from none to almost a fifth. Overall, approximately 11 per cent of observed teacher-pupil communications were of this type. Task supervision questions were observed less often than task supervision statements. Once work was under way, teachers tended to spend no more than three per cent of their time supervising work by means of questions, and the amount of time varied very little across the three years.

Feedback on work

This includes verbal comments or non-verbal feedback, as in the form of marking. We sub-divided such feedback into three types: neutral, praise and criticism. These judgements were frequently accompanied by directives which tell the children how to correct or improve their work.

Over a tenth of teachers' time was involved in giving neutral feedback about work. In each year, there were some teachers whose use of neutral feedback statements was much higher or lower than the average (11.5%), some teachers communicating in this way for one-quarter of all observed time and others for barely two per cent. Positive feedback, in the form of praise about work, was observed very infrequently (1% overall), and over the three years there was a decrease in the amount noted.

In addition to giving verbal feedback, teachers often spent considerable amounts of time marking children's work. Marking carried out in the presence of the children was observed more frequently in the third year than in other years, whereas verbal feedback decreased from year two to year three.

Approximately two-fifths of the teachers' time, as observed in the classroom, was taken up with contacts about the work the children were doing, or intending to do. A fairly large proportion (12%) was given over to neutral feedback, and similar proportions were devoted to the substantive content of tasks, and to their supervision. In all areas, there were marked variations between teachers in their use of different kinds of communications.

MATERIALS AND RESOURCES

The teachers in the sample drew upon a variety of different resources for their lessons. Many made use of duplicated worksheets or workcards, though blackboards were utilised by approximately half the teachers. The proportion of teachers drawing upon textbooks for ideas in mathematics (73%) was considerably greater than the proportion using their own ideas and experience (46%), but in language this relationship was reversed.

Half of the teachers who spoke about art and craft said they drew ideas for lessons from current projects within the school. A few mentioned using children's ideas, though it has been noted already that such ideas were rarely taken up in teaching sessions. Some used visits as sources of ideas in this area, and nearly two-thirds (63%) saw such visits as an important stimulus for project work. The teachers quite frequently made use of the environment beyond the classroom; 63 per cent took children out to work in the playground, the park or local streets. They also ventured further afield on day trips to theatres, museums, cinemas, historical sites and, for longer periods, on school journeys. Seventeen per cent of teachers overall had taken their classes to the theatre or cinema by the end of the first term in each year, and another 40 per cent had taken groups of children. Nineteen per cent had visited a museum with their classes, and a further three per cent had made two such visits.

DIFFERENT CURRICULUM AREAS

The teaching of reading

The vast majority of teachers made use of reading schemes, though the use of such schemes declined slightly over the three years. In the first year all teachers used at least one scheme, and most made use of more than one. By the third year, however, a sizeable minority (19%) reported that they either used no schemes at all or only for a minority of children. This figure probably represents the percentage of teachers who, by the third year, considered their children to be competent enough to choose their own books outside the range of a graded reading scheme. It may also reflect an increasing trend, over the last few years, away from the use of published reading schemes and towards an emphasis upon the use of individual children's books.

Eighty-nine per cent of second year teachers reported that they listened to all of the children read. Most of the remaining teachers concentrated either on the poorer readers, or on all except the better ones. Most children read to their teachers individually though, in a few classrooms, the teachers preferred to group children for reading, or to read around the class.

Observation showed that the amount of time teachers spent on hearing children read fell steadily from just over five per cent in year one to almost two and a half per cent in year three. This can perhaps be explained in terms of the children's overall increase in competence and experience in reading as they moved up the school. In the third year, half the teachers did not hear any children read during observed sessions, though they may have done so when the observer was not present.

Teachers provided their children with experience of a range of books by regularly reading stories to them. This activity frequently took place at the end of the school day or, sometimes, at the end of another teaching session. This usually involved the whole class. Overall, three per cent of classroom time was taken up with storytelling, though the proportion increased from just over two and a half per cent in year one to four per cent in year three.

Slightly more than half the teachers reported that they made use of other adults to assist with hearing children read and, in approximately three-quarters of the classrooms, children were expected either to be reading or working quietly whilst the teacher listened to readers. In the remaining classrooms the main body of the class would be working normally.

More detailed observation of quiet reading sessions in year three showed that teachers spoke more frequently to boys and heard them read more often than girls (57% boys, 43% girls). Communication with individual pupils was more common than for other curriculum areas observed and conversely there was very little communication with the whole class; less than for any other single activity.

Just under a tenth of teachers' time when hearing reading was spent talking to pupils about the content of their reading books. Teachers more commonly gave pupils information than asked questions (64% versus 36%). It appeared, however, that pupils needed little direction or supervision in reading sessions. Only 13 per cent of teacher time was devoted to telling pupils what to do, whereas the equivalent figure for mathematics sessions was 31 per cent. Routine management also took up only a small percentage of time in reading sessions (15%). This was similar to other areas of the curriculum, with the exception of art and craft, where more time was given over to routine directions concerning materials. For just over a quarter of the time during reading sessions teachers did not communicate with pupils at all.

The teaching of language

Almost all the teachers (95%) taught language as a separate subject but, of these, nearly half also included it in project work. Areas such as creative writing, storytelling, poetry, comprehension, spelling and grammar were covered in language work. Seven teachers also explicitly included oral work. Unlike mathematics, most teachers did not rely on a particular textbook for their language work, and a few used none at all. The most popular texts, in terms of the number of teachers who named them, were the 'Sound Sense' series (34%) and the Science Research Associates (S.R.A.) workcard series (25%). Children of different abilities were given different work according to their capability in 80 per cent of classes. Somewhat surprisingly, teachers of mixed-age classes did not tend to vary the work substantially for pupils of different ages.

A number of teachers stressed that language came into all areas of the curriculum, being particularly linked with project, history and aesthetic work. Observations of third year language sessions showed that 75 per cent of contacts were between teachers and individual pupils, which is more than for all other curriculum areas taught singly, apart from quiet reading sessions. Interactions with groups were very infrequent (8%). Boys were asked twice as many supervisory questions as girls and also more questions unrelated to work. In language work, teachers spent more of their time interacting with pupils than in any other curriculum area apart from mathematics.

The teaching of mathematics

This included all types of number, spatial and practical mathematical work. As already noted, most teachers used textbooks, and drew on several different schemes. The most frequently used texts were the 'Fletcher' series, used by 40 per cent, followed by 'Maths Adventure' (31%), and the 'Scottish Primary Maths' workbooks, used by one-fifth of teachers. Although most teachers followed one book as their main source, few worked right through any book. Practical equipment, such as scales and counting rods, was used by two-thirds of the teachers, and one-fifth watched television or listened to radio programmes with their classes. Only 15 per cent of teachers did not vary the work they presented to children of different abilities. Mathematics work was set more frequently for individuals than for groups.

Teachers varied in their overall strategies for mathematics teaching. The use of guidelines has already been reported. Some teachers worked through schemes, such as the Scottish Primary Mathematics series, covering different topics each time they occurred in the workbook. Others preferred to take an area at a time – say weight – and draw from different texts and a variety of materials.

A substantial minority (28%) of the teachers stressed the importance of giving the children experience of practical work in mathematics. Just under 10 per cent were dissatisfied with the resources available for mathematics work in their schools. Seventeen per cent who incorporated mathematical work into other areas of the curriculum – particularly project work – emphasised that the children should be taught that mathematics was involved in many areas of their lives.

Although more than two-thirds of teachers' communications in mathematics sessions in year three were directed at individual pupils, they talked to groups of pupils more frequently than during other sessions. Questioning was also a more common feature of mathematics lessons (13%) than of lessons in other areas (between 5% and 9%). A quarter of teachers' questions were directed at the whole class. In comparison with other curriculum areas, in mathematics sessions, teachers devoted more time to discussions concerning the work itself and its supervision (31%, compared with 13% to 29% for other curriculum areas) and less time to routine matters (14% compared with 15% to 23% for other areas).

The teaching of project work

Some form of project or topic activity was included in the curriculum of most classes (86%). A wide variety of subjects were covered during project work. These included: mathematics, language, art, science, history, geography, drama, physical education, music, religious education, environmental studies, social studies, and current affairs. These subjects were taught in many combinations. However, the areas most commonly included in project work were geography, history and science. The average number of projects completed over the year was three. Specific textbooks were used by less than half the teachers for project work and, even then, they tended to be referred to only occasionally. Library books were a more common resource, both for the children's use and as a source for teacher-produced worksheets or cards, and discussions. It was for project and topic work that teachers made most use of educational visits, and a substantial minority (38%) followed television and radio programmes.

In contrast to language and mathematics work, only a minority of teachers (33%) varied the work for pupils of different ability in project sessions. Thus, usually all the pupils were given the same work when the whole class was involved in one project. In just under half the classes, pupils worked on individual projects as well as, or instead of, class projects. The subject matter for these was chosen either by the pupils themselves, the teacher, or by both together.

Some teachers stressed the use of project work to integrate different areas of the curriculum; others emphasised its importance in enabling children to express their own ideas and interests. A few teachers stressed that project work had a beneficial effect upon children who were not normally interested in other areas of the curriculum. A small number of teachers, however, felt restricted by a lack of resources or guidance for project activities, or a lack of emphasis on project work in the school's policy. Project sessions involved a higher amount of teacher communication with the whole class than any other area apart from art. Boys were questioned considerably more than girls concerning non-work issues and, apart from during art and craft sessions, the amount of time discussing routine matters was the highest (18%). Teachers also spent more than a quarter of their time not communicating with any pupils in project sessions. Housekeeping activities (general organisation and preparation of materials around the classroom, not involving communication with pupils) took up more of their time (11%) than in any other sessions, apart from art and craft. Although there was little difference between project and language sessions in the overall amount of time teachers devoted to work discussion, they only asked half as many questions directly about work during project sessions.

The teaching of art and craft

The majority of teachers (77%) integrated art and craft into project or other ongoing work. More than three-quarters of these, however, also taught separate art lessons. A variety of media and techniques were offered by teachers, and more than a third made particular reference to the importance of giving children some experience of working in different media and of using varying techniques. Nonetheless, the most popular activity was painting, closely followed by drawing. Needlework was included as part of the pupils' activities by 63 per cent of teachers and three-dimensional work was mentioned by more than half. Textiles, printing and clay work were experienced in a substantial minority of classes. The teachers were fairly equally divided into those who tended to give all the pupils the same activity to do and those who provided several art activities within one session.

Ten teachers particularly mentioned courses at teachers' centres as providing source material for their art work. However, the most popular source, mentioned by nearly half the teachers, was project/topic work. The teachers' own ideas and experience were also important for a substantial minority (37%), whereas a few teachers obtained ideas directly from their pupils.

In third year art and craft lessons, comments were directed to the whole class more frequently than during other sessions. Teachers devoted more time to routine matters and less to the content of the work than for any other curriculum area observed. Routine statements were also more frequently directed to the whole class than during other sessions. The use of questioning during art sessions was extremely rare (5% of all observations).

More housekeeping activities were observed during art (13%) than during other lessons, and teachers did not communicate with pupils during 35 per cent of all observed sessions. This was considerably more than in any other curriculum area.

The teaching of physical education

More than 70 per cent of teachers stated that their PE work was organised to promote the acquisition of specific skills (including body skills of control, balance and co-ordination and activity-related skills such as ball skills). Over half the teachers indicated that they structured their physical education sessions, although only 23 per cent mentioned that they included a preliminary warming up time at the beginning. A thematic approach, for example travelling, was adopted by a minority (17%). The content of sessions varied. Outdoor games was the most popular activity in terms of the numbers of teachers who included these in their physical education sessions (86%). Just under three-quarters of teachers reported that they regularly made use of large apparatus.

Observations during sessions involving more than one curriculum area

When mixed-activity sessions were observed in year three, the majority of teacher interactions were with individual pupils (84%) and very few comments were directed to the whole class (4%). Teachers also talked more frequently to boys than to girls, particularly during the supervision of and feedback concerning pupils' work.

Less teacher time was devoted to talking about the content of pupils' work during mixed-activity sessions than during sessions involving any single curriculum area (with the exception of art). Teachers devoted one quarter of their time to supervising pupils, approximately the same as they devoted during project and topic sessions.

Monitoring of pupils was a more frequent occurrence in mixed-activity than during language, mathematics, project, art or reading sessions (9%, compared with 5% to 6% for all the others). In addition, the teachers' overall level of communication with pupils was lower in sessions where pupils were working on various different curriculum areas, than was the case during mathematics, language and quiet reading sessions. It was, however, still higher than for other single activity lessons.

SUMMARY

In this chapter we have described the curriculum that we observed in the classrooms of our sample schools. In doing this we have examined the strategies of the teachers, their interactions with pupils and any differences we found between difficult curriculum areas. For all curriculum areas, communication with individual pupils was more common than communication with the whole class or with groups – with more than two thirds of all contacts being devoted to individuals. Boys had more contact with their teachers than girls in all subjects, particularly in sessions where more than one curriculum area was covered.

6

Pupils' Progress

We have already described many aspects of the 50 schools and the characteristics of their heads and teachers. In this chapter the focus turns to the pupils attending the sample schools. First, we examine the pupils at the time of their entry into junior schools. We then discuss the relationships between children's attainments in different areas over the duration of the study.

THE CHARACTERISTICS OF THE PUPIL SAMPLE

Our analyses have confirmed that pupil intakes to the sample of 50 schools included in the Project were representative of junior age pupils in the Authority as a whole. In comparison with children nationally, however, the pupil sample is bound to reflect the characteristics of children living in an inner city area. Thus, the percentage of children from one parent families, ethnic minority groups, those using English as a second language, and those receiving free school meals, are probably higher than figures for the country as a whole. Unfortunately, it is not possible to compare our pupils with national figures directly except for the free meals factor. At the start of the study nearly 31 per cent of the pupils received free school meals, compared with under 21 per cent nationally (Chartered Institute of Public Finance and Accountancy (CIPFA) figures for 1980/81).

Language and ethnic background

Overall, 40 per cent of the pupils were from black and other ethnic minority groups - a reflection of the ethnic composition of the inner London population as a whole. The largest ethnic groups were those of Caribbean backgrounds (nearly 13%) and those of Asian backgrounds (7%). At entry nearly 16 per cent of children did not use English as their first language, according to their teachers' reports. A total of 34 different languages (other than English) were identified by class teachers as the first language spoken by individual children in the pupil sample. The total may have been higher because, in a few cases, teachers could not identify the language spoken by particular children. The most commonly spoken language, amongst the sample, was Greek, followed by Bengali/Sylheti, Urdu, Turkish and Gujerati. Nonetheless about half of the pupils who did not use English as a first language were assessed as fully fluent in speaking English by their teachers. Of the total sample eight per cent of children were classified as not fully fluent in English at entry to junior school.

Parental occupations

The majority of the children's mothers were economically inactive, that is, not in paid employment (59%). This reflects the child care responsibilities taken on by the mothers of these pupils, the majority of whom had two or more children. Of the working mothers, roughly equal proportions were in non-manual as were in manual work. In contrast to the fathers of the pupil sample, only three per cent of mothers were in skilled manual work (the equivalent figure for fathers was 35%). Overall, if those pupils whose fathers were absent are excluded, the majority of children were drawn from manual, or work-ing class, backgrounds (61%). This proved to be fairly representative of the social class composition of the economically active population of inner London.

In the first year of the study, six per cent of pupils' fathers were in long-term unemployment. By the third year of junior school, however, the proportion of unemployed had risen to ten per cent. Moreover, if fathers who were absent (and for whom no occupational data were available) are excluded from the calculations, it is clear that a sizeable minority of pupils were from homes where the father was unemployed (8% of pupils in the first year and 13% in the third year). This latest figure is very similar to the male unemployment rate in the summer of 1983 (around 14% in inner London). This increase in the incidence of unemployment in the families of our sample reflects the general deteriorating economic situation in London during the 1980s, and its impact on jobs.

A much higher percentage of fathers than mothers were absent from their child's home. Thus, at age seven, 17 per cent of children were in families where the father was absent, compared with only two per cent in homes where the mother was absent. Over the next three years the percentage of children in families where the father was absent increased to nearly a quarter, but there was very little change in the percentage of children in homes where the mother was absent.

Income levels

In terms of income levels, the only measure that could be collected (without intruding into the personal life of families) was the child's eligiblity for free school meals. This provides some indication of low family income. Nearly 31 per cent of the pupils were eligible for free school meals at the start of the Project and, by the third year, this had risen to about 40 per cent. This reflects the increase in pupils from one parent families and those whose fathers were unemployed. Thus, over the period of the study there was a general deterioration in the economic circumstances of a sizeable minority of the sample. This finding is in line with those reported by Hunter et al 1985, on increases in disadvantage amongst London school children.

Family size

Family size can have an influence on the level of family 'resources' (both financial and those of parental attention) available for individual children. The majority of the sample were from families with two children (nearly 43%) but 16 per cent were only children, and 18 per cent were from larger families (with four or more children). In terms of position in the family, the largest groups were first born (40.2%), and only one in ten children were fourth born or later.

Nursery and infant experience and age of entry to school

The majority of children had experienced some form of nursery education (nearly 73%). However, there was much variation in the amount of time spent in nursery class or school. Some children had attended only part-time for one or two terms, whilst others had several terms of full-time experience. Fourteen per cent of children had experienced the equivalent of only one term, or part of a term in a nursery class or school. Seventeen per cent had attended for more than one, but less than three, terms. In all, a quarter of the children had spent four or more terms in some form of nursery education. More than 62 per cent of the sample had entered school before they were five, and nearly one in ten before the age of four years eight months (see Figure 6.1). A minority of children (17% in all) had not entered school until they were more than five years and one month old.

There was marked variation in the amount of time that children had spent in school infant departments. Nearly a third of the children had spent only 28 months or less in infant school, whilst a third had 35 or more months of infant experience. The length of time spent in infant school was very closely related to pupils' age. Those who were born in the autumn term had experienced significantly more time in infant school than had their summer born peers. This in part reflects the ILEA's policy of admitting pupils to infant school in the term of their fifth birthday.

Figure 6.1: Differences between pupils in terms of age at entry to school

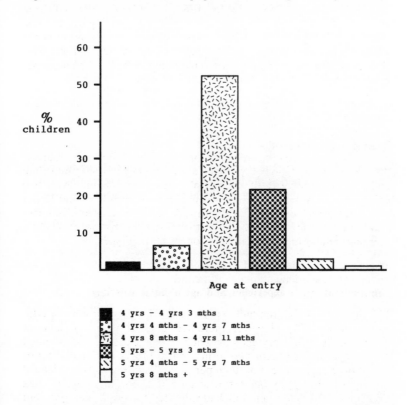

Age at entry

■	4 yrs – 4 yrs 3 mths
▦	4 yrs 4 mths – 4 yrs 7 mths
▨	4 yrs 8 mths – 4 yrs 11 mths
▨	5 yrs – 5 yrs 3 mths
▨	5 yrs 4 mths – 5 yrs 7 mths
□	5 yrs 8 mths +

Handicaps and health problems

Class teachers provided details of any handicaps or health problems experienced by the children who were members of their classes at the end of the first year. In their teachers' view, the vast majority of pupils (87%) had no problems, although it is likely that some children may have had problems of which teachers were unaware. A minority of children, around one in 14, were identified as having problems with hearing, sight or speech. Two per cent of the sample had hearing problems, and five per cent poor eyesight. Less than one in a 100 was reported to have a speech defect. These difficulties might be expected to be related to educational outcomes if left unattended.

Serious physical diseases, such as leukaemia or epilepsy, affected only a handful of pupils (around 10 in all) and asthma was reported in only 15 cases.

The pupils were assessed in various cognitive areas at entry to junior school. In addition, details about their behaviour at entry were collected from class teachers. This information was obtained to provide a baseline against which progress of individual children in later years could be assessed, and to ensure adequate account could be taken of differences in the characteristics of the intakes received by the 50 schools. Only by assessing progress, is it possible to take account of the enormous differences in pupil attainment which are evident even at the start of junior education.

Reading and mathematics

Marked differences in the reading and mathematics skills of individual pupils were identified at the beginning of their junior schooling. Thus, in terms of the reading assessment (where the maximum score possible was 91), the average score was 46 points. However, a quarter of the sample obtained scores of 24 points or lower, and a quarter scored 68 or more. This represents a very marked variation in reading ages, exceeding one year four months. Some children had reading skills equivalent to children aged over eight years four months, whereas others were experiencing major difficulties.

In mathematics, a similar range of attainment was identified. In this case, the maximum score possible was 40 points. A quarter of the children scored more than 29 marks, and a quarter obtained 19 or fewer marks. The average for the sample was 24 points – equivalent to the attainment of the average seven year old. These results are in broad agreement with the findings of the Infant School Project undertaken by the Thomas Coram Unit in ILEA infant schools. This study also identified marked differences between pupils at entry to nursery and at entry to infant education in terms of reading related skills (see Blatchford et al, 1985).

Writing

As with other cognitive assessments, there were also marked differences between children in terms of writing skills in the first year. Experienced junior teachers assessed the children's work in terms of quality of language and ideas, and more technical aspects such as legibility, use of punctuation and length. Differences were identified between children's performance in both qualitative and technical aspects (and the two were found to be quite closely related at this stage).

Some children's work (around 18%) showed a sophisticated use of language, a sense of audience and use of adjectives, adverbs, similes or metaphors. Nearly half of our sample's stories showed some sense of audience and read fairly well, though pupils generally used rather pedestrian language. A third of the children, however, showed little or no sense of audience in their work, used little variety in their language and produced stories which were difficult to read. In all, 16 per cent of pupils produced written work with a clear storyline – well expressed and clearly developed ideas which were well connected. At this age, however, in 31 per cent of pupils' written work, the storyline was unclear or absent, and ideas were sketchy and not well connected. A measure of maturity (a scale related to the 'sense of other people') showed that the majority of first year children showed little or no sense of other people in their writing (in terms of thoughts, motivations or characterisation).

The vast majority of children (86%), though, produced very legible work in their first year and, at this stage, most continued to use a clear, well-formed print script. There were differences, however, in the use of punctuation. Over 57 per cent made minimal or no use of punctuation, whereas only a fifth generally used capitals and full stops correctly. A minority made use of more sophisticated punctuation in the first year of junior education.

There were also marked differences between pupils in the word length of stories produced. Over a quarter of children wrote 115 words or more, but a quarter wrote less than 52 words. Only three children wrote nothing. The average length for first year writing was 88 words.

Behaviour

Information was collected about children's behaviour in school using the 'Child at School' schedule. This was completed on an individual basis for each child by their own class teacher. The behaviour schedule measured three aspects of disturbance – aggression, anxiety and learning problems. (See Kysel et al, 1983, for details of this instrument.) It is, of course, possible for a child to be assessed as having more than one type of behaviour difficulty. Substantial variation between children was identified in terms of the teachers' assessments of behaviour. Figure 6.2 shows the percentage of pupils assessed as having any kind of behaviour disturbance (over 17%). Learning problems were more common (affecting 13%) than those of either aggression or anxiety. Less than four per cent of pupils in our sample were assessed as aggressive, while nearly six per cent were rated as anxious.

At entry to junior school, therefore, there were marked variations in the cognitive skills and behaviour of pupils in the sample. These differences indicate the importance of studying the progress and development of individual pupils. Only by taking account of attainment at entry was it possible for us to look at the effects of schooling on pupils' progress over the junior years. We now examine the pupils' progress and attainment over the course of the Project and discuss the relationships between children's attainments in different areas over the junior years. It is important to investigate the strength and the consistency of these relationships, so as to know how much weight to place on a pupil's attainment at any one stage in her or his junior school career.

Figure 6.2: The incidence of different kinds of behaviour difficulties

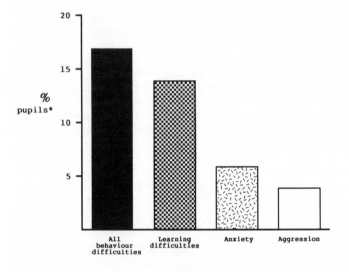

Autumn year 1

*The figures were based on class teachers' assessments.
It was possible for children to be assessed as
experiencing more than one kind of difficulty.

COGNITIVE DEVELOPMENT DURING THE JUNIOR YEARS

Reading attainment

Correlation techniques were used to examine the relationships between children's performance in reading over the three years. Correlations are usually expressed in the form of a figure between 0.01 and 0.99. The closer the figure to 0.99 the stronger the relationship between two measures. When the figures are preceded by a minus sign, as for example – 0.61, this indicates an inverse or negative relationship between the measures. It is not always easy to judge the significance of a particular correlation, but a useful guide is that a positive correlation of 0.5 indicates that up to one quarter of the variation in one measure can be explained, statistically, by the other measure. The results indicate that reading attainment in one year was highly related to reading attainment in later years. This means that a child's performance in reading at the start of junior school was a good predictor of her or his performance three years later (r=0.80).

Thus, of those children who were below average readers at entry to junior school (scoring in the bottom quarter of the distribution), the majority (64%) were still below average (in comparison with their peers) at the end of the third year. Similarly, of those children recorded as above average readers in their first year, 70 per cent again obtained above average scores (in the top quarter of the distribution) in the summer of the third year. Furthermore, 87 per cent of the children who obtained reading scores in the lowest quarter of the distribution in both the first and the third year summer assessments (and who were present for the London Reading Test (LRT) used throughout the Authority in the fourth year) achieved LRT scores at or below the 'cut-off' recommended for individual special needs screening at entry to secondary school.

Mathematics attainment

Significant positive relationships were identified between children's performance over different years in the written mathematics assessments. These relationships, however, were not quite as strong as those identified for reading. Thus, although initial performance in the written mathematics assessment gives a very good idea of the child's likely performance in mathematics after three years of junior education (r=0.75), there is rather more possibility of change. This may be because mathematics is more likely than reading to be influenced by the school as well as the home. In reading, the influence of home in buying or borrowing books and in the amount read by parents is important whereas parental involvement in mathematics in the home may be less evident (see Sammons et al, 1985).

Sixty per cent of pupils whose mathematics scores were below average in the first year also scored below the average level in the third year summer term assessment. Of those above average at the beginning of the first year, 63 per cent were again above average at the end of the third year.

Writing

Relationships between individual pupils' performance in the writing tasks taken in different years were weaker than those found either for reading or for mathematics. (The correlation between the first and the third year assessments of the quality of language and storyline was 0.60.) This result suggests that, during the junior years, there is rather less predictability in children's writing performance over time than in their reading or mathematics attainment. Of those children present for both the first and the third year writing assessments, only 46 per cent of those whose work was assessed as below average in the first year also produced work which was below average in the third year. Of those whose work was above average in the first year, 62 per cent produced above average work in the third year assessment. This indicates that there was greater change in the quality of writing produced by those who were below average than those who were above average. Poor written work in the first year of junior school, therefore, does not necessarily always predict poor written work at a later age.

A number of measures indicated the increase in maturity in children's writing over the three year period. In the first year, 44 per cent of children showed little or no awareness of the personality, motivations or emotions of other people in their written work. By the third year, this figure had fallen to only 11 per cent. There were also improvements in technical aspects of writing. In the first year, 57 per cent of pupils used little or no punctuation in their work, whereas by the third year the equivalent figure was only 25 per cent (see Figure 6.3).

Figure 6.3: Increase in maturity in pupils' writing between years 1, 2 and 3

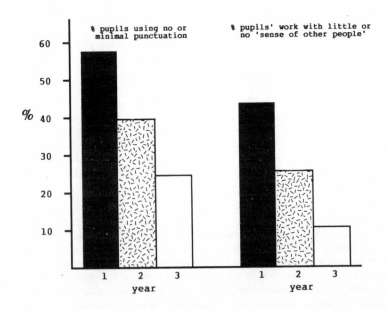

The children's stories revealed interesting insights into their views of the world and attitudes towards their homes, schools and peers. Stories often reflected the central role that school played in the children's lives. They focused on understanding school work and getting it right, and on relationships with teachers and other children. Occasionally, the children wrote about punishments for misdemeanours. In the third year, one child wrote the following in a story about a magic jumper:

> I ran back but I was still late. I got into my classroom and the teacher stared at me. You see they are very strict about lateness in our school. I'd forgotten about the jumper. I was so scared so I put it on. My teacher said 'why are you late?' I wished I could be a fly on the wall and ... Oh no what had I said. I became a fly on the wall. My teacher couldn't believe it and said she must have been dreaming.

For further details of the children's writing see Bunch (1984) or Strachan and Sammons (1986).

Practical mathematics attainment

For a sample of the children, performance in practical mathematics tasks was assessed in each year. The test covered five different skill areas – number, weight, volume, length and sets. As with performance in the written mathematics assessment, children who achieved high scores in the practical assessment in one year tended to achieve highly in later years. The relationships, however, were not as strong as those identified in reading or in written mathematics ($r=0.57$ between the first and the third year assessments). Of those children who were below average in the first year, nearly half also obtained below average scores in the third year assessment (scores in the bottom quarter of the distribution). In all, 49 per cent of children whose work was above average in the first year, again produced above average work in the third year.

Overall, therefore, change appears possible for both those initially doing well and those initially having difficulties. Considering different aspects of practical mathematics, there was greater consistency in children's performance in practical tasks involving number work ($r=0.46$ between the first and third year assessments) than in other areas. This could be due to the more frequent practice children have in number work, whereas other practical mathematical areas are usually covered less often. Performance in weighing tasks showed the lowest consistency over three years ($r=0.10$).

Oracy

An oracy (speaking skills) assessment was included to broaden the measures of pupils' language achievement included in the study. Five scales were used – a holistic impression mark, a task-specific impression mark, measures of verbal and non-verbal performance features, and one scale for the structural (lexico-grammatical) features of speech. The assessments were designed to judge communicative effectiveness, and have been described in Gorman and Hargreaves (1985). Oracy was assessed on only one occasion at the start of the fourth year. It was not possible, therefore, to examine the relationships between oracy performance in different years.

However, because assessments of several different aspects of children's oral skills were included, it was possible to analyse relationships between these different aspects. The results show that there was a strong relationship ($r=0.82$) between general oral performance and the child's ability to fulfil the requirements of the different tasks (the specific assessment). The quality of the children's performance in terms of the language and ideas used was also closely related to general verbal performance ($r=0.73$). However, there was a much weaker association between the non-verbal performance features (such as the use of eye-contact, gesturing and orientation to the listener) and the general assessment. A similarly weak relationship was identified between the lexico-grammatical features of speech and the general assessment ($r=0.48$). Thus, a child's ability to communicate effectively with others – measured by the general assessment – was not related strongly to the structural aspects of her or his speech. Children can be good communicators even if they do not speak 'correctly'.

NON-COGNITIVE DEVELOPMENT DURING THE JUNIOR YEARS

In this section we examine various aspects of children's non-cognitive development during the junior school years. As with the cognitive outcomes, we investigate the strength and consistency of relationships over time.

Behaviour

Class teachers assessed the pupils' behaviour at the beginning and end of each school year, using the 'Child at School' schedule. As reported earlier three possible types of behaviour disturbance were identified: aggression; learning difficulties; and anxiety. In order to be assessed as having disturbed behaviour, a child had to be rated highly on one or more of these three aspects. Overall, the percentage of pupils assessed as having disturbed behaviour remained fairly stable in different years, at around 17 per cent. Teachers rated each pupil on three aspects of learning behaviour: interest in work; perseverance; and concentration. In all years, approximately 60 per cent of pupils were described as keen to learn, although the number dropped slightly from the first to the third year (63% in year 1 to 59% in year 3). Conversely, only a relatively small percentage of pupils were assessed as showing a lack of interest in their work (approximately 12% in each year).

Pupils' perseverance with work was not rated as highly as their interest in work. Nonetheless, approximately half the pupils were assessed as able to persist with their work, even when faced with difficulties. Teachers' ratings of pupils' concentration increased marginally throughout the year. When teachers first met pupils, just under a half of pupils were seen as able to concentrate, usually, or for all of the time. At the end of the year, this description was ascribed to rather more than half. Just over a quarter of pupils in all years, however, were rated as being easily distracted from their work.

Of all problems experienced by pupils in the classroom, learning behaviour difficulties were noted most frequently by teachers. However, there was a slight fall in the percentage of pupils identified as having learning behaviour problems over the three years – from around 13 to around 11 per cent.

Two-thirds of pupils were perceived as happy and contented by their teachers, whereas only ten per cent were seen to be unhappy, anxious or worried. Most pupils were also viewed as sociable and friendly. In each of the three years the proportion of pupils rated as solitary and withdrawn declined between the autumn and summer terms. Pupils were also assessed on their ability to cope with new situations or people at school. More than half the pupils were perceived as showing confidence in this respect, the proportion increasing throughout the year. A minority of pupils (20%), however, were thought to show difficulties in such situations.

In the main, teachers were very positive in their ratings of pupils' acceptance of discipline within the classroom. Under ten per cent of pupils were viewed as disobedient, in comparison to more than three-quarters who were seen as co-operative. Teachers, in general, did not assess many pupils as having problems of an anti-social nature. A small number (fewer than one in ten) were perceived as indulging in frequent bullying or spitefulness towards other pupils, and only slightly more as being irritable or quarrelsome. Thus, on each occasion that assessments were made, learning behaviour difficulties were identified most commonly. Aggression was usually the least frequently noted behaviour problem. In the first two years more pupils were assessed as disturbed at the beginning of the year than at the end. The reverse was true for aggression in all three years. The proportion of anxious pupils, in contrast, remained fairly stable over the three years.

In general, behaviour was more stable in the second year (as measured by the correlation between autumn and summer ratings) and least stable in the first year. Of the three sub-scales, anxiety was generally less stable (the average correlation over the year between autumn and summer ratings was 0.69) than either aggression (average $r=0.74$) or learning difficulties (average $r=0.75$). It seems, therefore, that teachers may have some subconscious idea of how many pupils there are with difficulties at any one point in time. It was interesting how a roughly similar percentage of pupils were rated as having one or other of the behaviour disturbances in each year. However, these pupils were not always the same. Changes in behaviour over time were also examined. Over 70 per cent of the sample had never been assessed as disturbed by their teachers, but nearly 30 per cent were rated as having shown some kind of behaviour problem during the first three years of junior school. Of these children, 13 per cent had behaviour problems in two or more years. However, only a very small minority were repeatedly assessed as disturbed in each of the three years (3%).

Attendance

Full attendance information was collected for every pupil in the sample for each term of their first three years at junior school. The attendance measure was based on the number of half days the pupils could have been present. From this information, the overall average percentage of time present in school was calculated.

Average attendance was very high in all three years (91.6%): 91.8 per cent in the first year; 91.2 per cent in the second year; and 91.7 per cent in the third year. This represents an average absence of 15 school days in the first and third years and 16 days in the second year. In all years, attendance was slightly poorer in the spring term than in other terms. There was, however, considerable variation amongst pupils. For example, a quarter of children were absent for fewer than six days, whilst a quarter missed more than 21 days in the first year. Individual schools also varied in the amount of pupil absence in each year. For example, in one school the average absence over one year was four-and-a-half days; in another it was 28 days.

The number of weeks in which each pupil's absence occurred was also noted. Thus, for example, for a quarter of pupils in year one, absences only occurred in four weeks of the school year, whereas for another quarter, 12 weeks of schooling were interrupted. The pattern for the junior years two and three was similar to that noted in the first year.

Attitudes

At the end of every year, the pupils' attitudes to school and various school activities were measured using the 'Smiley' form, a five-point scale ranging from very positive to very negative. This used happy and sad faces to represent each point on the scale (see Stoll and Sammons, 1988).

The 'Smiley' form included items concerned with how pupils felt about various curriculum areas, and other classroom activities. From this collection of data, a fascinating picture emerged of the range of attitudes the pupils possessed, and of how these attitudes and feelings changed over time.

Looking at the curriculum areas, certain patterns were revealed as the children grew older. First, as a general rule, a considerably higher proportion of pupils expressed a liking for the work than those expressing dislike. For example, in all years, more than half the pupils liked mathematics, whereas only a quarter held an unfavourable view of the subject. The only exception to this rule was in the writing of poetry. By the third year, more pupils expressed dislike of this activity than expressed approval. There was also a general tendency for both very favourable and very unfavourable attitudes to diminish gradually over the three years. This was usually accompanied by an increase in neutral responses. Although pupils were generally positive about most activities, some proved much more popular than others (see Figure 6.4).

Figure 6.4: Attitudes to selected curriculum areas

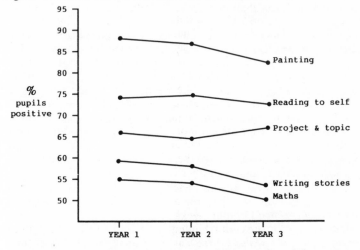

Reactions to specific mathematical activities such as doing sums and weighing and measuring were more favourable than those to the global term 'maths'.

Reading activities, in general, were more favourably rated than story writing, although reading to the teacher declined in popularity from year one (69%) to year three (48%). However, 'reading to yourself' remained at a high level of popularity, with almost three-quarters of pupils expressing a positive view and only 10 per cent not liking the activity. Although listening to the teacher read stories was less popular in the second and third years (63%) than in year one (80%), it was still a classroom activity appreciated by the majority of pupils.

Projects and topic work were the only activities that not only remained popular, but actually increased in popularity. Although pupils were not quite as positive as they were for, say physical education or painting, there was a reduction in the percentage of pupils with negative views towards project work, from 21 per cent in year one to 13 per cent in year three.

Physical education and games remained very popular throughout the entire period. Approximately 90 per cent of pupils in each year reported that they liked these activities, but even with these two very similar curriculum activities, there were interesting differences. For example, the proportion of pupils who reported liking games 'a lot' slipped by approximately five per cent from year one to year three (89% to 84%), whereas the comparable figures for physical education showed a drop of nearly 18 per cent (90% to 72%).

Painting and drawing and, particularly, modelling were two of the most popular curriculum activities, with between 80 and 90 per cent of pupils expressing liking for them each year. Those with a negative view represented less than five per cent of the sample.

Playing musical instruments was also much enjoyed by approximately three-quarters of the pupils. However, singing was not as popular. Although just over half the pupils (53%) liked singing in the first year, by year three only 44 per cent still had a positive attitude and 36 per cent expressed dislike. Furthermore, variations between schools ranged from one school where nearly 90 per cent enjoyed singing to another where only 16 per cent held a favourable view. Although movement and drama declined in popularity over the three years (from 60% to 51%), they were still activities enjoyed by more than half the sample.

Almost all pupils in each of the three years were extremely positive about going on visits and outings.

Other attitudes related to pupils' work
In addition to being asked how they felt about the different kinds of work they did, the children were also asked questions about their relationships with their teachers: how they felt about showing work to their teachers; and whether they asked their teachers for help. It seems that, generally speaking, the children found their teachers very approachable. The proportion of pupils who seemed less than keen either to ask for help or to show their work, tended to be small (ranging between 12% and 17%, and between 7% and 12% respectively). Pupils were very positive about showing good work to the headteacher, particularly in the first year. They also reacted favourably to the idea of working with other children in the classroom. Approximately two-thirds liked to work with their peers, whereas a small number (15%, falling to 10% in year 3) expressed dislike.

School rules

The pupils' attitudes towards school rules provided an insight into their behaviour at school. Although only a small and decreasing number of pupils reported that they approved of school rules, most pupils were not actively keen to break them (see Figure 6.5). As children became older, they also tended to adopt a more neutral attitude towards school rules.

Figure 6.5: Pupils' attitude to school rules

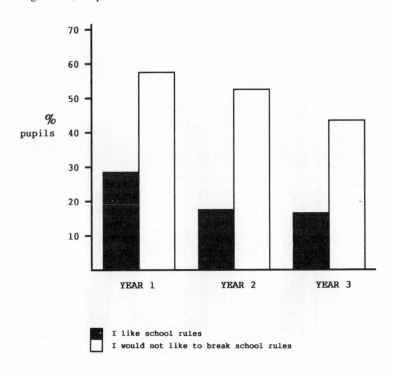

Getting into fights

There were mixed reactions when pupils were questioned about their attitudes towards getting into arguments and fights at school. Apart from year two, when almost as many pupils reported enjoying arguments as reported not liking them (approximately 40% for each), most pupils said that they did not like getting into fights. In line with attitudes towards most curriculum areas, the number of pupils with a neutral attitude to arguments also increased over the three years.

The pupils' view of school

At the end of each school year, we asked pupils, 'How do you feel about school?' Although less than half in all years were positive in their attitude, the number of pupils who did not like school had declined by year three. These figures were supported by an examination of children's attitudes just prior to transfer to secondary school.[1]

The results of our analyses of pupils' attitudes show that, overall 'school' is less favourably viewed by pupils than many of the activities which they actually do at school.

Figure 6.6: Pupils' attitude to school

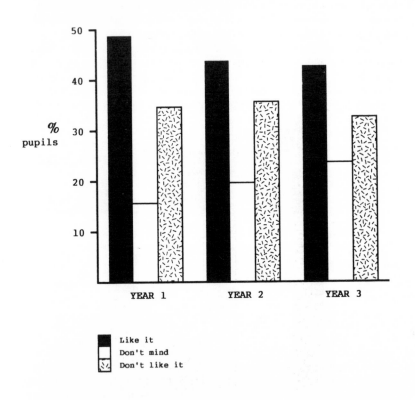

---

(1) Immediately after secondary transfer, however, there was a substantial increase in the proportion of the sample who had a positive view of school (see Runham, 1985)

Self-concept

The children's self-concept was assessed at the end of the third year. It was not studied earlier because of the difficulty young children have in completing self-report questionnaires. The instrument used consisted of a series of questions based on the 'Child at School' schedule. These questions were concerned with the child's perception of her or himself in terms of four areas - anxiety, aggression, learning and behaviour (for a description of the 'Me at School' assessment see Sammons & Stoll, 1988).

Only a small percentage of pupils (3%) perceived themselves as always or usually anxious. The percentage who saw themselves as aggressive was only a little higher (4%). However, slightly more children saw themselves as usually or always having some problems concerned with learning (6%). Eight per cent of children thought that they were usually or always naughty in their behaviour at school. Our results show that, in general, the majority of children had fairly positive self-concepts.

A very high percentage saw themselves as usually or always keen to learn new things. A smaller number, but still over half, felt that they always or usually persevered with difficult work. Concentration on work, however, appeared to be somewhat more elusive. Forty per cent of pupils admitted to experiencing frequent difficulty with concentration, (see Figure 6.7).

Figure 6.7 – Pupils' rating of their own learning behaviour

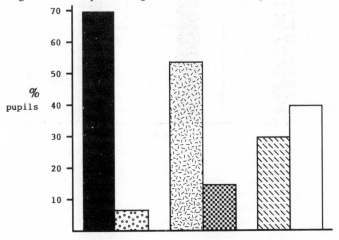

I am usually keen to learn
I am usually not keen to learn
I keep going if work is difficult
I give up easily if work is difficult
I can concentrate on my work and am not easily distracted
I find it hard to concentrate on my work and am easily distracted

Pupils saw themselves as slightly less-well adjusted than did their teachers. In particular, far fewer pupils indicated that they felt confident about facing new situations or new people at school (see Figure 6.8).

Figure 6.8: Pupils' adjustment – self ratings

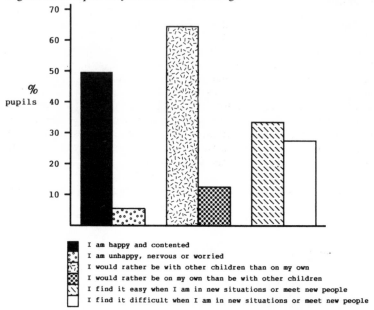

I am happy and contented
I am unhappy, nervous or worried
I would rather be with other children than on my own
I would rather be on my own than be with other children
I find it easy when I am in new situations or meet new people
I find it difficult when I am in new situations or meet new people

The pupils also did not see their behaviour in as positive a light as did their teachers. Only 53 per cent felt that they always or usually did what they were told. There was also a discrepancy between the children's perceptions of their behaviour and how they thought their teacher perceived their behaviour. Only 38 per cent thought their teachers viewed them as well-behaved!

With regard to their behaviour towards their peers, pupils, once again, were less positive about themselves than were their teachers. More rated themselves as 'sometimes kind and helpful, sometimes spiteful' and 'sometimes easy-going, sometimes irritable', although some children (8%) admitted to regular bullying. There was another discrepancy between how the pupils perceived themselves and how they thought other people (their peers) saw their behaviour. Whereas over half reported that they were kind and helpful to their peers, only 38 per cent thought that other pupils found them to be so!

Amongst the items on the self-concept scale, a fairly marked relationship (r=0.62) was found between the child's assessment of their own behaviour and their perception of their teacher's assessment. This is much higher than that found between children's perceptions of their teacher's assessment and the teacher's assessment itself (r=0.31).

Cognitive areas

As might be expected, there was a fairly strong relationship between children's attainments in both reading and writing in each year. (The correlations ranged between 0.69 and 0.74.) Children who obtained high scores in reading also tended to produce writing which was assessed highly in terms of the quality of language and ideas. (It should be pointed out that the writing was assessed by independent markers who were unaware of the children's reading performance.) In the third year summer assessments, for example, children whose writing was of below average quality had an average reading score of only 33 raw points. Those whose writing was above average quality had a mean reading score of 76 points (see Figure 6.9).

Figure 6.9: Relationships between pupils' reading and writing performance over time*

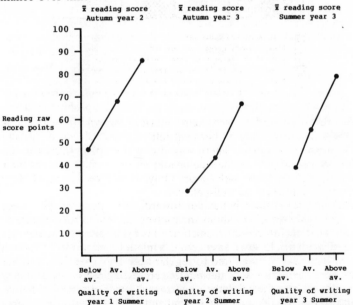

* Due to the use of another version of the ERT in the Autumn of the third year (to take account of the increase in children's ages) the distribution of scores differs.

Oracy was also quite strongly related to reading and to writing attainment. Thus, for example, in considering attainment in the third year summer reading assessment and that in oracy (assessed one term later), it was clear that the communicative effectiveness of speech was positively correlated with reading attainment (r=0.63). The correlation between communicative effectiveness of speech and the quality of children's writing was r=0.57. The lexico-grammatical features of speech were, however, less closely related to reading (r=0.48) and to writing (r=0.43), in line with the findings noted earlier. These results suggest that, in general, there were relationships between children's attainments in different aspects of language usage, but the associations were stronger between reading and writing than between speech and reading, or speech and writing. This may be because oracy is not usually treated as part of the formal curriculum and some very effective speakers do not perform well in reading and writing tasks in the classroom. There were also positive correlations between performance in mathematics and in oracy, but these were weaker than relationships between reading and oracy (r=0.59 for the general measure of communicative effectiveness and mathematics attainment).

Children's performances in the written and practical mathematics assessments were quite closely related, in each school year. The relationships were stronger in the second and third years than in the first year (r=0.55 in the first year, compared with r=0.69 in the autumn of the third year). It is interesting to note that the relationship between practical and written mathematics seems to have been more marked amongst pupils in the later junior years; earlier test results were only weakly related.

There was also a strong relationship between attainment in reading and in the written mathematics assessment. This relationship remained fairly stable in each year (correlations ranged between 0.70 and 0.81). The association was closest in the summer of the third year (r=0.81). Again, it seems that performance in different areas of learning is more closely linked in the later junior years. Mathematics and writing achievement was somewhat less closely related (correlations ranged between 0.55 and 0.60).

Performance in practical mathematics and reading and writing, however, were only weakly related in the first year (r=0.43 between practical mathematics and reading, and r=0.28 between practical mathematics and writing). In later years the correlations were rather higher but still not very strong. These results suggest that performance in practical mathematics is less closely tied to writing or reading abilities especially for younger children, and may be a function of the oral administration of the practical assessments. Furthermore, although information about oracy and practical mathematics performance was only obtained for a small number of pupils (because both assessments were conducted on two separate sub-samples), the results suggest that performance in these two areas tend to be related (r=0.58). Such results indicate the value of educational assessments which do not require pupils to possess high levels of competence in reading and writing. These forms of assessment may reveal children's strengths in cognitive areas which are not always apparent in reading and writing-based tasks. Our findings clearly have important implications for the ways in which pupils are assessed in school.

Non-cognitive areas

There was a weak but significant relationship (r=0.29) between pupils' self-concepts and their behaviour in school. Comparing similar items on each scale, the strongest relationship (r=0.35) was found for the item assessing pupil happiness. Generally, items which related to aspects of pupils' learning also showed significant correlations, while those relating to the child's personality, the lowest correlations. The anxiety subscales related less well (r=0.10) than the aggression and learning difficulty subscales (r=0.25, and 0.28 respectively). It seems, therefore, that there is a link between pupils' perceptions of themselves in school and their teachers' assessments. However, the relationships are not strong, showing that teachers and pupils often vary greatly in their perceptions.

Pupils' attitude to school, and to aspects of school, were also found to be only weakly related to self-concept (correlations with all self-concept items were below 0.30) and to the aggression subscale of behaviour (correlations with the aggression items were all below 0.21).

Children who were assessed by teachers as disturbed on the aggression subscale in both the second and third years differed significantly from those not assessed as disturbed in either year, on two aspects of their self-concept. These were: their poorer assessment of their own behaviour; and their more negative view of their teacher's perception. Those who were assessed as disturbed also had significantly more negative attitudes to school. However, they did not differ in their attitudes to other aspects of the school, nor in their attitudes to relationships with the teacher. Attitude to school was not found to be related to school attendance in any year.

RELATIONSHIPS BETWEEN COGNITIVE AND NON-COGNITIVE OUT-
COMES

We also used correlation techniques to establish whether any relationships existed between the cognitive and non-cognitive outcomes.

Relationships between behaviour and attainment

Assessments of pupils' behaviour and of reading and mathematics were carried out on four occasions: in the autumn of years one, two and three, and in the summer of year three.

For both reading and mathematics attainments, the correlations with the overall behaviour rating reduced over time. The correlations with reading were higher than the correlations with mathematics on all occasions except the last. The stronger relationship between behaviour and attainment in the earlier years (found for reading and mathematics) show that behaviour and attainment were more closely linked for younger children.

Writing quality showed a similar decrease in its relationship with behaviour over time. Writing quality showed comparable, though slightly lower, correlations with behaviour to mathematics (decreasing from 0.48 in the summer of year 1 to 0.42 in summer of year 3).

The behaviour subscales (learning difficulties, anxiety and aggression) when examined separately, showed differing correlations with each of the cognitive attainments. In each case, the learning difficulties subscale was, not surprisingly, more closely related to attainment than were the other two subscales.

For these three areas of attainment, the reduction in the association with the overall behaviour rating over the three years appears to be mainly due to a decreasing correlation with learning difficulties. Writing quality was also related most closely to the learning difficulties subscale and least closely to the aggression subscale. These correlations showed a systematic decrease over time.

Oracy, as measured by the 'general assessment' scale, had a correlation of 0.35 with the overall behaviour rating (in summer year 3), of 0.39 with the task specific rating and 0.43 with the verbal rating.

The correlations reported, whilst giving evidence of a link between cognitive attainments and behaviour, are not sufficient in themselves to allow investigation of the causal relationships, if any, between the two measures. It is likely that learning difficulties are antecedents to lower than average progress on cognitive attainments, and equally, that low attainment would reinforce a low rating on any of the behaviour subscales, and in particular, on learning difficulties. Alternatively, the association between the two measures could be an artefact of a common relationship of both the measures to aspects of the pupils' background. It is shown, in the next chapter, that both reading and writing were related to pupils' social class and sex, that mathematics was related to social class, and that behaviour – and in particular learning difficulties – was related both to social class and to sex.

To explore the relationship between reading and learning difficulties in more depth, statistical techniques based on the use of structural equations methods were used. (See Mortimore et al 1986b for full details.) Specifically, the following questions were addressed. Does low reading attainment in one year predispose learning difficulties in the next year, given a child's current learning difficulties? Do learning difficulties affect reading attainment in the following year, given the child's present reading attainment? Is there any evidence that these relationships continue over a time period of more than a year? Do any relationships, observed over a period of one year, change? For example, is there change from the first to second, or the second to third years?

Reading was found to affect the assessment of learning difficulties subscale a year later, given the learning difficulties measured in the previous year. Thus, lower reading attainment tended to result in greater learning difficulties at a later age. However, no relationship was identified between these measures over a period of more than a year.

Learning difficulties, however, also affected reading attainment a year later, when account was taken of initial attainment (in the same year). The relationship was again found to be constant over both periods – year one to year two, and year two to year three. Learning difficulties tended to affect later reading performance but no relationship between these measures was found over a period of more than a year.

Overall, therefore, we find evidence that pupils with a higher rating in learning difficulties in a given year tended to make less progress in reading over the following year. Similarly, pupils with lower reading scores in a given year tended to show an increase in the severity of learning difficulties in the following year. These findings suggest that pupils' reading attainment and behaviour at school are linked, in a complex way; each influences the other. Poor reading tends to encourage poor behaviour, and poor behaviour leads to poor reading.

Relationships between attitudes and attainment

Attitudes to reading, mathematics and writing had small but positive relationships with attainments in the same area in the same year. There was a slight increase in the strength of these relationships between the first and third years. Of the curriculum areas studied, the highest relationships between attitudes and attainment occurred for writing and reading.

Our data indicate that the relationships between attitudes and attainment were very much lower than those between behaviour and attainment. They also suggest that attitudes were almost independent of attainment for junior age pupils. This means that pupils' attitudes are not necessarily a good predictor of their achievement at this stage.

Relationships between attendance and attainment

In the first year, children with high absence rates from school tended to have lower attainments in reading (r=-0.20), mathematics (r=-0.15) and in writing (r=-0.12). These relationships, though significant, were nevertheless very weak. In later years the relationships were found to be even lower.

Relationships between self-concept and attainment

Our analyses showed that there was a weak positive relationship between children's self-concepts and their cognitive attainment (in reading, mathematics and writing) in the third year, those with higher attainment tending to have a more favourable self-image.

SUMMARY

In this chapter we have shown that there were marked differences between the pupils in our sample at the point of their entry to junior schools. Some children experienced no social or economic disadvantages. Others, however, were living in families with a low income or in very difficult circumstances. A few had serious health problems or handicaps. Likewise, in terms of their experience of education up to this stage, some were reading, writing and understanding mathematical concepts at levels much above the average for their age. Others had already demonstrated learning problems. Similarly, some pupils were positive about schools and reflected this in their behaviour; a few were already showing signs of considerable difficulties in their behaviour in school.

We have also reported the relationships between children's attainments in different areas over the duration of the study. It was found that, whilst reading at one age was a good predictor of reading at a later age, mathematics and writing were subject to greater change. A major finding on oracy was that children could be good communicators even if they did not speak 'correctly'. Where children's behaviour, attitudes and attendance were concerned, we showed that – in general – junior school pupils were positive. It seems that behaviour and attainment are linked, and that the relationship is two-way. We draw attention, however, to the finding that pupils believed their teachers to have a more negative view of their behaviour than the pupils felt was deserved.

7

Different Groups

In the last chapter we examined the overall progress and development of the sample of pupils we were following. Here we will identify and compare the progress and development of different groups of children.

Children included in our sample were drawn from a wide variety of backgrounds. Some lived in families which were advantaged in material terms, while others were living in very difficult circumstances. Such differences in circumstances can have a considerable impact upon pupils' educational outcomes (see Essen & Wedge, 1982, or Sammons et al, 1983). As noted earlier, there is growing evidence that, within London, the incidence of disadvantage is increasing (see Hunter et al, 1985).

Educational research has frequently demonstrated that social background and income are good predictors of cognitive attainments among primary pupils (see reviews by Rutter & Madge, 1976, or Mortimore & Blackstone, 1982). Family variables – such as size and birth order – also appear to be related to educational outcomes (see Marjoribanks, 1979).

The strength of differences due to race has been debated extensively in recent years, and evidence of underachievement by children of some ethnic minority backgrounds is a cause for serious concern (see Essen & Ghodsian, 1979; Rampton, 1981; Swann, 1985; Eggleston et al, 1985; Mabey, 1985). Differences in achievement amongst pupils of primary age have also been found to be associated with sex, differences usually being found in favour of girls at this stage (see Maccoby & Jacklin, 1980; APU, 1981, 1982).

It should be stressed that, although differences in achievement have been identified for children of different social class, sex or ethnic groups, the causes of such differences are seldom clear (see Mortimore, 1983). Moreover, although there is evidence that such factors are related to cognitive attainment, their relationship to progress has been studied less frequently. In addition, relatively little attention has been paid to variations in the non-cognitive outcomes of education for different groups of pupils.

In furtherance of the Authority's Equal Opportunities policies, we investigated the strength of differences in a variety of cognitive and non-cognitive measures due to social class, sex and race. We also paid attention to variations caused by age (a factor which has been neglected in many studies) because this may be an area of educational disadvantage not always recognised in the classroom. Many analyses have been undertaken to investigate the strength of relationships between family factors (family size, position in the family, parental language) and attainment and progress in cognitive and non-cognitive outcomes. These relationships, wherever they were found to be statistically significant, have been taken into account in analyses of progress and school effects. Moreover, all background factors found to be important in previous studies have been included when assessing the effects of age, sex, class or race on individual attainment and progress. Other home-based factors have also been investigated for the sub-sample of pupils involved in the home interview study. The results of this work have been reported by Sammons et al, 1985, and Varlaam et al, 1985. The aim of the analyses of these factors is to establish their impact on the educational prospects of children from different backgrounds. Particular care has been paid to the relative progress made by children from particular groups when account is taken of attainment at entry into junior education.

DIFFERENCES ACCORDING TO AGE

Although it is well known that attainment in cognitive assessments is related to age (such that the majority of tests take into account a pupil's age in the standardisation of results), rather less attention has been given to the long-term prospects of pupils within the same year group who are the youngest members of the class. The studies which have investigated age effects have tended to look at attainment and have not examined non-cognitive outcomes. Most were also conducted over 15 years ago. (See, for example, Williams, 1964; Freyman, 1965 or Thompson, 1971.)

The majority of educational studies have controlled for the effects of age, when comparing children's attainments in cognitive areas, by using standardised test results. Although correct, this procedure obscures the size of differences in actual attainment within a year group which may have an impact upon teachers' assessments of pupils' ability and performance in class work. It is not always easy for a teacher to take into account pupils' ages when comparing work, especially in year-based classes. For this reason, variations in junior pupils' attainment and progress due to age have been investigated in detail. Full account has been taken of other background factors – including mother's and father's occupations; eligibility for free meals; family size and position; nursery experience; fluency in English; sex and race – when estimating the effects of age in analyses of individuals.

Cognitive outcomes

Reading attainment
Highly significant differences between the mean scores of sample children born in the autumn, spring and summer terms were identified at each assessment of reading (see Table 7.1).

TABLE 7.1: Average raw reading scores at each assessment by term of birth

	Reading assessment			
Term of birth	Year 1 autumn	Year 2 autumn	Year 3 autumn	Year 3 summer
Autumn	51.4	66.3	43.1	54.9
Spring	46.5	64.7	41.1	53.0
Summer	40.8	59.1	36.8	47.9
overall average	46.2	63.4	40.4	52.0

In each year, the youngest children (summer born) performed less well in reading than those born in the autumn. Thus, at entry to junior education nearly 33 per cent of pupils born in the summer, compared with only 19 per cent of those born in the autumn term, obtained scores in the bottom quarter of the distribution. These proportions remained remarkably consistent over time, such that, at the end of the third year, 32 per cent of the summer born group, but only 21 per cent of the autumn group, obtained reading scores in the bottom quarter of the distribution. Analysis of London Reading Test (LRT) results for the fourth year revealed a similar pattern. Thirty-two per cent of the summer born group, but only 21 per cent of their autumn born counterparts, scored fewer than 35 raw points in the LRT. This score was the 'cut-off' recommended for individual special needs screening at transfer to secondary school. Children who score below this level are likely to have difficulty in coping with reading material used in the first year of secondary schooling.

Taking into account all other background characteristics, the month of birth made a highly significant difference to the statistical explanation of variation in children's reading attainment. This represented a difference of 13 raw points compared with an overall mean of 46 in terms of the first year assessment between the oldest children (born in September 1972) and the youngest (born in August 1973).

Reading progress
In analysing progress, account was taken of pupils' initial attainments in reading at entry to junior school. The first assessment acted as a baseline for the measurement of progress over the next three years. In contrast to attainment, reading progress was not related to pupil age. Thus, the gap in performance between older and younger pupils neither increased nor decreased during the junior years.

Mathematics attainment
At each assessment, age was highly significantly related to mathematics attainment (as can be seen in Table 7.2).

TABLE 7.2: Average raw mathematics scores at each assessment by term of birth

	Mathematics assessment			
Term of birth	Year 1 autumn	Year 2 autumn	Year 3 autumn	Year 3 summer
autumn	25.9	25.6	30.3	28.2
spring	24.7	24.6	29.6	27.3
summer	22.3	22.5	28.0	24.5
overall average	24.3	24.3	29.3	26.7

As with reading, a much higher percentage of summer than of autumn born pupils obtained scores in the lowest quarter of the distribution (34% compared with 19% respectively) in the first year. These figures remained very similar in later years (the equivalent figures for the summer of the third year were 31% and 18% for the two groups).

Taking into account all other background factors, the difference in attainment between the oldest and youngest pupils in the sample (those born in September 1972 and in August 1973, respectively) reached five raw points in the first year compared with a mean of 24 for the whole sample. This difference remained highly statistically significant throughout the junior years.

Mathematics progress

Once account was taken of initial mathematics attainment, age did not make a significant contribution to the explanation of variations in pupils' progress during the junior years. As with reading, attainment at entry was used as the baseline against which to assess progress in mathematics over the following three years. As expected, initial attainment accounted for the majority of the variation in progress (53%) but the figure is lower than that for reading, indicating that mathematics performance is more susceptible to change than is reading performance, over the junior years.

Writing attainment

Pupils in the sample completed an exercise involving creative writing in the summer term of the first, second and third years. The two assessments of quality of language and of ideas were closely related (r=0.80) and were combined, therefore, to give an overall measure of the quality of writing for each child at each assessment.

Analyses provided strong evidence that, within a year group, month of birth was related significantly to writing performance. In the first year writing assessment, there was an average of a half-point difference between summer and autumn born pupils in the quality of writing (the assessment being based on a nine point scale). This difference – which favoured the older group – remained fairly constant in later assessments. The percentage of pupils whose writing was assessed as below average in quality also differed according to term of birth, though the differences were less marked in the third, than in the first year assessment (see Figure 7.1).

Figure 7.1: Quality of writing by term of birth (years 1 and 3)

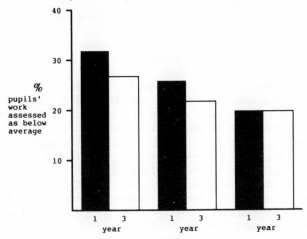

Variations in the length (in words) of children's writing were also related to age. This difference, when account was taken of other factors, remained highly significant in all years. On average, summer born children produced stories 70 words long in the first year while autumn born children produced stories of average 90 words. In the third year, the equivalent figures were 224 compared with 256 words. There was also a difference in various technical skills, such as use of punctuation, in favour of the older members of the year group.

Writing progress
There was no evidence that age affected progress in the quality or the length of writing between the first and the third year. Thus, although the gap in attainment remained highly significant, it did not increase or decrease over time.

As expected, the quality of writing produced in the first year was the most important factor related to progress over the three years. Nonetheless, it accounted for only 32 per cent of the variation in third year attainment. For length of writing, first year length accounted for 15 per cent of the variation in length of third year stories. These figures, though highly significant, are considerably weaker than those identified for reading or mathematics progress. Writing performance appears to be more susceptible to change over the junior years than performance in reading or mathematics.

Practical mathematics
As with performance in the written mathematical assessments, there was evidence that age was related to performance in practical mathematics. The practical assessments were conducted with a sub-sample of pupils, due to the one-to-one administration of the test. Age was related to overall performance in practical mathematics in the first year, but some differences emerged when the five skill areas (weight, number, volume, length and sets) were considered separately. It appeared that performance in number work was significantly affected by age. Younger pupils attained less highly than their older peers. However, there were no significant age related differences in the volume, length, weight or sets assessments. A similar pattern of results was identified for the second year assessment.

In contrast to the first and second year assessments, age was related to performance in weighing activities in the third year, but no longer to number work. Differences which were identified were in favour of the older pupils but these were small and not statistically significant. Thus, in contrast to the results in written assessments, age did not have a significant impact upon all practical mathematics performance tasks. In practical tasks, age differences related mainly to number work in the first and second years, but in the third year assessment number work performance was no longer affected.

Oracy
Oracy was assessed on only one occasion for a sub-sample of pupils (as discussed earlier) in the autumn term of the fourth year. In marked contrast to findings for other cognitive areas, age was not found to be related to performance in any of the five oral assessments (there were some trends in favour of older pupils but all were small and none reached statistical significance). It appears that the ability to communicate effectively though speech was not related to variations in age of less than one year, the age range within the Junior School Project sample. It is, of course, highly likely that age would be related to performance in a sample of pupils of more varied age.

Relationships between cognitive outcomes

In general, there was little evidence that age had an impact upon the relationships between pupils' performance in different cognitive areas, or over time. Children of all ages who performed well in one area tended to do well in other cognitive areas. The major exception to this rule was the relationship between reading and oral skills. The association between reading and oral skills was significantly closer for older children in the year group. The correlation (adjusted for reliability) for the autumn born group was 0.70 compared with a lower figure of 0.55 for the summer born group.

The implications of this result for methods of assessing children's skills and abilities are again important. The inclusion of oral assessments of pupils' work may help to give a fairer judgement of the performance of younger members of an age group because children's abilities to communicate effectively were not significantly related to age, in contrast to the other cognitive assessments.

Teachers' assessments of pupils' ability
Teachers were asked to assess each child's ability in terms of a five point scale ranging from well above average to well below average on four occasions. There were significant differences between summer and autumn born children in the proportions rated as below and above average ability. These differences were always in favour of the oldest children. Summer born children were consistently more likely to be judged as of below average ability than were their autumn born counterparts (see Table 7.3).

TABLE 7.3: Percentages of children assessed as above and as below average ability by their class teachers, according to term of birth*

Term of birth	% rated above average	% rated below average
Autumn born	35.4	21.8
Spring born	31.3	28.6
Summer born	25.4	32.7
All pupils	27.7	26.3

* based on teachers' assessments made in the autumn term of the second year.

Further analyses of teachers' assessments of ability are given later. These suggest that teachers were influenced in their assessments primarily by children's reading, writing and mathematics attainment. The significant gap in attainment in these areas due to age thus seems to influence class teachers' judgements of ability. It appears that teachers did not take full account of the effect of age differences on attainment when judging children's ability.

Analyses of the Verbal Reasoning (VR) band to which the sample children were allocated at the end of junior schooling also indicated that a higher proportion than expected of the summer born group were allocated to band three and a lower than expected proportion to band one. Correspondingly, a higher than expected proportion of autumn born children were allocated to band one and a lower than expected proportion to band three (see Table 7.4).

TABLE 7.4: Percentages of children allocated to verbal reasoning bands by term of birth*

Term of birth	Band One %	Band Two %	Band Three %
Autumn	24.2	54.8	21.0
Spring	22.7	55.0	22.3
Summer	18.4	54.3	27.3
All pupils	21.8	54.7	23.5

*(Over the Authority as a whole, the expected percentage of pupils in band 1 is 25%, band 2 is 50%, and in band 3 is 25%. Amongst our sample, however, a slightly higher percentage were allocated to band 2 and a lower percentage to bands 1 and 3 than expected.)

In comparing children's actual verbal reasoning scores with the band ascribed by their schools, adjusting results for age at test, it was clear that a higher proportion of summer born children who were predicted (on the basis of age adjusted test score) band one were actually allocated to band two. Furthermore, a higher proportion of children who were predicted band two were allocated to band three than was the case for the autumn born groups (see Table 7.5).

These results give cause for concern. It seems that, within a year group, teachers find it difficult to take full account of the impact of age in judging children's abilities. Because VR band is important in the secondary transfer process, and secondary schools frequently use it as an indicator of pupils' abilities, there is a danger that summer born children may be disadvantaged. Class teachers may need to pay particular attention to age differences even within a year-based class when assessing children's work and ability.

TABLE 7.5:
Percentages of pupils allocated to a lower verbal reading band than predicted by their test score (adjusted for age), according to term of birth

Term of of birth	% Pupils allocated to lower band than predicted by test score
Autumn	4.0
Spring	6.5
Summer	12.1

Non-cognitive outcomes

Behaviour
The investigation of information about pupils' behaviour in school, indicated that, on each occasion, a higher percentage of summer than of autumn born pupils were assessed by their class teacher as having some kind of difficulty (see Figure 7.2).

In all, 23 per cent of summer born pupils, compared with only 13 per cent of their autumn born classmates, were assessed as having some kind of difficulty in behaviour by their first year class teachers. Thus, age had a significant impact upon behaviour in school. Again, the youngest members of the year group were at a disadvantage. It is

Figure 7.2: Percentage of pupils assessed as having behaviour difficulties by term of birth (years 1, 2 and 3)

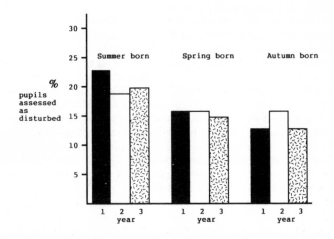

likely that this relationship may be due, at least in part, to the association between behaviour difficulties and low cognitive achievement (discussed in Chapter 6). It has already been demonstrated that summer born children performed less well than autumn born children in nearly all of the cognitive assessments. Poor attainment may lead to behaviour problems or reinforce them, but it is also likely that poor behaviour has an impact upon attainment in school.

Comparisons of pupils who were assessed as having some kind of behaviour disturbance in two or more years, demonstrated that 16 per cent of summer born pupils, in contrast to only 10 per cent of autumn born pupils, had difficulties. Overall, it seems that behaviour difficulties were more common and more persistent for younger members of the age group.

Taking a combined measure of behaviour over three years, and controlling for sex and all other background factors, the month of birth still made a highly significant contribution to the statistical explanation of pupils' behaviour in school during the junior period.

Attendance

Age was not found to be significantly related to children's attendance at school in any year. In all years, average attendance was very good (exceeding 90%) irrespective of term of birth. Thus, in contrast to cognitive and other non-cognitive outcomes, age did not influence school attendance during the junior years.

Attitudes

A comparison was made of attitudes to the three curriculum areas in which marked age differences in attainment had been identified. Age was found to be unrelated to attitudes to either reading or writing. However, for attitude to mathematics, age differences were identified. These occurred in the second and third year assessments and were particularly marked in the third year. At this stage, 31 per cent of the youngest (summer born) group compared with only 19 per cent of the oldest (autumn born) group had an unfavourable view of mathematics. It is possible that this poorer view of mathematics was related to the lower attainment of younger pupils in this area. However, there was also a gap in both reading and writing attainment due to age, but no age-related variations in attitudes to these curriculum areas were identified.

Individual analyses, taking into account sex and background factors indicated that month of birth was highly significantly related to pupils' attitude to mathematics in the third year.

Differences related to age were also identified in pupils' general attitude to school. These differences were most marked in the third year. At this stage, 37 per cent of summer born, compared with only 28 per cent of autumn born pupils, had a negative view of school. In line with our earlier findings for other outcomes, individual level analyses indicated that age made a highly statistically significant contribution to the explanation of the variation in pupils' attitudes to school.

Self-concept

An examination of the children's response to questions administered verbally, indicated that age was not related to self-concept. Younger children were not more likely than older members of the year group to have an unfavourable view of themselves in school.

Relationships between non-cognitive outcomes

In contrast to the findings about the impact of age upon the relationships between the different cognitive outcomes, no differences were identified in the relationships between non-cognitive outcomes according to age. The links between behaviour and attendance, and between behaviour and attitudes, did not differ for autumn and summer born children. Neither were there any differences, according to age, in the relationships between attitudes and attendance. The patterns of relationships mirrored those for pupils as a whole (described in the last chapter).

Relationships between cognitive and non-cognitive outcomes

Again, very few differences were identified, according to age, in the relationships between cognitive and non-cognitive outcomes. As with pupils as a whole, behaviour in school was closely linked to attainment in the various cognitive assessments in each year for both summer and autumn born pupils. Learning difficulties were more closely related to attainment than those of aggression or anxiety. Attitudes were only very weakly related to cognitive outcomes for all pupils and no differences were identified according to age.

The relationships between behaviour difficulties and reading attainment was somewhat weaker for summer born pupils in the first year of junior school ($r=0.49$) than for the older members of the age group ($r=0.55$ for their autumn born peers). In the first year, anxiety and attainment were also more closely linked amongst the older members of the year group. In later years, however, these differences were much reduced.

It seems, therefore, that although older pupils achieved more highly than younger members of the year group and were less likely to be assessed as having behaviour difficulties at entry to junior school, the link between attainment and behaviour was somewhat stronger for older pupils.

The influence of infant school experience

There was a close and highly statistically significant relationship between a pupil's age and the length of time she or he had spent in infant school. For example, prior to transfer, summer born pupils had an average of only 26 months infant school experience. Spring born pupils, in contrast, had an average of 31 months, while autumn born pupils had an average of nearly 35 months experience of infant education. Expressed as a correlation, this relationship between month of birth and months in infant school was also found to be very marked ($r=0.83$).

The link between age and length of infant experience reflects policies on the age at which children are encouraged to enter infant school (usually the term of their fifth birthday, in this Authority). Due to this, summer born children, in general, spend far less time in infant departments or schools prior to transfer into junior education than do the older members of their year group. It appears that summer born pupils tend to suffer the double disadvantage of being the youngest members of a class and of having substantially fewer months of infant education, in comparison with their autumn born peers.

In considering the relative importance of age and length of schooling, Russell & Startup (1986) have noted that, in practice, it is a little difficult to tell which of the two theories is better supported by the data. This is because in Britain, length of schooling is so highly related to age.

Analyses indicated that length of infant school experience was weakly, but significantly associated with reading and mathematics attainment at entry to junior school. These relationships were stronger in the first than in later assessments, suggesting that length of infant school experience is a more important influence upon attainment for pupils at transfer into junior education than is the case in the second and third years.

The relationships between infant school experience and cognitive attainments were, in part, a function of age, because age was so strongly linked to length of infant schooling. Nonetheless, infant experience remained significantly, though weakly, related to reading and mathematics performance, even when account was taken of pupils' age at test.

When account was taken of the impact of age, sex and other background factors upon reading and mathematics attainment, length of infant school experience was found to have a significant but small impact upon attainment in the first year reading assessment, but the relationships were not significant in later assessments. For mathematics, length of infant experience had an impact in both the first and second year assessments, but no effect in the two third year assessments.

The length of infant school experience was not, however, related to pupils' progress over three years in either reading or mathematics. This finding is in line with those reported earlier on the impact of age, which indicated that age did not affect junior pupils' progress in these two cognitive areas.

SUMMARY

We have identified differences in attitudes to school, a greater incidence of behavioural difficulties and a marked gap in reading, writing and mathematics attainment between the younger and older members of the year group who formed our sample. These differences indicate that younger children are at risk of experiencing greater difficulties in adjustment to junior school. The results of the analyses suggest that it is important to promote teachers' awareness of the impact of age differences within year-based classes of pupils. In particular, it appears that, within a year group, the younger children have usually had significantly less infant school experience than other groups, and that this helps to account for age differences in attainment at entry to junior school. These results are of especial significance because recent work indicates that age-related differences in achievement can continue throughout formal schooling and on into higher education (see Russell & Startup, 1986).

DIFFERENCES ACCORDING TO SOCIAL CLASS

Having presented our findings on the impact on children's progress and development of age differences, we now review the effects of social class.

Cognitive outcomes

In assessing the impact of social class upon attainment, it must be emphasised that the broad scale developed by the Registrar General neglects many important aspects about the child's home, relationships with parents and life style (see the discussion by Bland, 1979; or Mortimore, 1983). Nonetheless, the scale is associated with many aspects of inequality, for example it has been shown to be linked with differences in health and morbidity (see Black, 1980). The strength of relationship between social class background and attainment throughout a child's school career has been tested in numerous studies, and work on our sample confirms the importance of this factor, even when account is taken of differences in parents' activities with their children, housing and income (see Sammons et al, 1985).

To assess the impact of social class upon pupils' attainment and progress in the junior years, information about both the mother's and the father's occupation was collected for the sample of pupils. Figures in Table 7.6 indicate the percentages of pupils in the sample with parents in the various social class groups.

TABLE 7.6: Social class classification of parents' occupations

		Mothers	Fathers
		%	%
Non-manual	I	1	3
	II	6	14
	III	12	8
Manual	III	3	35
	IV	10	8
	V	6	7
Long term unemployed		1	6
Not in paid employment		59	2
Absent		2	17

(Children for whom no information was available are excluded.)

Overall, the majority of children were from working class homes, a reflection of the social class composition of the inner London population. (A more detailed discussion of pupils' social class backgrounds was given in Chapter 6.)

Reading attainment and progress
Both mother's and father's occupations were highly related to reading performance at entry to junior school. In considering the relative influences of the mother's and the father's social class, the high percentage of mothers who were not in paid employment (59% of those for whom data were available) needs to be borne in mind. Moreover, the proportion of children for whom no occupational information was known was much higher for mothers (25.5%) than for fathers (17%). The fact that only just over a quarter of mothers had an occupation-related description reduces the potential of this variable for the statistical explanation of children's attainments, since it is likely that mothers classified into the economically inactive (not in paid employment) group may have had very different employment histories.

The average first year reading scores are shown in Figure 7.3 for groups classified by their father's social class.

Figure 7.3: Average raw scores in reading by social class (year 1)

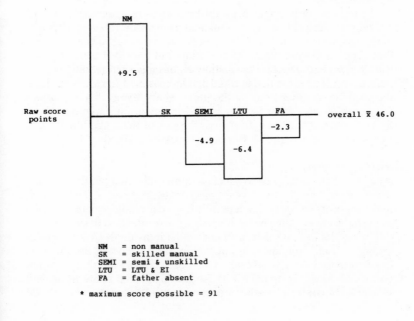

```
NM    = non manual
SK    = skilled manual
SEMI  = semi & unskilled
LTU   = LTU & EI
FA    = father absent

* maximum score possible = 91
```

In assessing the impact of social class upon attainment and progress in cognitive areas full account was taken of other factors, including ethnic family background, fluency in English, family size and birth order, eligibility for free school meals, experience of nursery education, sex and age. We chose this set of variables from analyses of the full range of background data to cover all the major factors which research has suggested may be influential. Therefore, differences between the social classes can be seen as 'net' of the impact of other factors.

Even having taken full account of other influences, a difference of 14 raw score points – which represents a gap of nearly ten months in reading age – was found between children with fathers in professional or intermediate non-manual work, and those with fathers in unskilled manual work.

The relationships between social class and reading attainment remained marked throughout the period of junior education, on all four occasions that reading was assessed. By the summer of the third year, the differences due to father's occupation had become even greater than at entry to junior school. At entry to the juniors, 20 per cent of those with fathers in semi- and unskilled work, compared with 41 per cent of their non-manual counterparts obtained reading scores in the top quarter of the distribution. By the end of the third year, 19 per cent of the semi- and unskilled manual group obtained scores in the top quarter of the distribution, compared with 46 per cent of the non-manual group.

In the London Reading Test, differences were again identified. In all, only 16 per cent of the non-manual group scored below 35 points in this assessment (the 'cut-off' recommended for special needs screening). The equivalent figure for the semi- and unskilled manual group was 28 per cent. The results of analyses of individual reading performance over time identified marked and increasing differences between the social class groups during the junior years, even when important relationships with other factors have been taken into account. These findings generally agree with the conclusions of the longitudinal study by the National Children's Bureau (see Essen & Wedge, 1982).

Reading progress
Analysis of the impact of social class upon individual pupils' progress in reading during the junior years was possible because of the longitudinal nature of the study. Each pupil's first year reading score was used as the basis for assessing her or his progress over the next three years.

The results indicate that, although some individuals change considerably, reading attainment at entry accounts for most of the variation in performance three years later. The social class of father's occupation continued, however, to have a statistically significant relationship with progress. In contrast, mother's occupation did not make a significant contribution to the explanation of differences in pupils' reading progress (this is likely to reflect the high proportion of mothers who were not in paid employment and, therefore, for whom no occupational data were available). Overall, children whose fathers were in non-manual work made significantly greater progress than other groups. The difference was four raw score points, compared with a mean of 54 and a possible maximum of 100 points for the whole sample in the summer of the third year. Children from manual backgrounds tended to make less progress in reading when account was taken of other factors and initial attainment at entry to junior school.

Mathematics attainment
The relationships between children's social class background and attainment in mathematics were investigated in the same manner as reading. Again, substantial differences between children of different social class backgrounds were identified at entry to junior school. In Figure 7.4, the mean raw scores of children from different social class groups are shown.

Figure 7.4: Average raw scores in mathematics by social class (year 1)

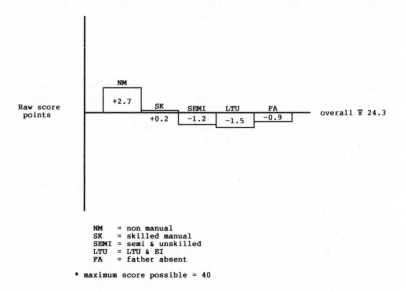

The results of the analyses of the relationships between mother's and father's social class, taking into account other background factors, indicate that both mother's and father's social class were significant.

Again pupils whose fathers were in non-manual occupations had significantly higher attainment than those whose fathers were in unskilled manual work. The difference in mathematics attainment between the professional and intermediate non-manual groups represented around nine months in terms of age – a very similar gap to that identified in reading. This pattern of differences remained at each of the four assessments of mathematics. For example, in the summer of the third year, children whose fathers were in professional or intermediate non-manual work obtained scores more than 7.5 raw points higher than those with fathers in unskilled manual work (compared with a mean of 27 points), when other background factors were taken into account. However, the differences in mathematics attainment between the social groups did not appear to increase over time. In the first year, 43 per cent of the non-manual and 23 per cent of the semi- and unskilled group obtained scores in the top quarter of the distribution. By the end of the third year the figures were little changed, at 42 and 22 per cent respectively.

Mathematics progress
In contrast to reading, progress in mathematics was not statistically significantly related to social class when the effects of initial attainment and other background factors were controlled. Thus, although the gap in achievement in mathematics between the social classes remained large throughout the junior years, it did not increase – in contrast to the results for reading.

Although social class was not related significantly to progress in mathematics, one socio-economic measure (eligibility for free school meals, an indicator of low family income) did have an impact upon both reading and mathematics progress. Children eligible for free meals made poorer progress than predicted given their initial attainment in both reading and mathematics.

These findings about the impact of social class suggest that home factors may be less important influences upon mathematics progress and attainment than upon reading. It seems likely that mathematics progress may be more affected than reading progress by school work because parents are likely to provide greater help at home with reading than with mathematics.

Writing attainment
Marked differences in writing performance (in terms of both quality and length) according to social class were identified in each year. Thus, 28 per cent of the semi- and unskilled manual group produced writing which was assessed as below average in quality in the first year, compared with only 18 per cent of the non-manual group (see Figure 7.5).

Figure 7.5: Quality of writing by social class (years 1 and 3)

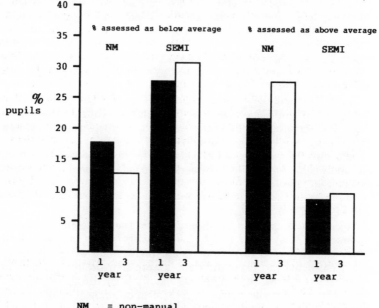

```
NM   = non-manual
SEMI = semi & unskilled
       manual
```

The analysis of the relationship between background factors and the quality and length of writing produced by pupils in their first year clearly indicated a significant relationship with father's social class. For quality (assessed on a nine point scale), the difference between the writing of children whose fathers were in non-manual work and those in unskilled manual work exceeded one point (compared with a mean of 6.2 and a maximum possible score of 10). In terms of writing length, children with fathers in non-manual work produced stories 22 words longer than the sample average (of 88 words), whereas the writing of those whose fathers were in unskilled manual work was 15 words shorter than the average. The pattern of relationships between social class and the quality and length of children's writing remained highly significant at each assessment.

Progress in writing
Father's social class was highly significantly related to progress in both the quality and length of writing, even when first year attainment was taken into account. As with reading, mother's social class did not make a statistically significant contribution to progress in this area.

Again, children whose fathers were in non-manual work made greater progress than those with fathers in unskilled manual work (a difference of nearly half a point in terms of the ten point quality assessment). However, those whose fathers were not working, or were absent, also made rather greater progress than predicted by their first year attainment. The non-manual children produced stories 32 words longer than expected (compared with a mean of 246 words), given their first year attainment.

It is clear, therefore, that in the formal language-based areas of the curriculum (reading and writing) pupils from non-manual backgrounds make greater progress than others over the junior years, in addition to their superior attainment at entry.

The implications of these social class differences in progress in reading and writing for children's careers in secondary school require serious consideration.

Practical mathematics attainment
Analysis of attainment in five different areas (number, length, weight, volume and sets) showed that children with fathers in non-manual employment tended to perform more highly than other groups in particular activities. These differences were statistically significant in two areas – volume and length – in the first year. In the second and third year assessments, however, significant differences in attainment were identified in volume, length and sets work. In the second year, differences were also identified in number work and, in the third year, in weighing activities.

Therefore, in addition to differences in attainment in the written mathematics assessment, some differences in practical mathematical skills were also related to social class background. Because the practical mathematics test measured several separate aspects of attainment (rather than one single aspect), it was not possible to assess progress in this area during the study.

Oracy
Father's social class was the only background factor which was significantly related to the oral assessments. It made a statistically significant contribution to the explanation of the general performance (holistic), task specific and verbal performance assessments. These three scales were themselves quite highly correlated. Pupils whose fathers were in non-manual work obtained significantly higher scores than other groups (a difference of nearly four points on the holistic measure of general performance, compared with an overall average of 21.5). In contrast, social class was not related to attainment in the lexico-grammatical or non-verbal performance scales. Further details of the the relationships between social class background and oracy are given in Ecob & Sammons (1985).

It appears that, as with all the other cognitive areas, oral attainment is related to social class background. In terms of general performance, the ability to fulfil the requirements of different kinds of speaking tasks (the specific assessment), and in the use of language, children from non-manual backgrounds had rather higher attainments. There were, however, no significant differences in non-verbal performance (the child's ability to involve her or his audience through eye contact and gesturing) or in the structure of speech (lexico-grammatical features).

Relationships between cognitive outcomes

Some differences in the relationships between performance in the different cognitive areas were found for pupils of different social class backgrounds. Thus, not only were there significant differences in attainment between social classes, there were also some differences in the way achievements in different areas were related. The correlation between reading performance in the first and the third year was slightly stronger for the non-manual than for the semi- and unskilled manual groups ($r=0.83$ compared with $r=0.75$). A similar trend was found for mathematics and writing attainments over time.

Analyses of the relationships between attainments in different cognitive areas indicate that, for reading and writing, the correlations between attainment in these two areas were weaker for the semi- and unskilled manual than for the non-manual groups. This was particularly noticeable in the first year (the correlation between reading and writing in the first year was 0.63 for the semi- and unskilled manual group but 0.76 for the non-manual group). It seems that, for children of semi- and unskilled manual backgrounds, performance in reading at a younger age was less closely related to their writing performance than was the case further up the school.

Analyses of the relationships between reading and mathematics attainment show that there was also a tendency for the correlations for the semi- and unskilled manual groups to be weaker than those for the non-manual group. In the autumn of the third year, the correlation was 0.67 for the semi- and unskilled manual group, but 0.77 for the non-manual group.

The association between reading achievement and oracy was much stronger for the non-manual ($r=0.63$) than for the semi- and unskilled or the skilled manual groups ($r=0.56$ and $r=0.40$ respectively). Thus, for working class children, reading attainment was less closely linked with the ability to communicate effectively when speaking than was the case for those in the non-manual group. A similar pattern was found for the relationships between writing and oracy when the social class groups were considered separately.

These results suggest that, for junior pupils from working class homes, oral skills may be relatively more developed than reading or writing skills, even though some social class differences were found for oracy. It will be important, therefore, to consider ways in which cognitive assessments can incorporate oral elements, so that children's achievements in verbal communications are taken into account in teachers' assessments of ability.

Teachers' assessments of pupils' ability
There were very marked differences, according to father's social class, in the percentage of pupils rated by their class teachers as above and as below average ability. In the autumn of the second year, 48 per cent of the non-manual, compared with only 25 per cent of semi- and unskilled manual group were rated as of above average ability. Only 16 per cent of the non-manual, but 32 per cent of the semi- and unskilled manual group, were rated as below average ability. By the third year, the differences were even greater.

As we have noted earlier there were significant variations between children of different social classes in terms of cognitive attainments. Since teachers' assessments of pupil ability were found to be strongly related to performance in reading, writing and mathematics, analyses were conducted to establish whether social class background was related to teacher judgements, while controlling for attainment in these three areas and for other background factors. The results indicated that, once account was taken of reading, mathematics and writing performance, social class background was still related to teachers' ratings of abilities. This effect, it must be emphasised, was small. It was, nonetheless, statistically significant and operated in favour of the non-manual group on each occasion.

It seems, therefore, that although teachers' judgements of ability were largely determined by children's attainments, on the whole, teachers tended to have a slightly more favourable view of those of non-manual backgrounds. Thus, higher teacher expectations may be one factor which contributes to the greater progress in reading and writing made by the non-manual group in comparison with other groups during the junior years. These findings also support those identified by other researchers (see the review by Pilling & Kellmer Pringle, 1978).

Non-cognitive outcomes

Relationships between non-cognitive outcomes and background factors were investigated using similar methods to those adopted for cognitive areas.

Behaviour

Analyses showed that socio-economic factors were highly related to teachers' behaviour assessments of pupils at entry to junior school. Both mother's and father's social class were significantly associated with behaviour ratings in the first, second and third years of junior school. According to their teachers' assessments, children from semi- and unskilled manual backgrounds had a higher incidence of behaviour problems in school. A comparison of pupils who were assessed as having some kind of behaviour disturbance on two or more occasions with those who were never assessed as disturbed, shows that differences between the two groups in socio-economic background were striking. In all, only ten per cent of disturbed, compared with 24 per cent of non-disturbed pupils, were of non-manual origins. In contrast, 23 per cent of disturbed children's fathers did not live with them, compared with 12 per cent of non-disturbed children. Thus, as with the cognitive outcomes of education, social class also appears to have an effect on non-cognitive areas.

Attendance

Overall, background factors were less strongly related to children's attendance than to their attainments (only around 12% of the variation in attendance compared with 24% of the variation in reading attainment, for example, was accounted for by background factors). On the whole, attendance in the junior years for children of all backgrounds was very good. Nonetheless, attendance in the first year of junior school was related significantly to social class. Children with fathers in non-manual work were absent for the least time, whilst those whose fathers were unemployed, economically inactive or absent, missed the most school time in the first year. However, those from semi- and unskilled manual homes were not absent for a significantly greater proportion of time than those of non-manual backgrounds. This is in contrast to relationships in the cognitive areas described earlier.

Mother's occupation was also related significantly to attendance. There was a tendency for children whose mothers were economically inactive or unemployed to be absent for a higher percentage of time than was the case for those whose mothers were in employment. This may reflect the difficulties working mothers have in obtaining time off work, which could explain why they were less likely than non-working mothers to keep children at home.

Children from low income families were also more likely to have poor attendance records than were other children. Those eligible for free meals were absent for around ten per cent of the time, whereas those not eligible were absent for only eight per cent of the time. These findings may reflect the link between ill-health and unemployment or low family income which has been noted in a number of studies (see Black, 1980).

Mother's social class did not make a significant contribution to the explanation of attendance in the second or third year, although father's social class and eligibility for free meals remained of importance. Taking into account all other background factors, in the third year, children with fathers in non-manual work were absent for around one per cent less of the time than others, compared with an average absence rate of 8.3 per cent.

Attitudes
Background factors accounted for only a very small percentage of the variation in pupils' attitudes towards mathematics, reading or towards school in any year. The analyses demonstrated that attitudes to curriculum areas and to school were related less strongly to pupils' backgrounds than was attainment in the various cognitive areas.

Social class was not related to children's attitudes to mathematics, to 'reading to yourself', or to general attitudes towards school in the first year. By the third year, however, father's social class was related significantly to attitude to reading. Overall, children whose fathers were in non-manual work expressed more favourable attitudes to reading. Children in this category did not, however, show more favourable attitudes to mathematics than did most other groups.

It appears that, amongst primary aged children, socio-economic factors were less powerful determinants of attitudes towards school or towards curriculum areas, than they were of cognitive attainment. This may be because attitudes are influenced more by teacher behaviour or school organisation and atmosphere than is attainment (an argument put forward by Reynolds, 1985). Alternatively, it may simply be that children's attitudes are much more difficult to measure and much less stable than attainment.

Self-concept
There were no significant differences between the social classes in pupils' self-concepts.

Relationships between non-cognitive outcomes

For all social class groups, first year behaviour was related significantly to behaviour in the third year. The link was strongest, however, for the non-manual group ($r=0.60$) and weakest for those whose fathers were in long term unemployment ($r=0.47$). This reflects the much higher incidence of behaviour difficulties in the first year amongst those whose fathers were unemployed, and the lower incidence in later years. For all groups, attendance in the first year was correlated with that in the third year, but the relationship was strongest for the skilled manual group and weakest for those from long term unemployed backgrounds ($r=0.53$ for skilled manual and $r=0.31$ for long term unemployed).

For all children, the attitude measures taken in different years were only very weakly correlated, attitudes to school and to curriculum areas clearly changing over the junior period. Nonetheless, the non-manual group exhibited greater stability in their attitudes to mathematics between the first and third year than other children. The correlation, however, remained very weak.

In the first year, behaviour and attitude to school were not significantly linked, except for the long term unemployed group where the association, though weak, was statistically significant ($r=0.15$). By the third year, behaviour and attitude to school were significantly, though weakly, related for all groups. The correlations were strongest for those of semi- and unskilled manual backgrounds and those whose fathers were not working.

Relationships between cognitive and non-cognitive outcomes

For each social class group in each year, behaviour was the non-cognitive measure most closely related to cognitive attainment, especially reading. This reflects the pattern identified for pupils as a whole. However, the relationship between behaviour and reading was much stronger in the second and the third year for the group whose fathers were not working.

Amongst first and second year pupils, the relationships between reading performance and behaviour was affected by social class background. By the third year, however, differences between the social classes were much smaller and were no longer significant.

Attendance and attainment were only very weakly related in each school year. Nonetheless, in the second and third years the correlations between attendance and attainment in mathematics were rather stronger amongst pupils from semi- and unskilled manual background, and reached statistical significance. Children from this group who were absent from school more frequently were likely to attain less well in mathematics than members of other groups.

Relationships between attainment in certain cognitive areas and behaviour and attendance thus differ in certain respects for pupils of different social class backgrounds. There were, however, no social class differences in the relationships between attitudes and attainment in different areas. For all groups, attitudes were very weakly and inconsistently related to attainment. No clear patterns were identified.

SUMMARY

In this section we have shown that the non-manual group attained more highly in the majority of cognitive areas. They also made greater progress than other groups in reading and in writing. A small but significant difference was found in teachers' assessments of ability, in favour of the non-manual group. Children whose fathers were in semi-and unskilled manual work, and those whose fathers were absent, were significantly more likely to exhibit behaviour difficulties in school. We found no clear differences according to social class, however, in attendance, attitudes or self-concept.

DIFFERENCES ACCORDING TO SEX

Following on from the analysis of progress by social class, we now describe the data that we have collected on the differences in the progress of girls and boys.

Cognitive outcomes

Both variations in attainment and, where possible, progress, have been explored for each of the cognitive outcome measures. The individual level analyses of attainment have taken into account the influences of a common set of background factors (mother's and father's social class, free meals, family size and position, fluency in English, ethnic background, nursery school experience and age). This means that we can identify whether there are any differences which are independent of the effects of other background factors.

Reading attainment
There were marked differences between the two sexes in terms of average reading scores at each assessment. For example, at entry to junior school, the average score for girls was nearly 51 raw points, but for boys the average figure was only 41 points. Moreover, only 17 per cent of girls, compared with 33 per cent of boys, obtained scores in the bottom quarter of the distribution at entry to junior school. In contrast, 31 per cent of girls, compared with 19 per cent of boys, obtained scores in the top quarter of the distribution. At the end of the third year, a very similar pattern was identified. Nineteen per cent of girls obtained scores in the bottom quarter of the distribution, compared with 31 per cent of the boys. Moreover, 31 per cent of girls and only 21 per cent of boys obtained scores in the top quarter of the distribution.

Analyses at the individual level showed that, taking into account all other factors, the raw scores of girls were significantly higher, and those of boys significantly lower than the average, at each assessment. In the first year, for example, this represented a difference of about five months in reading age in favour of girls. The effects of sex upon reading attainment are illustrated in Table 7.7.

TABLE 7.7: Effects of sex on reading attainment at each assessment

Adjusted deviations in raw score points			
	Girls	Boys	Overall average	Difference
Year 1 (autumn)	+4.0	-4.1	46.1	8.1
Year 2 (autumn)	+3.6	-3.8	63.5	7.4
Year 3 (autumn)	+2.4	-2.5	41.0	4.9
Year 3 (summer)	+3.2	-3.4	52.6	6.8

(All analyses are adjusted for the effects of sex, age and all other background factors. Therefore, the effects of sex are expressed, net of other factors.)

In terms of the London Reading Test (LRT) results, a similar pattern of sex differences was identified. Girls were much less likely than boys to score below 35 points (the 'cut off' recommended for special needs screening at secondary transfer). In all, 19 per cent of girls, compared with nearly 32 per cent of boys, obtained LRT scores of below 35. These results, therefore, provide no evidence of a significant closing of the gap in reading achievement between boys and girls during the junior years. Our findings, on the importance of sex as a factor influencing reading attainment, support those of the APU Language Survey (1981) which also indicated, in a national sample, that girls' attainment was superior to that of boys.

Reading progress
Analyses of progress in reading, however, indicated that sex did not have a significant effect on progress in addition to the effect on reading attainment. Thus, when account was taken of reading attainment at entry, girls did not make greater or less progress in reading over the junior years than boys. The reasons for the differences between the two sexes in reading attainment are not easily explained. It is possible that girls enjoy reading activities more than boys and that this causes them to spend more time than boys in private reading at home or at school (see APU, 1981, for details of reading preferences). Alternatively, girls may perceive reading as an area in which it is acceptable to excel, or they may receive more adult encouragement in their reading than boys. In the section on non-cognitive outcomes, the behaviour and attitudinal data are examined to test whether differences in behaviour and in attitudes to reading were also associated with pupils' sex.

Mathematics attainment
Figures in Table 7.8 show the average raw scores in mathematics for the two sexes at each assessment.

TABLE 7.8: Average raw mathematics scores at each assessment by sex

	Girls	Boys
Year 1 (autumn)	24.6	24.0
Year 2 (autumn)	24.5	24.0
Year 3 (autumn)	29.4	29.2
Year 3 (summer)	27.5	25.8

In contrast to reading, sex was not related significantly to mathematics attainment at entry to junior school. Taking into account other background factors in the individual level analyses, very little difference in attainment was identified in any assessment except that made in the summer of the third year. At this stage, however, sex had some effect on mathematics attainment, although the differences between the two groups just failed to reach statistical significance. Although small, (just over one raw point), the sex difference in mathematics attainment in the summer of the third year was in favour of the girls. Our results provide no evidence, therefore, that girls' performance in the mathematical skills included in this test declines with age, at least during the junior years. If anything, girls had marginally higher achievement than boys in the later junior years. We recognise, however, that this may not be true in areas of mathematics not included in this test.

Mathematics Progress
Interestingly, given commonly held beliefs about girls' underachievement in mathematics, it was found that, when initial attainment was controlled, sex had a statistically significant impact on progress in mathematics (p=0.02). This difference was in favour of girls, who made slightly more progress than the boys over the first three years in junior school. This result indicates that girls were not underachieving in mathematics during the primary years and, in terms of mathematics attainment, they did not transfer to secondary school disadvantaged in comparison with their male peers.

Writing attainment

Sex was related highly significantly to the length of children's writing in the first year of junior school. The differences between the sexes in the length of stories written was 21 words (compared to the average of 88 words), in favour of the girls. More importantly, the work of the two sexes differed significantly in the first year, in terms of quality of language and ideas. The difference was more than half a point (compared with an average of 6.4 points). Overall, in the first year only 20 per cent of girls' writing was assessed as below average in terms of quality of ideas and language. This compares with a figure of 33 per cent for the boys. A very similar result was found in the third year. In all, 19 per cent of the girls', compared with 27 per cent of boys' writing, was assessed as below average on this occasion. There were also significant sex differences in most of the technical measures for example in legibility and the use of punctuation.

As with reading, therefore, the girls' attainment in writing was markedly better than that of the boys. This again confirms findings by the APU (1982) that girls tend to achieve more highly than boys in language-based areas. In both the second and third year writing assessments, girls' writing was found to be significantly longer than that of the boys and was again assessed more highly in terms of quality. It appears, therefore, that girls' initial superiority in writing performance was maintained during the junior years.

The children's writing contained many examples of sex-stereotyping in the roles and behaviour that were ascribed to men and women, especially their parents (see Bunch, 1984). Mothers were almost always portrayed at home, doing domestic jobs and interacting with the children: 'I did not tell my mum but when she was cleaning my room she found it'. In contrast, frequent references were made to fathers returning from work. It is perhaps a reflection of the present economic climate, however, that a percentage of children appeared to be aware of, and value, the concept of having a job.

Girls and boys also attributed different (and stereotypical) activities to their own sex. Boys frequently mentioned football and fighting, whereas girls described playing on the swings or slide, shopping, talking or just 'playing'. They also mentioned crying when they were upset more frequently than did boys. If boys admitted to crying, they tended to qualify the reaction in some way:

> 'He got so frustrated that he sat down and cried and cried which was unusual for Peter for he was a strong man'.
>
> (Adrian).

> 'I began thinking to myself 'why do people think I'm being horrible' and sat down on my bed and began crying'.
>
> (Patricia).

Writing progress
In terms of progress, however, although on average girls' writing was significantly longer than that of boys (by 34 words compared with a mean of 246), in the summer of the third year sex did not make a significant contribution to the explanation of this variation in length. Similarly, sex was not related to progress in terms of quality of third year writing (when quality of first year writing and background factors were controlled). Therefore, girls did not make greater or less progress than boys in creative writing over three years, although differences in attainment remained apparent.

Practical mathematics attainment
No sex differences were identified in any of the three years in which practical mathematics assessments were conducted, either in overall performance, or in the specific skills measured by the different areas covered by the test. Therefore, in neither written nor practical tasks was there any evidence of underachievement by girls in mathematics during the junior years.

Oracy attainment
Sex was not related to performance in any of the five scales used to assess children's oral skills. Moreover, no significant differences between the sexes in their performance in different types of speaking activity were identified. Therefore, although girls had higher achievement than boys in two of the language assessments (writing and reading) they did not have superior attainments in all language-based activities. Again, this result supports the conclusions reached by the APU's work on oracy (see Gorman et al, 1984).

Relationships between cognitive outcomes

There were few differences between girls and boys in the relationships identified between different cognitive areas, within or across years. Thus, even though the overall reading attainment of girls was higher, for both sexes performance in reading or in mathematics at entry to junior school was a good predictor of attainment in that area for both sexes three years later. For the quality of writing assessment (in which, as a group, the boys' attainments were significantly lower than those of the girls, in each year), the first year assessment was a rather better predictor of third year writing attainment for girls than for boys ($r=0.67$ and $r=0.58$ respectively). It appears that boys' writing performance was more changeable than that of girls during the junior years.

There were some minor differences between the sexes in the relationships between writing and mathematics attainment. In each year, the relationship was slightly weaker for boys than for girls, and this may reflect the girls' superior writing performance. Some boys who attained poor assessments for their creative writing may, nonetheless, have achieved highly in mathematical work. Conversely, the relationship between practical mathematics and writing attainment was much weaker for girls than for boys, in the third year. The practical assessment did not require writing skills and it seems possible that, amongst older pupils, those girls who score highly in writing do not necessarily do as well in practical mathematics (r=0.38 for girls compared with r=0.58 for boys).

Interestingly, the general oracy assessment and reading attainment were more strongly correlated for girls (r=0.67) than for boys (r=0.58). This result suggests that speaking skills were more closely related to performance in reading for girls than for boys. This may possibly be due to the absence of sex differences in oral work, but their presence in the reading assessments.

Overall, therefore, there were some differences between the sexes in the ways different aspects of cognitive attainment were related. Nonetheless, in general, for both boys and girls, early performance remains a fairly good predictor of later attainment during the junior years of schooling.

Teachers' assessments of pupils' ability

Overall, a higher percentage of girls than of boys were assessed as above average ability by their teachers, at each assessment (see Figure 7.6). Analyses of the relationships between children's attainments in cognitive areas and teachers' ratings of ability, indicated that reading,

Figure 7.6 Percentage of pupils assessed as a) above b) below average ability by sex (years 2 and 3)

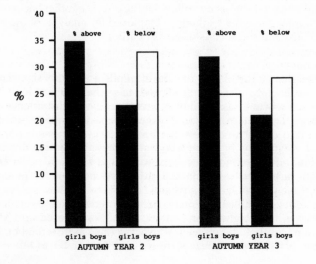

writing and mathematics performance were strongly related to teachers' judgements. As has been demonstrated, girls were achieving significantly more highly than boys in reading and in writing. When account was taken of children's attainments in these three areas, no significant difference between the sexes in teachers' assessments of ability were identified. Surprisingly, when account was taken of attainment, the small difference between the two sexes in ability rating was consistently in favour of the boys (though these results were not statistically significant).

Comparisons of the two sexes in terms of verbal reasoning band allocated indicated that, as might be expected given their superior attainment at the junior level, a higher percentage of girls than of boys were allocated to band one (26% of girls compared with 18% of boys). Conversely, a lower percentage of girls than of boys were allocated to band three (19% of girls compared with 29% of boys).

Analyses of children's test scores, adjusted for age, indicated that neither sex was more or less likely than the other to be allocated to a higher or lower band than predicted by test scores. In all, eight per cent of girls and eight per cent of boys were allocated to a higher band than predicted by their VR score, and a very similar percentage of both sexes were allocated to a lower band than predicted. These results suggest that, at the junior level, the sex of pupils did not have a significant impact on teachers' judgements of pupils' ability, and there was no evidence of a consistent bias towards either sex.

Non-cognitive outcomes

Relationships between sex and behaviour, attitudes, and self-concept were investigated whilst controlling for the effects of other background factors, using the same methods as employed for analyses of the influence of age and social class discussed earlier.

Behaviour
Our analyses indicated that the sex of pupils was highly significantly related to teachers' assessments of children's behaviour in school. Girls were less likely to be assessed of as having behaviour disturbance than were boys. The pattern of sex differences in behaviour ratings remained pronounced on each occasion that behaviour was assessed. Furthermore, a comparison of pupils who were assessed as having disturbed behaviour on two or more occasions with those who were never assessed as disturbed, revealed marked differences between the groups in terms of the percentages of girls and boys. Thus, of those assessed as having behaviour difficulties on two or more occasions, the percentage of boys was much higher than that of girls (63% compared with 37%). In contrast, of those pupils who were never rated as disturbed by their teachers, a higher percentage were girls (56%) than boys (44%). The

results of our analyses support findings of differences between the sexes in the incidence of behaviour difficulties reported by Chazan & Jackson, 1974; and Varlaam, 1974.

Therefore, it appears that the sex of pupils is related to non-cognitive outcomes, such as behaviour in school, as well as to cognitive attainment. As noted earlier, attainment and behaviour were quite closely related. It is possible that part of the relationship between sex and behaviour may be due to boys' poorer attainment in certain cognitive areas. If poor attainment has an adverse impact on behaviour, boys' poorer achievement may account for their greater risk of behaviour disturbance. Alternatively, if poor behaviour has a detrimental impact on later attainment, then boys' poorer behaviour may account for some of the differences in cognitive outcomes between the sexes. However, what is perhaps particularly surprising is that, despite better attainment and better behaviour, there was no evidence of over-expectation of girls by teachers. With both age and class, the superior group was favoured by teachers. We might have expected, therefore, to find the same trend operating with girls.

Attitudes
Analyses revealed no significant relationship between pupils' attitude to mathematics and sex, in any of the three years for which information was obtained. Thus, there was no evidence that girls have a less positive view of mathematics than boys during the junior years.

Sex was not related significantly to attitude to reading in the first or the second year. By the third year, a small but statistically significant difference between the two sexes in attitude to reading was apparent. Girls had a marginally more favourable view than boys at this stage. Both groups, however, had a generally positive view. Given the absence of a relationship between attitude to reading and sex in the first and second years, it seems unlikely that differences in attitudes between the two sexes could explain the markedly higher attainment of girls compared with boys in those years. Moreover, there were no differences between the sexes in attitudes to writing, another cognitive area in which differences in attainment were noted.

In contrast, sex was related highly significantly to the attitude to school expressed by children in each of the three years. In each year, boys expressed a less positive view of school than the girls. For example, in the third year 32 per cent of boys rated their feelings about school very negatively. The equivalent figure for girls was only 17 per cent. Conversely 27 per cent of girls but only 19 per cent of boys had a very positive view. At the junior level, therefore, boys are more likely than girls to be disenchanted with school.

The reasons for sex differences in attitudes to school are not clear. Although poor attainment by boys might be expected to lead to less favourable attitudes to school work and to school in general, sex differences in attitudes to curriculum areas were weak or non-existent (as described above). It is possible that the tendency for boys to have a higher incidence of behaviour difficulties may have affected their attitudes to school. But it is equally possible that less favourable attitudes to school led to behaviour problems. However, as reported earlier, amongst the whole sample, relationships between behaviour and attitudes were rather weak.

Attendance

Sex was not related to attendance in the first, second or third year of junior school. The generally higher attainments of girls in certain cognitive areas were not due to better attendance at school. Moreover, although boys tended to have poorer behaviour and less favourable attitudes to school, they were no more likely than girls to be absent from school.

Self-concept

As with attitudes to school, girls were found to have significantly more positive self-concepts in relation to school than boys. This may reflect the nature of some of the items relating to naughtiness included in the questionnaire. The boys were more likely than the girls to admit to naughtiness and irritability and also were more likely to think that the teacher perceived them as being naughty. However, they were less likely than the girls to rate themselves highly on items concerned with personal anxiety. As noted in the discussion of behaviour, there was a highly significant difference between the two sexes in teachers' assessments of behaviour in school. Overall, in each year, teachers assessed a higher proportion of boys than of girls as having behaviour problems.

Relationships between non-cognitive outcomes

Although, in general, the relationships between the various non-cognitive outcomes were similar for girls and boys, there were a few differences in the second and third year. For girls, attitude to school was more closely linked to attitude to mathematics than was the case for boys in the second year ($r=0.55$ for girls compared with 0.48 for boys). A similar pattern was identified for the link between attitude to writing and attitude to school in the second year ($r=0.50$ for girls, $r=0.44$ for boys). There was no difference between the two sexes, however, in the stability of attitudes over time. For both groups, relationships were very weak. As with pupils as a whole, attitude to mathematics was more stable than attitude to reading or to writing, for both girls and boys.

Behaviour and attendance were weakly but significantly linked for girls and boys, in the first year. By the third year, the relationship was no longer significant for girls but remained of significance for boys (though it was very weak, r=0.11). First year attendance was a better predictor of third year attendance for girls than for boys (r=0.52 for girls, r=0.45 for boys). Thus, it appears that poor school attendance in the first year amongst girls is slightly more likely to be related to poor attendance in later years of junior education.

Relationships between cognitive and non-cognitive outcomes

It has already been demonstrated that behaviour difficulties in school were more common amongst boys than amongst girls throughout the junior years. However, the link between behaviour and attainment in both reading and in mathematics was closer for girls than for boys in the first and second years. The association for both groups was, however, strongest at entry to junior education. Analysis of the three areas of behaviour difficulties indicated that anxiety and attainment in reading and in mathematics were more closely linked for girls than boys. Although girls as a group had significantly higher attainment in reading, similar attainment in mathematics, and were rated as having fewer behaviour problems, where behaviour difficulties related to anxiety were identified, the link with attainment was stronger for girls than for boys.

SUMMARY

Our data have revealed marked differences between girls and boys in reading and writing attainment, but not in progress, throughout the junior years. In mathematics, however, differences in attainment were slight, but girls made greater progress than boys over the junior years. There were no sex differences in oracy. Girls tended to have more positive attitudes towards school and more favourable self-concepts. Marked differences were identified by class teachers between the two sexes in behaviour in school. Boys were more likely than girls to be assessed as having behaviour difficulties.

DIFFERENCES ACCORDING TO RACE

Having looked at age, social class and sex, we now turn to an examination of the effects of race on the progress of the pupils.

Cognitive outcomes

Reading attainment
Results of analyses of the effects of ethnic background and fluency in English upon reading attainment at entry to junior school indicate that

both factors were highly significant. Thus, children who were not fully fluent in English, according to their class teacher, obtained markedly lower reading scores than those who were fully fluent. The effect of being a beginner, or at the second stage of fluency in English, was a reduction in reading scores by between 14 and 23 raw points, in relation to the overall mean of forty-six. For a description of the definition used to determine pupils' stage of fluency in English see Kysel (1982).

The effects of ethnic background were more complicated. Even where fluency in English and other background factors had been controlled, certain Asian groups performed differently from others. For example, those who spoke Gujerati performed better than average in the reading test, whilst those speaking Punjabi had poorer reading attainment. However, because the numbers of Asian children in different language groups were often small (eg Gujerati = 14 in year 1, Punjabi = 10) results on differences between sub-groups of Asian children should be treated with great caution. Children of Caribbean, Greek and Turkish family backgrounds obtained lower reading scores than those of English, Scottish, Welsh or Irish (ESWI) backgrounds. Those of Chinese family backgrounds (only 17 in all) had higher scores than those of other ethnic groups, when all other background factors had been taken into account.

In both the second year and the third year reading assessments, ethnic background and fluency in English remained highly significant. There was no evidence, therefore, that the impact of these factors decreased over the junior years. For reading attainment, the pattern of initial differences remained fairly stable over time.

Reading progress
Relationships between ethnic family background, language fluency and childrens' progress in reading over three years were explored. It was found that both factors had a statistically significant impact upon progress. Children of Caribbean backgrounds and those of Asian backgrounds made significantly poorer progress than other groups, even when account was taken of initial attainment. Children who were not fully fluent in English at entry to junior school also made significantly poorer progress in reading over the three years. The poorer progress of minority ethnic groups in reading supports the results of previous research (see Rampton, 1981 or Mabey, 1981, 1985) which indicated that the gap in attainment between English and Caribbean children increases over time. Amongst the present sample, however, it also appears that Asian children as well as Caribbean children made poorer progress in reading over the junior years. The size of these differences are given in Table 7.9.

TABLE 7.9: Effects of ethnic background and fluency in English upon reading progress over three years

Effect in raw score points*

Caribbean	-3.4
Asian	-4.5
Incomplete fluency in English	-3.7

Overall average = 53.8

* (Analyses adjusted for all background factors, including age, sex, social class, initial attainment, test reliability and the clustered nature of the sample. Due to the small sample of Asian pupils it was not possible to examine separately the progress of different language sub-groups.)

Mathematics attainment
For mathematics attainment at entry, analyses also identified highly significant relationships with ethnic background and with fluency in English. Again, there was variation in the achievements of different sub-groups of Asian children. Those who spoke Bengali tended to have lower scores than those who spoke Gujerati (a difference of 5.5 raw points compared with an average of 24.3). Children who were of Caribbean and of Turkish origins also tended to obtain lower scores (2.6 and 1.5 points respectively below the average). A consistent pattern of differences between the different ethnic groups in mathematics attainment was also identified in analyses of asessments in later years. Thus, as a group, in the summer of year three, Caribbean children's attainments were 4.5 points below the average of 26.8 raw points, and Turkish and Greek children were nearly two points below. In contrast, Gujerati-speaking Asian pupils (a small group) scored nearly three points above the average. This pattern of ethnic differences was very similar to that identified in the first year.

Mathematics progress
Although the gap in mathematics attainment remained marked throughout the junior years for children of different ethnic backgrounds or with different levels of fluency in English, there was no evidence of an ethnic or fluency effect on progress in mathematics. Controlling for initial attainment, neither Caribbean or Asian children made significantly poorer progress than their peers. This result is posi-

tive because it indicates that differences in the performance of children from different ethnic backgrounds do not increase over the junior years in mathematics, in contrast to the results for reading.

Writing attainment
There was no significant relationship between ethnic background and writing performance in the first year in terms of quality or length. In contrast, fluency in English was highly related significantly to both length and quality of writing. In the summer of the third year, however, it was found that ethnic background was related significantly to the length of writing, with the various Asian groups, those of Caribbean and those of Turkish backgrounds tending to produce shorter pieces of work. There were, however, no significant differences between ethnic groups in terms of quality of ideas and language expressed in their written work. Again, fluency in English was related significantly to quality, but no longer had an independent impact upon length of writing.

An examination of the children's writing revealed no evidence of racist attitudes or racial stereotyping. This does not necessarily mean that they did not exist, or that the children were unaware of such attitudes. However, we found that racial issues were not reflected in their writing during the junior school year (see Bunch, 1984).

Writing progress
When progress in the quality of writing was analysed, no relationship was found with ethnic background, although the effects of fluency in English just reached significance. Thus, taking account of first year writing quality, children who were not fully fluent in English made slightly poorer progress over the three years than did children who were fully fluent (by around half a point on the ten point quality scale). For progress in the quantity written over three years, controlling for length of first year writing, it was found that ethnic background did not have a statistically significant effect. These results indicate that, in terms of quality of writing, ethnic background was not related to attainment or to progress during the junior years. This is in contrast to the findings for reading and for mathematics attainment. As might be expected, however, children not fluent in English are disadvantaged in attainment in writing as well as in reading and mathematics.

Practical mathematics
There were few significant relationships between achievement in practical mathematics tasks and either ethnic or language background. Children of Asian background performed slightly less well than other groups in the volume tasks. Fluency in English was only related to attainment in activities related to work with sets. Overall, however, the relationships were not strong.

Oracy

As stated earlier, the oracy assessments were designed to judge the communicative effectiveness of children's speech, and assessors did not penalise pupils who used non-standard English. Results from the analyses indicated that ethnic background was not related to perfor- mance in any of the five scales used to assess the oracy sample. Interest- ingly, fluency in English, as assessed by teachers, was not related to pupils' speaking skills. The reasons for this may be due to an improvement in pupils' abilities to speak English over the junior years (the fluency assessment was made in the first year of junior school, whereas the oracy assessments took place in the fourth year). Alterna- tively, the ability to use standard English forms may be more closely related to reading achievement than to oral skills. These findings show that in some language areas – oracy and quality of writing - there were no significant differences between children of different ethnic backgrounds. For reading and mathematics attainment and for prog- ress in reading, differences were identified. The reasons for differences between the measures of attainment and of progress in reading, rather than in other areas of language, are not yet clear.

Relationships between cognitive outcomes

Due to the longitudinal nature of the Junior School Project, it was possible to compare relationships between children's attainments in different cognitive areas within and across years separately for three groups: Caribbean, Asian, and English, Scottish, Welsh and Irish. (Due to the small numbers of pupils in other ethnic groups and the small numbers in separate Asian language groups, it was not feasible to examine results separately for these pupils.) The results revealed that, for all groups, reading attainment at entry was a very good predictor of attainment three years later, though the correlation was highest for the Asian group ($r=0.87$ for Asian, $r=0.79$ for Caribbean, $r=0.78$ for others).

In the quality of writing, however, it was found that, for the Asian group, the association between attainment in the first and the third year was much weaker than for the other groups ($r=0.43$ for the Asian, $r=0.71$ for the Caribbean, $r=0.59$ for the others). This indicates that performance at entry to junior school does not give as good a prediction of later attainment for Asian children as for others. This was almost certainly related to the numbers of Asian pupils who were not fully fluent in English at entry, and whose writing skills in English would, therefore, have been limited, but who progressed over the next three years in both written and spoken English. There were no differences between groups for the inter-relationships of mathematics and other cognitive areas.

There was no consistent pattern of differences between the three groups in terms of the relationships between reading and writing attainment, in any year. For oracy, however, (in which there were no significant differences in the overall performance of children from different ethnic groups) the relationship between reading attainment and communicative effectiveness in speaking was less strong for the Asian than for the other groups ($r=0.49$ for Asian, $r=0.69$ for Caribbean, $r=0.59$ for others). This was also true of the relationships between writing and oracy when the three groups were compared.

Teachers' assessments of pupils' ability
At each assessment, a higher percentage of English, Scottish, Welsh and Irish than of other pupils were assessed by their class teachers as of above average ability, and a smaller percentage as of below average ability (see Figure 7.7).

Figure 7.7: Percentage of pupils assessed as a) above b) below average ability by ethnic group (years 2 and 3)

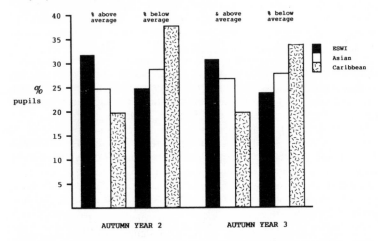

As noted earlier in this chapter, class teachers' ability ratings were found to be related strongly to children's attainments in reading, writing and mathematics. Individual analyses of ability ratings, once other background factors (including sex, age and father's social class) and attainment in these three areas had been controlled, indicated that ethnic background was no longer related to ability ratings. From our data it appears that teachers were not biased against those of ethnic minority backgrounds, when judging pupils' abilities.

Analyses of the relationship between VR Band allocated and ethnic background also revealed marked differences (see Table 7.10).

TABLE 7.10: Percentages of pupils allocated to verbal reasoning band one, two and three by ethnic background

	Band One %	Band Two %	Band Three %
Asian	9.9	49.5	40.6
Caribbean	13.2	49.1	37.7
ESWI	24.7	56.7	18.6
All pupils for whom VR band and VR test score obtained	21.8	54.7	23.5

In a large part, these differences were due to performance in the verbal reasoning test. For the vast majority of pupils, the band to which they were allocated and that predicted by test score were the same. However, the agreement was somewhat lower for the Caribbean group (78% for Caribbean compared with 86% for ESWI and 89% for Asian pupils). There appeared to be a tendency for some Caribbean children, predicted as band one on the basis of test score, to be assigned to band two by their school. Due to the very small numbers of pupils involved, it is not possible to test the statistical significance of this tendency but the figures are presented in Table 7.11.

TABLE 7.11: Percentage of pupils allocated to a lower verbal reasoning band than predicted on the basis of test score by ethnic background

	% Pupils predicted VR Band One assigned Band Two	% Pupils predicted VR Band Two assigned Band Three
Caribbean	31.4	16.5
ESWI	11.5	7.1

N of Caribbean predicted Band One, 35; Band Two = 103
N of ESWI predicted Band One, 217; Band Two = 494

(Due to the small numbers of Asian pupils for whom data were obtained it was not possible for this group to be included in these analyses.)

The implications of this finding are disturbing, given the use of VR bands in the secondary transfer process, and may suggest the possible existence of subconscious racism in the operation of the banding procedures for some children.

Non-cognitive outcomes

Behaviour
Overall, there was a higher incidence of behaviour difficulties in school (according to class teachers' assessments) amongst the Caribbean than amongst other groups. Thus, using the criterion of being assessed highly in terms of the behaviour scale (where a high score signifies greater difficulties) in two or more of the three years, nearly 20 per cent of Caribbean, compared with 12 per cent of Asian and 11 per cent of other pupils, were highly rated. The most common form of behaviour difficulty for all groups was associated with learning behaviour problems – rather than aggression or anxiety. In all, nearly 14 per cent of the Caribbean, compared with only five per cent of Asian and eight per cent of English, Scottish, Welsh and Irish pupils were rated highly on the learning difficulties sub-scale.

Much of the relationship between ethnic background and behaviour was accounted for by other factors (it has already been demonstrated that father's social class, sex and eligibility for free meals made a significant contribution to the explanation of variations in behaviour). Nonetheless, taking a combined measure of behaviour over three years, analyses at the individual level indicated that, when controlling for the influence of all other background factors, Caribbean pupils were assessed as having greater behaviour difficulties. This effect, though statistically highly significant, was nevertheless small in comparison to the effects of pupil sex, father's social class, or eligibility for free meals.

It is likely that the higher incidence of behaviour difficulties in school (as assessed by teachers) amongst Caribbean pupils, may be due, in part, to the significant link between attainment, especially in reading, and behaviour (discussed in the last chapter). It has already been shown that the Caribbean group had significantly lower attainments at each assessment than ESWI pupils, though not in comparison with Asian pupils. Controlling for first year reading attainment removed the relationship between pupils, race and teachers' behaviour ratings. It thus appears that lower attainment was related to behaviour, especially learning behaviour difficulties, and that the higher incidence of behaviour difficulties identified amongst Caribbean pupils in the sample over a three year period was possibly attributable to this factor, rather than to race. Controlling for attainment, however, did not remove the significant relationships between sex, free meals, and father's social class and behaviour. These factors continued to have a statistically significant impact. Nonetheless, the link between attainment and behaviour is complex and no clear conclusions can be drawn from these results.

Attendance
Differences in attendance were identified during the junior years according to ethnic background. In each year, children of Caribbean background were present for a higher percentage of the time than the ESWI group, whilst children of Asian backgrounds were, on average, absent for a higher percentage of time (see Table 7.12).

TABLE 7.12:
Average percentages of time absent in years one, two and three by ethnic background

Ethnic group	average % time absent		
	Year 1	Year 2	Year 3
Asian	11.7	11.6	10.6
Caribbean	7.1	8.2	6.1
ESWI	9.1	9.5	9.0

Taking into account all other background factors, sex and age, analyses at the level of the individual pupil indicated that these differences in attendance were highly statistically significant for the Caribbean group, and were largest in the third year. At this stage, Caribbean children were absent for 3.3 per cent less time than the average for the sample as a whole (8.3%). This represents just over one week's extra attendance in the school year. Although Asian children, as a group, tended to have the poorest attendance, this trend was not statistically significant when other background factors were taken into account.

Attitudes
Overall, there were a few statistically significant differences in the attitudes of children from different ethnic backgrounds. Asian children tended to have more favourable attitudes towards mathematics in the second and third years and towards school in the first and second years. For those of Caribbean backgrounds, more favourable attitudes towards mathematics were identified in the first year, and more favourable attitudes towards reading in the third year. The ESWI group tended to have the least favourable attitudes to school.

Self-concept

Asian children tended to rate themselves significantly more favourably at the end of their third year in junior school than other children. There was, however, no evidence to suggest that Caribbean children had poorer self-concepts in relation to the school environment. (This finding is in contrast to some earlier research which suggested that black children had poorer self-concepts than their white peers – see, for example, Wylie, 1963; Proshansky & Newton, 1968, but is in agreement with the arguments of Stone, 1981).

Relationships between non-cognitive outcomes

In most respects, the pattern of relationships between the different non-cognitive outcomes was very similar for children of different ethnic backgrounds. Over time, successive behaviour ratings were more closely related than was attendance. Attitudes measured at different points in time were very weakly associated for members of each ethnic group. Nonetheless, some differences were identified.

Behaviour ratings in different years were much more closely related for both the Caribbean and the ESWI groups than for the Asian group. The correlations between the first and third year behaviour assessments (autumn) were 0.64 for the Caribbean, 0.56 for the ESWI and 0.41 for the Asian groups. Thus, not only was the incidence of behaviour difficulties generally lower for the Asian group, there was also greater variation amongst individuals in their behaviour over time.

For attendance, differences between the groups were also identified. The relationship between first and third year attendance was weakest for the Asian group (who had the poorest attendance record in each year) and strongest for the ESWI group. For Caribbean children (who, as a group had the best record of school attendance in each year) the correlation, though significant, was rather weaker ($r=0.59$ for ESWI, $r=0.34$ for Caribbean, and $r=0.02$ for the Asian group between first and third year attendance). It is clear that, for individual Asian pupils, the record of attendance in the first year of junior education is not a good predictor of attendance in later years. For other groups, however, first year attendance is more likely to be related to future attendance.

As with the patterns described for pupils as a whole, attitudes to school and to curriculum areas in different years were very weakly associated. In general, however, attitudes to school, to mathematics and to writing were rather more closely linked for the Asian than for other groups. It appears that, as a whole, Asian pupils tend to have more positive attitudes to school and some curriculum areas, and also that their attitudes tended to be slightly more stable over time.

Relationships between cognitive and non-cognitive outcomes

As noted earlier difficulties associated with learning behaviour were more common (according to teachers' assessments) amongst the Caribbean than amongst other groups. Analyses of the relationship between attainment in reading and the assessment of children on the learning sub-scale of the behaviour scale indicated that the relationship was strongest for the Caribbean and weakest for the Asian groups in each year (see Table 7.13).

TABLE 7.13: Correlations between reading attainment and learning behaviour by ethnic background

	Reading & learning behaviour difficulties		
	Asian r	Caribbean r	ESWI r
autumn year 1	-0.51	-0.61	-0.58
autumn year 2	-0.43	-0.61	-0.55
autumn year 3	-0.53	-0.56	-0.55

A similar pattern was identified for mathematics and for the quality of writing in the second and third years. In each case, the attainments of Caribbean children were much more closely linked to learning behaviour than was the case for the Asian group. Our results show that behaviour was more closely linked to attainment in cognitive areas for the Caribbean group, followed by the ESWI group. The relationships were weakest for Asian pupils.

SUMMARY

The results of examining differences in educational outcomes according to pupils' race and language background, indicate that there were significant differences in some areas of cognitive attainment, specifically reading and mathematics, both at entry to junior school and in later years. Moreover, we found small but significant differences in progress in reading, with the Caribbean group making poorer progress than predicted by first year attainment. Differences, however, were not identified for writing or oral skills.

It also appears that the effects of race varied for the non-cognitive outcomes of education. The incidence of behaviour difficulties was higher (though still recorded only for a minority) amongst Caribbean children, in their class teachers' assessments. This relationship, however, was apparently due to poorer attainment (behaviour and attainment being closely linked). In contrast, we found that the Caribbean group had better attendance and Asian pupils poorer attendance during the junior years. On the whole, attitudes varied little, but the Asian group tended to have more favourable attitudes to school and to mathematics, whilst Caribbean children had more favourable views of reading. We found no evidence that minority groups had less positive self-concepts than their white peers, and the Asian children actually had more favourable views of themselves in school than others.

OVERVIEW

In this chapter we have demonstrated the importance and complexity of the relationships between background factors, sex and age and children's attainment, progress and non-cognitive development. In particular, age, social class, sex and race, were all found to be related to attainment, and in some cases to progress and non-cognitive development. Our analyses demonstrate the need to take full account of such factors before examing school effects on pupils' educational outcomes.

8

Teacher Expectations

The previous chapter has detailed the progress of different groups of pupils as they moved through the years of junior schooling. In this chapter we will discuss the phenomenon of teacher expectations and examine our data for evidence of differential expectations for any of these groups.

Every class room inevitably contains pupils of differing personalities, abilities and backgrounds. Previous research findings demonstrate that, for some teachers at least, the expectations they have for their pupils can influence the children's future academic performance and self-perception (see, for example, Pilling and Kellmer Pringle, 1978; and Meyer, 1982). Nash (1973) suggests that the teachers' behaviour is affected by their expectations, and 'somehow the teacher's mental attitudes to the child are ... being communicated ...' (p.12). Thus, different pupils may be presented with quite different psychological environments by their teachers.

Inevitably, many predictions about pupil achievement are based on past experience and may well reflect accurate teacher expectations. Furthermore, as Brophy and Good (1974) pointed out, not all teachers will allow their expectations to interfere with their ability to treat pupils appropriately. Some studies, however, have shown that certain teachers do treat children differently according to differential beliefs about them (see Pilling and Kellmer Pringle, 1978). We have been able to consider whether teacher behaviour, particularly in terms of individual contacts with pupils, varied towards different groups of children. These groups are defined by age, sex, social class, ethnic background, perceived ability and behaviour.

AGE DIFFERENCES

It has been shown in the last chapter that the attainment of younger pupils within a year group was generally poorer than that of their older peers, although there was no difference in their progress in cognitive skills. Teachers, however, were found consistently to have judged pupils born in the summer months as being of lower ability and having more behaviour difficulties. Younger pupils themselves also were found to have a less positive view of school than their older peers.

Pidgeon (1970) has suggested that teachers 'know' that older children are capable of doing more advanced work and – albeit subconsciously – expect more from them. In order to test out this theory, teachers' communications with pupils of different ages were analysed. The youngest pupils (those born in the summer term) were found to have received the least feedback on their behaviour, whilst the oldest received the most. This is surprising, given that the youngest pupils were rated as having the most problems and were also observed to be distracted from their work more frequently than the older ones. This finding suggests that Pidgeon's explanation may need to be adapted. It may be that teachers have expectations of pupils' behaviour in that they 'know', subconsciously, that older pupils are more mature. They may be less prepared, therefore, to accept disobedience from older children.

Teachers also listened to autumn born pupils read more frequently than they listened to their younger peers, even though the older children scored more highly in the reading assessments and were rated as being of higher ability. No other statistically significant differences in interaction, however, between teachers and pupils of different ages were identified.

In mixed-age classes covering more than one year group, less than a third of the teachers reported that they usually gave younger and older pupils different work in language and mathematics sessions. In project work, only nine per cent of the teachers took age into account when planning work. Given that younger children achieve less well in the cognitive assessments, it is likely that they may be even more at risk in mixed-age classes where all the pupils are given the same work. However, it is also possible that older pupils are held back because work is pitched at too low a level for them. This could also occur in single-age classes where all pupils work on the same task.

SOCIAL CLASS DIFFERENCES

The influence of pupils' background upon teacher behaviour in the classroom has concerned researchers for some time (see Pilling and Kelmer Pringle, 1978, for a review). Opinion is divided. Some studies have found no social class effect (Nash, 1973; Murphy, 1974; Croll, 1981). Others, however, indicate that social class is one of the major sources of expectations teachers hold for their pupils (Goodacre, 1968; Barker Lunn, 1970; Dusek and Joseph, 1983) and that teachers' behaviour can vary according to a child's background. For example, Sharp and Green (1975) found that pupils whom teachers regarded as more 'successful' were given greater attention than other children. These pupils invariably came from a 'good area'. The influence of social class may not always be relevant, particularly if teachers know little about a child's home circumstances. Nonetheless, other cues such as speech, physical appearance and eligibility for free school meals, may also be indicators of social class.

The fact that pupils from non-manual backgrounds had higher attainments in most of the cognitive assessments and made more progress in reading and writing has already been pointed out. They were also rated by their teachers as of higher ability, even after account had been taken of their attainment. Those from unskilled manual backgrounds and from homes where the father was absent were perceived by their teachers as having a greater incidence of behaviour problems. Thus, it appears that some teachers have different expectations of pupils from different social class backgrounds, irrespective of the children's performance on cognitive assessments.

Teachers' contacts with pupils were observed systematically at set periods throughout each observation day. In the second year, observation time over three days totalled four and a quarter hours, almost the equivalent of one whole day's teaching time. During this time the average number of individual contacts between teachers and each pupil was approximately eleven. This covered a wide range, with one child experiencing only one contact, whereas at the other extreme, a teacher communicated with a particular pupil on 63 occasions. Children from one parent families had, on average, just over 15 contacts with the teacher, a figure which is half as much again as that for the non- or skilled manual backgrounds.

There was no significant difference between groups in the number of discussions they had with the teacher about the content of their work. The non-manual and those of skilled manual backgrounds, however, were told significantly less often how to set about and organise their work. There may have been less need for teachers to supervise these latter pupils' work, given their higher attainments in the cognitive assessments.

There was only one significant difference between the social class groups in the frequency with which they were observed reading to their teachers. Pupils whose fathers were not working read to their teachers more often than those who lived with only one parent.

Teachers spent a significantly greater proportion of their time discussing non-work (routine) matters with the pupils whose fathers were absent. This is in line with their ratings of these pupils' behaviour. Routine comments included, for example, advice on the use or location of materials, telling pupils where and with whom they should be sitting, and feedback on behaviour, whether positive, neutral or negative. The particular emphasis on behaviour control also related to the poorer concentration observed amongst pupils in the father-absent group.

Thus, teacher expectations did not appear to affect their behaviour with regard to the depth of discussion on work-related issues. However, in line with their perceptions that pupils who did not come from non-manual backgrounds were less likely to be of above-average ability, teachers devoted more time to the supervision of these pupils' work.

SEX DIFFERENCES

There is already considerable evidence of differences in teacher action towards, and judgements of, girls and boys (Palardy, 1969; Good and Brophy, 1971; Whyte, 1983). The reinforcement of sex-stereotyping in the classroom has also been referred to as part of the 'hidden curriculum' (Serbin, 1983). Thus, teachers may well be completely unaware of their own behaviours that encourage and sustain stereotyping and that, subsequently, may have an effect upon the academic progress and behavioural development of girls and boys.

It will also be seen that girls had higher attainments in reading and writing throughout their junior schooling and slightly higher attainment in mathematics by the third year. There were few other sex differences in pupil performance or progress. Although it did not reach statistical significance, teachers tended to rate boys' ability slightly higher than that of girls, when account was taken of their attainments in cognitive areas. This was surprising, because boys were consistently assessed as having more behaviour difficulties, and were also found to be less positive in their attitude to school. They were also observed to be less involved with their work by the field officers.

The I.L.E.A's Primary Record Summary, completed by teachers at the end of infant school, and at the end of the first and second junior years, was examined for all children individually. Significantly more girls than boys were rated as demonstrating marked ability in the four areas of written language: personal statements; factual statements; imaginative writing; and using information from various sources of reference. Conversely, more boys were rated as showing serious and persistent difficulties in these areas. For mathematics, the only difference was noted at the end of the second year, when more girls were rated at the later stages of development in work involving operations with whole numbers. This is in line with our finding of better progress by girls in mathematics.

Differences, once again in favour of girls, were also found in the stage of reading development reached, particularly at the end of the second year. By this year, significantly more girls could, in the opinion of their class teachers, follow a narrative, appraise material critically, and skim and scan material. They also showed more proficiency in the use of dictionaries, indices and other reference sources.

A similar difference was noted in favour of girls in records of pupils' creative abilities, particularly in dance, drama and music. For art and craft work, there was a slight variation. More boys at the end of infant schooling had difficulties, but there were also more boys showing a particular flair in two and three-dimensional work. In the junior years, differences in teachers' records of boys' and girls' art work were not significant.

Analyses show that teachers communicated more at an individual level with boys than with girls. This was found to be true for both female and male teachers. Differences were greatest in the third year when it was found that female teachers gave boys relatively even more attention.

The major difference concerned a greater use of criticism and neutral remarks to individual boys about their behaviour. This difference was not related to the sex of the teacher. Teachers also communicated more with boys on a non-verbal level, using both facial gestures and physical contact, and teased them more frequently. The extra behaviour control comments to boys are not surprising, given the teachers' lower assessments of boys' behaviour and the boys' tendency to be distracted more often from their work, as seen in the classroom observations. Another possibility is that the boys' poorer behaviour and attitudes to school may be related to, and exacerbated by, their treatment by teachers in the classroom. Thus, perhaps, pupils are reacting to the way they are treated by their teachers, as well as teachers responding to pupils' behaviour.

There were also differences between the sexes in their contact with teachers on work-related issues. Boys were given more work supervision, particularly in the form of extra feedback. Girls, however, received significantly more praise from teachers. Although there was no consistent pattern, there was some suggestion that teachers discussed the factual content of the work more frequently with the boys. There was no difference, however, in the frequency with which teachers heard girls and boys read throughout the day, although in sessions specifically designated for quiet reading, teachers heard more boys than girls read.

Overall, it appears that the main difference in teachers' classroom contact with girls and boys was in the greater number of negative comments, referring to their behaviour, made to boys. Boys also received more communication in general, and work feedback in particular, from their teachers. Given their poorer performance in cognitive areas this is perhaps not surprising. As far as positive work feedback was concerned, however, girls received more. It is interesting that teachers tended to rate the boys slightly more favourably than the girls in terms of ability, when account was taken of individual pupils' performance. Perhaps teachers were being influenced by the generally livelier behaviour of boys.

School Matters

ETHNIC DIFFERENCES

It has also been suggested that teachers' expectations for pupils may be influenced by pupils' ethnic background. Thus, the Rampton Report (1981) proposed that the performance of ethnic minority children might be affected by low teacher expectations due to negative stereotypes about the abilities of such groups. The Swann Report (1985), whilst not rejecting the conclusions of the interim Rampton Report, suggested that the issues involved are complex and merit considerably more research. Eggleston et al (1985) reached similar conclusions to those of Rampton about the educational and vocational experiences of young people of different ethnic groups in the secondary school context. However, an alternative interpretation was offered by Short (1985), who suggested that teachers' expectations might have been influenced by their experience of ethnic minority groups in the classroom.

The Junior School Project found no relationship between teachers' ratings of pupils' ability and the children's ethnic background, once account had been taken of other background factors and attainment. Ability ratings, however, were strongly related to pupil attainments. These attainments were lower in reading, writing and mathematics for Caribbean and some Asian pupils than for other pupils. This suggests, as indicated at the beginning of this section, that for pupils from all ethnic backgrounds, teacher expectations appear to be tied to specific knowledge of previous attainment and performance in the classroom.

A number of differences between pupils of different ethnic backgrounds have already been described. It has been demonstrated that, as a group, Caribbean pupils were rated by their teachers as having more behaviour problems, particularly those connected with learning difficulties. Caribbean pupils' attitudes to reading, however, were more positive than those of other pupils. The same was found for the positive attitudes of Asian pupils to mathematics. Within the classroom, however, Asian pupils were observed to concentrate less upon their work than were other pupils.

Given these differences, it was important to establish whether there were any differences in teacher behaviour towards pupils of different ethnic origins. Using the same sample of pupils who had been selected for observation, and for whom data on ethnic background was available, it was possible to investigate differences between Caribbean, Asian, ESWI and 'other' pupils, to see if any variations in teacher behaviour towards particular groups could be identified. All the observations took place within the classroom.

Teachers were found to have had more individual contacts than the average with Caribbean pupils (average for Caribbean pupils = 13.8, average overall = 10.9) than with other children. There was no difference between groups in the amount of teacher contact related to work discussion, supervision or feedback. However, it was found that teachers talked significantly more often to Caribbean pupils about non-work matters.

Children of Caribbean background also received more neutral and negative feedback on their behaviour than did other pupils. This could be due to teachers' poorer perceptions of the behaviour of this group, as evidenced in the 'Child at School' ratings. (These behaviour ratings were, however, closely linked to attainment, especially for the learning sub-scale.) Teachers also listened to Caribbean pupils read significantly more often than Asian pupils, and slightly more frequently than all the other children. This possibly relates to the poorer progress in reading identified for the Caribbean group. The extra attention in reading may also be responsible for Caribbean pupils' more positive attitudes towards reading in the classroom.

It is, perhaps, surprising that, overall, teachers spent significantly less time hearing Asian pupils read than other children, given the Asian pupils' lower attainments in the reading assessments. It seems, however, from observation of individual pupils, that other adults were used more often to help hear Asian pupils read in the classroom. This may have reflected policies in the particular schools in which Asian pupils were concentrated. Additional resources for second language work tended to be available in these schools.

There was some variation, therefore, in teacher behaviour towards pupils of different ethnic origin. The particular differences (teachers heard Caribbean pupils read more often and devoted more time to non-work contacts with them) suggest that teachers were attempting to meet the individual needs of those pupils. It is clear, however, that no simple explanation of the influence of teachers' behaviour on pupil performance is possible. The data supply no evidence to support the view that teachers were withholding attention from any ethnic group. In fact they appeared to go out of their way to attend to black and ethnic minority pupils. This evidence is positive though, quite clearly, it is not definitive. Expectations can be transmitted in subtle ways and it is possible that it was precisely through such differences in teacher attention that teachers were signalling differential expectations.

ABILITY DIFFERENCES

Most studies of teacher expectations, and the ways in which these may be mediated within the classroom, have concerned the effects of such expectations upon pupils of different abilities (see, for example, Rosenthal and Jacobson, 1968; and Barker Lunn, 1971). Burstall (1968) found that pupils taught by teachers who believed that low ability children were able to learn French achieved better results than those whose teachers thought that such children would not be able to do so.

More recently, attention has focused on teacher behaviour in the classroom. Studies have varied in the extent to which differences in the behaviour of teachers towards high and low ability pupils have been observed. Some researchers have noted higher rates of contact with children of above average ability, more praise for correct responses, less criticism for incorrect responses, and greater opportunities to contribute in class (see the reviews by Brophy, 1983; and Galton and Delafield, 1981). Others, however, reported no differences. Alpert (1974), for example, found as much 'good' teaching with the least able reading group as with the most able. Previous research, therefore, has produced no firm conclusions on the extent to which teacher behaviour varies towards different groups of pupils.

A sub-sample of pupils in the present survey were selected for observation on the basis of their first year test scores. Eight pupils were observed in each class: on the basis of their assessments two were chosen as above average, four as average, and two as below average.

Overall, we found that pupils of below average ability had a higher number of individual contacts with their class teachers. This contrasts with the findings of other research quoted above. Teachers were also found to talk with the low ability pupils significantly more often about their work and to listen to them read more frequently. The less able pupils were also given more feedback on their work than more able children.

When eight teachers' contacts with a sub-sample of 80 pupils were examined in some detail, it was discovered that they criticised the higher ability pupils' work significantly more often than they criticised that of the lower ability children. Conversely, they praised the less able pupils' work more frequently than they praised that of more able children. These results are contrary to the findings of most other studies (see the review by Brophy, 1983). It is possible that teachers are less prepared to accept poor work from pupils they believe are capable of producing a high standard. These eight teachers, however, showed themselves to be supportive and encouraging of good effort by those pupils they saw as being generally less able. This was confirmed in notes, written after visiting one of the eight classes: 'He doesn't expect just one standard, however, and is probably more likely to praise a good try from a poor attainer than a much better try from one more able'.

It may be, however, that this seemingly positive approach to pupils considered less able demonstrates the limited expectations that teachers hold for them. Dweck and Repucci (1973) have argued along such lines in their study of girls being taught woodwork. Boys – seen as more suited to the subject – were criticised more often than girls who, in turn, were praised. The real meaning of such praise, however, may be that the performance is poor, or that expectations are lower.

On average, teachers made significantly more non-work comments to low ability pupils. These included both extra routine instructions and more neutral and negative remarks related to their behaviour. This is likely to reflect the significant relationship between teachers' ratings of pupils' behaviour and their ability, even after pupils' attainment had been taken into account. Furthermore, as a group, lower ability pupils spent less time involved in work activities. The relationship between ability and behaviour will be explored in more detail later in this section.

Differences were also identified in the ways teachers organised work and seating. Most teachers prepared different levels of work in mathematics and language according to pupils' abilities. Children were also seated according to their ability for at least some of the time in a quarter of classes.

It is possible that teachers' expectations may be influenced, at least in part, by the judgements of previous teachers. An examination of teachers' records of the progress of individual pupils showed that pupils rated as above average ability, at the beginning of the second year, were significantly more likely to have reached a further stage of development in their reading work. For example, by the end of the first year 59 per cent of the high ability pupils knew how to use a dictionary whereas the same was true for only 18 per cent of low ability pupils.

Within the classroom it appeared that, in the main, teachers responded to the needs of lower ability pupils by giving them extra support with their work and hearing them read more often. Teachers also talked to these children more frequently about their behaviour, in line with their lower assessments of these pupils' behaviour and the poorer concentration of low ability pupils observed by field officers. There was no evidence, therefore, that teachers skimped in the giving of attention. However, as was noted earlier, low expectations may be transmitted in very subtle ways.

BEHAVIOUR DIFFERENCES

Teachers make judgements about not only the ability and work habits of pupils, but also about their behaviour. In teachers' statements of aims, intellectual objectives are seen as no more important than those concerning pupils' personal and social development. Behaviour control is also seen to be an important aspect of classroom management. Much previous research has, generally, neglected the importance of behaviour when studying differences in teacher action towards various groups of children. It was decided, therefore, to examine whether teachers' behaviour varied towards pupils perceived by them as well or poorly behaved.

Teachers devoted significantly more individual attention to pupils they had rated as poorly behaved. In contrast, well-behaved pupils received more teacher contact in groups than predicted. The teachers also initiated fewer of their discussions with poorly-behaved children and more with well-behaved pupils. Calling across the room occurred more frequently with children perceived as naughtier. Either the teachers called across to pupils who were not getting on with their work, or these pupils called out to get teacher attention, rather than going up to their teachers or putting their hands up.

Teachers spent significantly more time on management and other non-work matters with poorly-behaved pupils. This included criticising their behaviour more frequently. Observations of the poorly-behaved pupils showed them to be more frequently distracted from their work than were their better-behaved peers. The extra non-work feedback given by the teachers, therefore, is likely to relate directly to pupils' behaviour in class. However, it was also found that teachers tended to praise the good behaviour of those pupils who were generally poorly-behaved significantly more often than that of their well-behaved peers.

Well-behaved pupils were much less likely to receive negative comments on their work than poorly-behaved pupils, although the amount of praise for good work did not differ between the two groups. In work discussions, teachers also tended to joke with and tease naughtier pupils more than other children. There was no difference between these groups of pupils in the frequency with which teachers heard them read, or in the amount of communication connected with the more detailed content of their work.

Overall, therefore, teachers' interactions with pupils they perceived to be different in terms of behaviour, tended to relate most closely to keeping the pupils 'on task'. It appears that teachers tried to achieve this end by using both positive, and negative control comments.

THE LINK BETWEEN ABILITY AND BEHAVIOUR

A link between teachers' assessments of pupil ability and pupil behaviour has already been noted. The findings also indicate that teachers differentiate children in respect of their behaviour as well as their ability. Galton and Delafield (1981) suggest that, if teachers are forced to make judgements about the ability of pupils who have similar attainment levels, they do so largely on the basis of pupils' classroom behaviour. Thus, it has been argued that those nominated as of the highest ability are the quietest, most obedient pupils, and those of the lowest ability are the noisiest, most disruptive children. We were able to compare teachers' ability and behaviour ratings for individual pupils. It became apparent that teachers could separate out their judgements of pupils' ability from those of behaviour. (This accords with the conclusions of Murphy, 1974.) Amongst pupils perceived as of high or of low ability, both poor and good behaviour ratings were recorded.

More detailed observations were made in eight second year classes. The sample of pupils was selected, from teachers' ratings, to represent four groups: well-behaved pupils of high ability (hereafter referred to as Group 1); poorly-behaved pupils of high ability (Group 2); well-be-haved low ability children (Group 3); and poorly-behaved low ability children (Group 4).

Although the pupils had been selected as being of high or of low ability, analyses of pupils' attainments in reading, mathematics and verbal reasoning showed variations amongst the groups. Attainment in reading was higher for pupils with no behaviour difficulties in both high and low ability groups. This supports the findings of a significant link between performance in cognitive areas and behaviour. Further-more, for children with no behaviour problems, early reading attain-ment was a good predictor of later performance. This was especially true for the high achieving pupils (Group 1). For mathematics, how-ever, the poorly-behaved, low ability pupils (Group 4) made less prog-ress than expected.

There was, however, no evidence of any difference between the Group 4 pupils (poorly-behaved and low ability) and other children in attitudes towards mathematics, reading, writing, school or towards doing what they were told in the classroom. At the end of the third year more Group 4 pupils than other children thought that their teachers perceived them as naughty, at least some of the time. This was not in accordance with their own view of themselves. Group 4 children did not see themselves as significantly naughtier than did members of any of the other groups.

Despite similar attitudes to work and broadly similar self-concepts to those of all the other groups, the poorly-behaved lower ability pupils performed less well than expected in the mathematics assessment at the start of the third year. Teacher behaviour towards these and the other pupils was compared, therefore, to establish whether the poorer progress of Group 4 related to any differences in aspects of teachers' communication with them.

There were more contacts between teachers and poorly-behaved pupils, particularly Group 4. The teachers initiated more communica-tions than expected with the two well-behaved groups, and less than expected with Group 2, the naughty high ability pupils. The reverse was true for pupil-initiated contacts, suggesting that teachers' ratings of pupil behaviour may be related to attention-seeking behaviour.

The content of interactions with teachers varied for the four groups. Group 1 pupils (well-behaved and of high ability) were involved in more work-oriented contacts and less routine contacts than predicted. The reverse was true for Group 4 pupils (poorly-behaved and of low ability). Galton et al (1980) found marginally less task interactions with low achievers. The present analysis, thus, supports this finding, but only when behaviour is not taken into account. Poorly-behaved low achievers were involved in less work contact than well-behaved low achievers. There was no difference between the four groups in the length of their individual contacts with teachers. For all groups, interactions lasting more than a few seconds formed less than ten per cent of all teacher-pupil contacts.

Analysis of different aspects of teachers' interaction with pupils showed that a higher number of negative comments were directed at the poorly-behaved pupils, but this was only significant for the Group 2 children. It is possible that teachers are less prepared to accept misdemeanours from children for whom they have high achievement expectations. The Group 4 and Group 1 pupils received more praise than the other children, with a particular emphasis on positive encouragement of Group 4 pupils' work and behaviour.

The teachers also seemed to vary the number of children they talked to at any one time according to the behaviour and ability of the pupils. Group 2 children (well-behaved, low ability) were spoken to individually significantly more often than all other groups. The difference was particularly noticeable in comparison with the well-behaved groups, who interacted more often with teachers in a group setting than did the poorly-behaved children.

Thus, Group 4 pupils did not differ significantly from the other pupils in most aspects of their communication with teachers. The data indicate, however, that they received more non-work contact than any other group. It appears that teachers made a particular practice of encouraging good effort from these low ability, poorly-behaved children, both in terms of their work and of their behaviour. Nonetheless, as has been argued previously, this does not deny the possibility that such behaviour transmits unintended messages to pupils.

From our analyses we have shown that, for the most part, teachers have accurate expectations for their pupils, based on past performance, previous experience and the knowledge passed on from other teachers. In general, the behaviour of teachers towards different groups of pupils in the classroom seems both to respond to, and take into account, individual pupils' needs. Teachers are obviously aware of and influenced by children's behaviour when they assess pupils' potential. However, they meet the needs of pupils with learning and behaviour difficulties in a variety of different ways.

Of most concern is the apparent lack of awareness on the part of teachers regarding the age of pupils. Younger pupils have been found to achieve less well in cognitive assessments, to exhibit more behaviour problems in school and to concentrate less on their work. It is, therefore, important that all teachers take these factors into account when they are working with pupils in the classroom.

For pupils of lower ability who also have behaviour difficulties, a greater emphasis on work rather than routine discussions may improve their performance, and also the way that they feel they are perceived by teachers. It was encouraging to see that teachers were supportive of pupils with learning and behaviour difficulties when they had made a particular effort. Nonetheless, praise was not commonly observed in classrooms for any group of children.

Two final points need to be made in relation to teachers' expectations of, and behaviour towards, different groups of pupils. First, a particular pupil may appear in a number of different groups. This has been illustrated in the analysis of pupils categorised according to behaviour and ability. It is also true for social class, sex, race and, as pointed out earlier, for age. Any pupil appearing in the less positive category of all or most of these dimensions may be more likely to be treated differentially. Even though the teacher may go out of her or his way to give individual attention to such a pupil, the effect of such interactions may be negative. If this is the case, the message transmitted by the interactions is likely to reinforce still further the lower expectations.

The second point is that much of this process may be subconscious. Teachers may feel they are doing all they can to divide their time between all their pupils in as fair a way as possible. They may be quite unaware of the different meanings that their behaviour could convey to pupils. Some may try to give particular attention to, or be especially nice to, specific groups (girls or black pupils) without realising that, by this very action, they may be indicating lower academic expectations. The work of Dweck and Repucci (1973) provides some illustrations of the paradoxical nature of teachers' praise for the inadequate work of some groups of pupils. In considering the effects of differential expectations transmitted in the classroom it must be remembered that, for children interacting daily over a period of a year with a teacher who has a low perception of their abilities, the inhibiting effect may be stultifying. In the same way, for one of the pupils about whom the teacher holds positive views, the effect will be stimulating.

SUMMARY

In this chapter we have discussed the phenomenon of teacher expectations. Drawing on the published literature we have examined our data to see if there was any evidence of differential expectations towards different groups. What we found is complex and we have attempted to interpret the data in a way that reflects the complexity yet leaves open an alternative view.

9

The Importance of School

THE NEED TO TAKE ACCOUNT OF SCHOOL INTAKES

In the last two chapters we have identified important differences in children's educational outcomes during the junior period. Such differences were found to be related significantly to a number of factors. Age, social class, sex and race each had an impact on cognitive outcomes. In most cases, differences in attainment identified at entry to junior school, continued throughout the junior years; in a few cases, change occurred. We also found that differences in non-cognitive outcomes varied according to age, social class, sex and race. These differences, however, were not necessarily consistent with those noted for cognitive outcomes. This complexity was mirrored in our discussion of teachers' expectations about pupils.

The first of the three main questions we asked in this Project was 'Are some schools more effective than others in terms of pupils' educational outcome when variations in the intakes of pupils are taken into account?' Our focus, therefore, is on the effectiveness of schools in promoting junior pupils' progress and develoment. In order to answer this question we had to find a way of comparing schools' effects on their pupils, while acknowledging the fact that schools do not all receive pupils of similar abilities and backgrounds. It will clearly be essential for us to take into account the relationships between pupils' background characteristics and their educational outcomes in our analyses of individual school effects.

There is strong evidence that schools vary considerably in the areas they serve and in the background characteristics of their pupils. Thus, Cuttance (1986) has noted 'the fact that school catchments are based on established patterns of residential settlement means that the intakes to schools vary enormously both within educational authorities and between them' (p.24). This is especially true at the primary level. (See Plowden, 1967; Little & Mabey, 1972; 1973; Sammons et al, 1983; for details of research into variation in schools' intakes.) The sample of junior schools included in our study was no exception. There were marked variations in the initial attainments, behaviour and background characteristics of pupils forming the intakes to these schools. Some of these many variations in the characteristics of the pupil intakes are described below.

Sex

At the beginning of the study, marked differences were identified between the schools in terms of the home background and individual characteristics of their first year junior intakes. Even in the balance of the sexes there was much variation. One of the schools was all female and, in three other schools, two-thirds or more of the first years were girls. In contrast, in another school only a third of the first years were female. This compares to a figure of 51 per cent girls for the sample as a whole. Such differences in the sex balance may have an impact upon teacher behaviour and interactions in the classroom, on the level of attainment, and on the extent of behaviour problems. As we demonstrated in Chapter 7, the incidence of behaviour problems was much higher amongst boys than amongst girls, while attainment in some cognitive areas was lower.

Ethnic and language background

As might be expected, given that members of black and ethnic minority groups lived within particular geographical areas of inner London (for example, the proportion of the population of Caribbean background is relatively high in Hackney and Lambeth, Asian families are most highly represented in Tower Hamlets, while Greeks tend to be concentrated in parts of Camden and Islington), children from particular ethnic minority groups were distributed differentially amongst the 50 schools. These distributions tended to reflect the geographical variations in the inner London population at large. Some examples of these differences between schools identified at the beginning of the project are shown in Table 9.1, although it should be noted that during the four years of junior schooling the numbers of children from minority ethnic groups increased considerably in some schools.

TABLE 9.1: Differences between schools in the ethnic composition of first year pupil intakes

	Asian	Caribbean	English/Scottish Welsh/Irish
	%	%	%
Average per cent all schools	6.8	11.8	59.0
Maximum per cent pupils any school	37.5	52.6	95.6
Minimum per cent pupils any school	0	0	22.0

In the case of children of Asian backgrounds, for instance, five schools had intakes with more than a fifth of pupils from this group and, in one instance, the figure was 38 per cent. In contrast, in 16 of the schools none of the first years were Asian. The average for the sample as a whole was seven per cent. Similarly, there were marked variations in the distribution of children of Caribbean backgrounds. One of the schools received over half, and a further six schools had over a quarter of first year pupils from this group. In eight schools, however, none of the pupils had Caribbean family backgrounds. Overall, for English, Scottish, Welsh and Irish pupils, variations were also in evidence. A total of 96 per cent of pupils was drawn from this group in one of the Project schools but, in another, the comparable figure was less than a quarter.

In terms of language background, in six schools more than a quarter of first year juniors were assessed as not fully fluent in English. These figures compare to eight per cent for the pupil sample as a whole. But in 13 schools, all pupils were fully fluent in English. The maximum percentage in any one school was, in contrast, nearly 42 per cent.

The data indicate the extent of differences in the ethnic, language and cultural mix of junior schools within the Authority, and highlight the tendency for particular groups to be concentrated in certain schools.

Social class composition
Father's occupation rather than mother's occupation was used to classify pupils into social class groups. This strategy was adopted for several reasons:
i) it conforms to the Registrar General's Classification and enables the results to be compared with those of other studies;
ii) a majority of mothers (59%) were not working in paid employment;
iii) of those mothers who were working, many may have returned to work at a lower level after having children;
iv) there was little relationship between mothers' occupations and children's attainments when fathers' occupations were taken into account. Moreover, the combination of mothers' and fathers' occupations did not increase the amount of variance in pupils' attainments which could be statistically 'explained'.

Differences in the social class composition of pupil intakes were also marked at the beginning of junior school (See Table 9.2).

In one school, nearly 67 per cent of the intake had fathers in non-manual work, but in four schools none of the first year pupils were of non-manual backgrounds. This compares with an average figure of around 25 per cent for the pupil sample as a whole. In another school 59 per cent of pupils were from semi- or unskilled manual homes. At the other extreme, in two schools none of the intake had fathers in this type of employment. The percentage for the pupil sample as a whole was fifteen.

In terms of children whose fathers were not employed at the start of the Project (either due to unemployment or economic inactivity, including students, disabled and retired persons), nearly a third of first years in one school were from families where the father was not in work, but in nine schools none of the first years' fathers were in this position.

TABLE 9.2: Differences between schools in the social class composition of first year pupil intakes

	Father's occupation			
	Non-manual	Skilled manual	Semi-unskilled manual	Not employed
	%	%	%	%
Average per cent all schools	20.0	28.0	13.6	7.0
Maximum per cent any school	66.7	67.7	59.1	32.4
Minimum per cent any school	0	4.8	0	0

One parent families
Half the first year intake in one school were from families where the father was absent and, in four other schools, more than a third of pupils were in similar circumstances. In contrast, in four different schools all of the intake lived with both parents and, in ten, more than 95 per cent of first years were in a similar position. As has been noted earlier (in Chapter 6), very few mothers were absent from children's homes, and there was no tendency for pupils whose mothers were absent to be concentrated in particular schools.

Income levels
The results of analyses of information about pupils' eligibility for free school meals show that there were significant differences between schools in the percentage of pupils entitled to them. In eight schools more than half the first years were eligible for free meals, but in five schools less than ten per cent qualified. This compares with an average

of 31 per cent of pupils in the total sample. The extremes ranged from a maximum of 59 per cent to a minimum of three per cent of pupils in this category. Thus, there were marked variations in the family circumstances of first year pupils. In some schools, a majority of pupils came from homes with a low income. Research by the National Child Development Study has indicated that poverty is an important educational disadvantage (see Essen & Wedge, 1982), as has research on educational priority (see Sammons et al, 1983).

Family size
Some studies have indicated that family size is a factor related to educational outcomes (see the review by Rutter & Madge, 1976). Children from large families, it is argued, achieve less well than those from small families. Amongst the sample schools there were differences in the proportion of children from families with four or more children. In six schools, more than 30 per cent of children were from large families – compared with a figure of 18 per cent for the whole sample. In contrast, in five schools, less than five per cent of the intake were from large families.

Nursery experience
Differences were also identified in the extent of nursery experience. In four schools, more than 80 per cent of first years – the vast majority – had some nursery experience, whereas in another four schools, over 80 per cent of first years had none.

Health and handicaps
There were also some variations between the schools in terms of the percentages of pupils identified as having health problems or handicaps in the first year of the Project. These differences tended to be smaller than those identified for other measures. For example, in one school, 41 per cent of pupils were noted to have some health problem or handicap and in another the figure was 30 per cent. However, for the majority of schools, more than 80 per cent of the children were said to have no such problems.

Changes over time
Overall, in inner London as a whole, there was an increase in the proportion of disadvantaged pupils during the early 1980s. This reflects the deteriorating economic climate which led to a rise in the percentage of pupils eligible for free meals and those with an unemployed parent – two factors which relate to educational disadvantage (see Hunter et al, 1985). The majority of our schools recorded an increase in the proportion of disadvantaged pupils amongst their intakes between 1981 and 1983. Thus, 30 schools recorded an increase, compared with only 11 that experienced a decrease. Table 9.3 illustrates the extent

to which the characteristics of the pupils changed in the sample schools. It shows the increase (between 1981 and 1983) in the percentage of pupils who were eligible for free meals; from one parent families; from large families; with fathers in semi- or unskilled manual work or who were unemployed; and those who were not fully fluent in English (all factors that relate to educational disadvantage).

TABLE 9.3:
Increase in disadvantage – extent of increase in the percentage of intake affected by selected education priority factors between 1981 and 1983

	Number of schools		
Educational Priority factors	Increase in % affected below 10%	Increase in % affected between 10%-20%	Increase in % affected above 20%
Free meals	13	7	14
Large family	20	3	1
One-parent family	16	12	5
Semi-/unskilled manual work	6	11	6
Unemployed	12	13	10
Not fluent in English	28	4	2

Overall, more than two thirds of schools in our sample had recorded an increase in the percentage of pupils pupils affected by four of the educational priority factors. These four factors were: eligibility for free school meals (a measure of low family income); one parent families; parental unemployment; and incomplete fluency in English.

Differences in attainment levels between schools
Many studies have shown that, for individual pupils, early attainment is a good predictor of later attainment, and a better predictor than measures of pupils' backgrounds, and our own findings reported in Chapter 6 support this view. Of course, background factors are themselves strongly related to early school attainment as we demonstrated in Chapter 7. Gray (1981a) has suggested that measures of attainment at entry to school are the best single predictors of children's later performance. Work by Hutchison et al (1979) has drawn similar conclusions. It is necessary, therefore, to take into account variation in

the attainment of pupils at their point of entry to junior school. This is the best single measure for controlling for variations in pupil intakes to school. It also provides a baseline against which to measure the progress of individual pupils through the junior years.

There were large differences between the average raw reading scores of the pupil intakes to the 50 schools. At one extreme, the average was 62.6 (the maximum score possible for a pupil was 91 in the first year) compared with only 17 points at the lowest extreme. The latter school was one of the most disadvantaged in the sample, in terms of the home backgrounds of children. Overall, for all pupils the average raw score was 46 points at entry to junior school.

For mathematics, there were also sizeable differences in average raw scores at the school level. The lowest scoring school had an average raw score of 18.3 points, compared with a average score in the highest scoring school of 29.3. The average for all pupils in the mathematics test at entry was 24, and the maximum possible score was 40.

At the school level, there was a very strong relationship between the mean raw reading and the average raw mathematics score of first year pupils (r=0.74). This means that schools whose first year intake tended to have a high average attainment in mathematics also had a high average attainment in reading. Conversely, those schools with intakes whose average mathematics score was low tended also to have a low average score. This, of course, reflects the relationships noted in our analyses of individual pupils' attainment in Chapter Six.

Differences in the behaviour of intakes to the schools
Teachers of pupils in the 50 schools varied considerably in their assessments of the behaviour of children in their classes. In four schools, 25 per cent or more of the pupils were rated as having difficulties (reaching a total of a third of children in one school). At the other extreme, no pupils were classified as disturbed in two schools and less than five per cent in a further seven schools. The average for schools as a whole was nearly 14 per cent of the junior intake at age seven. There was a negative relationship between the percentage of pupils assessed as disturbed and average reading and mathematics attainment at the school level. This indicates that schools that received first year pupils with a low average attainment at entry were likely to receive a higher proportion of pupils with behaviour difficulties. This, itself, is likely to reflect the strong link between attainment and behaviour for individual pupils.

We have shown that there were marked differences between pupils at the point of entry to junior school. Some children experienced no social, economic or family disadvantages, but other children were living in families with a low income, or in difficult circumstances. A substantial minority of children were experiencing three or more disadvantages, which have been shown to increase the risk of low educational performance. A few children had some health problem or handicap. We have already reported (in Chapter 7) on the strength of relationships between pupils' backgrounds and their educational outcomes. Our findings point to the need to take full account of differences in intakes when comparing the effects of individual schools on the progress and development of their pupils. Past studies of school differences, however, have been criticised on the ground of the paucity of their intake measures, or the crudity of the measures used (see the criticisms of measures used to control the characteristics of school intakes in school differences research, made by Gray, 1981b). Moreover, Gray and Jones (1985) have argued that the 'major weakness of many of the studies has been their failure to control adequately for differences in the prior attainments and home backgrounds of pupils at different schools' (p.106).

Without proper controls for the importance of school intake it is not possible properly to compare like with like. Thus, recent research by Marks et al (1983, 1986) illustrates the dangers of neglecting to measure differences in intakes adequately. This led to misleading results in studies of school and LEA differences in examination results (see criticisms of Marks' research by Gray, 1983; Gray and Jones, 1983; Goldstein, 1984). In addition, Gray and Hannon (1985) have shown that even the HMI's interpretation of schools' examination results is seriously flawed because of the failure to control for the effects of differences between schools in their intakes.

HOW SCHOOL EFFECTS CAN BE STUDIED

We have included a wide range of measures of pupils' educational outcomes in our investigations of school effects. This is in contrast to most past studies of such effects (see the reviews by Cuttance, 1980b; Purkey and Smith, 1983). Although we agree that 'An exemplary school should produce high achievement in basic academic skills, literacy and numeracy' (Ralph & Fennessey, 1983, p.690), the present study did not limit itself to a narrow focus on pupils' achievement in the three 'Rs'. Other areas are also considered by us to be important. Our analysis of teachers' aims for their pupils has demonstrated that, in addition to intellectual aims, teachers considered social and personal areas of equal importance (see the description of class teachers' aims in Chapter 5). As Widlake (1980) commented in a discussion of what made some primary schools effective, 'success, at one level, is easily observable in primary schools. The children are seen to be happily involved in meaningful activities and their attainments in the basic subjects can be assessed. They are interested and interesting; literate and numerate, as well as sociable and articulate' (pp. 116-117). In order to take into account the variety of aims of primary education, therefore, the Project has considered school effects on a range of both cognitive and non-cognitive outcomes. In this way a fairer assessment of the general effectiveness of schools can be obtained. In addition, the relationships between school effects on different kinds of educational outcomes can be explored, and the particular strengths and weaknesses of individual schools can be assessed.

In this study, because of the known importance of age, sex, social class, race and language background, and family circumstances, the analyses of school effects have taken into account each of the background factors identified as influential. Membership of an individual school has been included as an additional characteristic for each pupil, because this may well have had an impact upon the child's progress and development. In this way the effects of background characteristics and of school membership are identified and separated out, whilst controlling for the effects of other factors simultaneously. Thus, the influence of school membership is estimated while account is also taken of children's background. All the analyses have been conducted at the most sensitive level, that of the individual pupil.

The effects of school membership on pupils' progress in the various cognitive areas (reading, mathematics, and writing) and upon attainment in the oracy and practical mathematics assessments are discussed first. The effects of school are described in terms of the amount of variation in pupils' progress over the junior years which is explained, in a statistical sense, by the school. This method allows us to compare the strength of school effects in general, with those effects due to background factors. We also describe the variations in the effect of being a member of a particular school. Here the sample schools are compared in terms of their influence upon pupils' progress in the different cognitive areas – for example reading progress. Finally, the effects of particular schools on different cognitive areas are examined, to see whether schools which have a positive effect on some outcomes also have a positive effect on other areas of pupil progress. Such a strategy enables the identification of schools which appear to be more effective than others in promoting good progress over the junior years.

School effects upon pupils' non-cognitive development (their attitudes, attendance, behaviour and self-concept) are then explored. Clearly, a simple concept of progress cannot apply to some of the non-cognitive outcomes (attendance and behaviour, unlike reading, are not expected to improve automatically over time), although it is possible to investigate whether change has occurred. Likewise, behaviour difficulties may either disappear or develop further during the junior years. For the behaviour measure, information was combined for all three years to give an overall measure of adjustment to school. This combined measure is used to indicate whether pupils in particular schools consistently showed more behaviour difficulties than expected. This approach reduces the effect of the assessment of a particular teacher in a particular year. To score highly, a pupil must have been rated as having difficulties in two or more years.

As with the cognitive outcomes, the size of the influence of school (in terms of the proportion of variance explained) is compared with the amount due to different background factors for each non-cognitive area. In addition, the effects of particular schools are investigated to see whether some schools were more effective than others in promoting good non-cognitive outcomes, once account is taken of the impact of pupils' backgrounds. The effects of individual schools on cognitive and on non-cognitive areas are then compared. Here the intention is to answer the question – are some schools more effective than others in promoting different kinds of outcomes?

THE IMPACT OF SCHOOL ON PUPILS' PROGRESS AND ATTAINMENT

Reading attainment and progress

Children's reading progress was examined over three school years, whilst taking account of initial attainment, sex, age and background factors. Our results describe the impact upon a child's progress over three years of being a member of one particular school in the sample, rather than of belonging to any of the other schools.

We found the school has a significant impact upon reading attainment. In all, nine per cent of the variation in children's reading attainment at the end of the third year was accounted for by the school as a factor. This figure is higher than that identified in previous studies of school effects. Thus, Gray (1981a), Reynolds (1982) and Rutter (1983) have described the possible range in the size of school effects, in published studies. As Rutter noted 'Jencks et al (1972) concluded that school variables accounted for a mere 2 to 3 per cent of the variance, a figure far below the estimated 50 per cent attributable to family background.' Rutter himself concluded that other studies have varied somewhat in the precise figures ... 'but with one exception ... all have agreed in finding that far more of the variance in pupils' attainment is attributable to family variables than to school variables' (p.3). Our results show that the size of the school effect on third year reading attainment was much greater than that due to background, when account is taken of initial attainment.

An important concept in the Junior School Project is that of progress. As we demonstrated in Chapters 6 and 7 (and as many other studies have shown), even at the age of seven there are marked differences between children in their attainments when they first enter junior school. Such differences are quite closely related to pupils' background characteristics. Nevertheless, there are variations between children in the amount of progress they make during the junior years, as we have shown in the last two chapters. It is of considerable importance, therefore, for all concerned with education to know whether the school a child joins at seven can have an impact upon her or his progress in later years. Does school membership help us to explain why some children make more or less progress than we would expect, given a child's initial attainment at the start of junior schooling?

When we considered this issue of relative progress over the junior years, we found that nearly 30 per cent of the variation in children's progress was accounted for by school membership and background factors taken together. (As Gray and Jones (1985) have noted, studies of pupil progress have 'explained' only about a quarter of the difference in progress pupils have made. The proportion of variance in reading progress 'explained' in the Junior School Project is, therefore, in line with the results of past research.) But, the school has much the larger effect. School attended is responsible for nearly a quarter (24%) of the variation in pupils' reading progress between the first and the third year of junior education.[1] In other words, the school was roughly four times more important in accounting for differences in pupil progress than background factors.

It should be remembered that, in these analyses (which were conducted at the more sensitive level of the individual child) the impact of a much wider variety of background factors than have appeared in most previous studies of school effects has been taken into account. Because of thorough control for background influences, it seems unlikely that the variation due to school membership found in this study would be accounted for by the inclusion of still further background factors (see Maughan et al, 1980 and Hutchison et al, 1979). Most studies of school effects (such as that by Coleman et al, 1966; and by Jencks et al, 1972) have examined attainment. But, as has been argued earlier, because of differences between schools in pupils' attainments, it is necessary to take into account each child's initial attainment or entry in order to examine school effects upon progress in a particular cognitive area. The effect of background characteristics upon progress is lower than that on attainment, because such characteristics are strongly related to initial attainment. Thus, for the pupils in our sample, school membership was of great importance. In particular schools, children made greater progress in reading than expected, given their initial attainment and background characteristics. In other schools, children made less progress than expected. For these pupils, therefore, it is clear that the school which they entered at age seven made a considerable different to their progress in reading over the next three years.

---

[1] The method of calculating progress effects due to school is outlined in the technical appendices of Mortimore et al (1986b), and is based on the method described by Plewis (1985).

The size of the effects of particular schools upon children's reading progress in terms of raw score points was calculated and compared. Our figures show that the difference between the school with the most positive and that with the most negative effect was a striking 25 points (see Table 9.4). This compares with an overall average for all children of just under 54 points on the third year summer reading test, and a range of possible scores of 0 to 100 points. This difference between individual schools in their effects on children's reading progress is of educational, as well as statistical, significance.

TABLE 9.4: The difference between the most and the least effective school in promoting pupils' reading progress

	Difference in raw score points*	% Difference from average
Most effective school	+15	+28
Least effective school	−10	−19
Overall average for sample	54	

*Maximum possible raw score on the third year reading assessment=100

Mathematics attainment and progress

We investigated school effects upon pupils' attainment and their progress in mathematics over the three years in the same way as for reading. As with reading, the school was found to account for a sizeable proportion of the variation in children's third year mathematics attainment when sex, age, background factors and initial attainment were taken into account. In all, 11 per cent of the variation was due to junior school membership. As with reading, therefore, the school a child entered at age seven had an effect upon mathematics attainment over the next three years.

The size of the school effect upon third year mathematics attainment is slightly larger than that found for attainment in reading over the same period. As with reading the effect of school membership is much greater than that due to background variables. More importantly, when relative progress in mathematics is considered we found that 26 per cent of the variation in children's mathematics progress was accounted for by age, sex, background factors and school membership. The school attended was responsible for most of this variation in relative progress (23%), while all the background factors combined, explained less than three per cent. In other words, school was roughly ten times more important than background as the determinant of progress in mathematics. When we turn to the size of the effects of individual schools upon their pupils' mathematics progress, striking differences between the sample schools were identified. As figures in Table 9.5 show, the difference between the most and the least effective school reached a total of 12 raw points. This compares with an overall average of just under 28 on the third year mathematics test and a range of possible scores from 0 to 50 raw points.

TABLE 9.5: The difference between the most and the least effective school in promoting pupils' mathematics progress

	Difference in raw score points*	% Difference from average
Most effective school	+6	+21
Least effective school	−6	−21
Overall average for sample	28	

* Maximum possible raw score on third year mathematics assessment = 50

It is also of interest to establish whether schools which had a positive effect on one cognitive area were also effective in other areas. In other words, were the schools which were more effective in promoting good reading progress also more effective in promoting mathematics progress? A measure of this relationship, given by a correlation, shows that there was a significant association – though not an overwhelmingly strong one – between the two areas of learning. Schools which were more effective in promoting progress in mathematics, tended also to have a good effect upon reading progress. Thus, it is clear that success in one of the basic skills is associated with success in the other. However, there were some schools which, from their pupils' outcomes, appear to have been more successful at teaching – or to have put more emphasis on – some areas rather than others.

Writing attainment and progress

To investigate progress in writing we adopted the same sorts of analyses as those used for reading and mathematics. Our results show that nearly half of the variation in the quality (in language and ideas) of children's third year writing can be statistically explained by sex, age, background factors and first year writing performance. As would be expected, initial attainment is important, but the school accounted for over 13 per cent of the variation in children's writing performance in the third year.

As with reading and mathematics, when initial attainment is included in the analyses, the influence of children's background characteristics (including sex and age) is much reduced. School membership also makes a significant contribution to the statistical explanation of variance in children's progress in writing over three years. Nearly 20 per cent of the variation in children's writing progress was accounted for by the school but under three per cent was due to background. In line with results for mathematics, the school was around ten times more important in determining progress in writing than background factors.

For progress in reading, writing and mathematics, therefore, we are able to conclude that the school is much more important than children's background characteristics, having between four and ten times more effect. We can conclude that schools do matter!

Turning to the effects of particular schools, Table 9.6 shows marked diffences between schools in their impact on writing, and the size of the effects in particular schools was substantial. Quality of writing was measured on a nine point scale with a range of 2 to 10 points.

TABLE 9.6: The difference between the most and the least effective school in promoting pupils' progress in writing

	Difference in raw score points*	% Difference from average
Most effective school	+1.7	+27
Least effective school	−1.3	−21
Overall average for sample	6.2	

* Maximum possible raw score on third year assessment = 10

Again, these results confirm that the particular school to which a child belongs can have a significant impact upon that child's progress in cognitive areas during the junior years.

In contrast to the significant relationships between school effects in reading and in mathematics, the associations between school effects on progress in these areas and progress in writing quality were weak. Thus, those schools which had a positive effect upon pupils' progress in reading did not necessarily have a positive effect upon progress in quality of writing. Schools with good effects on mathematics progress, however, showed a weak, but statistically significant, effect on progress in the quality of writing.

Our results suggest that, in some schools, there may have been a special emphasis on particular curriculum areas. Nonetheless, schools which have a negative effect upon progress in one cognitive area do not usually have a positive effect upon other areas. All the correlations, though weak, were in a positive direction.

Oracy attainment

Because oracy (speaking skills) was assessed on only one occasion it was not possible to look at progress in this area. However, school effects upon oral attainment were examined in the same way as other cognitive outcomes. In all, ten per cent of the variance in children's attainment in the general assessment was attributable to background factors, sex and age, and 27 per cent was due to school membership. Thus, the school which a pupil attended was found to have had a highly significant impact upon children's ability to communicate effectively through speech. This impact was greater than that due to individual children's characteristics of background, sex and age.

We found a similar pattern of results for the specific and the verbal performance assessments, and the non-verbal and lexico-grammatical assessments. (For a description of the oracy assessments, see Gorman and Hargreaves, 1985.) In all cases, the school was responsible for a much higher percentage of the differences between pupils in their attainments than that due to background factors, sex and age. Thus, the individual school attended can promote – or have an adverse effect upon – pupils' abilities to communicate effectively in speech. Some schools apparently pay greater attention to oral work in the junior curriculum than others, whether directly or indirectly.

As with other outcomes, we compared the size of the effects of particular schools on the two oracy assessments for which school membership had the largest effects (the general and the verbal assessments) (see Table 9.7). It is clear that marked differences between the most and the least effective schools existed. Thus, for the general assessment, the most effective school added nearly six raw points to children's performance whilst, in the least effective school, scores were nearly five points lower than predicted. This compares with a average of 21.5 points on the general assessment. For the verbal performance assessment (where the average score was ten points) scores were raised by 3.5 points in the most effective school, but were 1.6 points lower in the least effective school.

Our analyses showed that the size of school effects upon pupils' performances in the specific and the general assessments of oracy were highly significantly associated. There were also strong positive relationships between school effects on the general and on the task specific and the verbal performance assessments. Schools which were good at promoting one particular aspect of oracy were, therefore, also good at fostering other aspects of verbal communication skills.

TABLE 9.7: Differences between the most and the least effective schools for pupils' oracy attainment

	Differences in raw score points*		% Difference from average	
	General assessment	Verbal assessment	General assessment	Verbal assessment
Most effective school	+5.7	+3.5	+27	+35
Least effective school	−4.9	−1.6	−25	−16
Overall average for sample	21.5	10.0		

* Maximum possible raw score on the general assessment = 35
Maximum possible raw score on the verbal assessment = 15

When we looked at the links between school effects on the oracy assessments and school effects on progress in reading and quality of writing, we found only a weak positive relationship. Thus, school effects on oracy are not generally related to effects on progress in other areas of the curriculum.

Some schools had a good effect on progress in cognitive areas and a good effect on oracy: other schools appear to have had a good effect on other cognitive areas but not on oral communication. However, it must be remembered that for oracy, school effects on attainment have been considered. There was no control for previous attainment in this area, therefore progress has not been measured. The absence of relationships between school effects on oracy and other cognitive areas may, in part, be due to the different aspects measured.

Practical mathematics attainment

Attainment in practical mathematics could only be examined for a sample of pupils in 20 schools. Because the assessment we used covered performance in five different areas it was not possible to examine progress for the overall measure. Nevertheless, it was possible to investigate the size of school effects upon pupils' attainment for the 20 schools, using the same methods we had adopted for investigating the other cognitive areas. Our analyses indicated that, overall, background factors, sex and age accounted for a smaller proportion of the variation in attainment for practical mathematics than for reading, mathematics or writing quality. There were differences, however, between the five areas of practical mathematics. Background factors, sex and age we found to be more important in accounting for pupil performance in the volume (nearly 17%) and less important for performance in the weighing assessment (only 6%).

The school, however, also made a significant contribution in accounting for variations in pupils' attainments in particular aspects of the practical mathematics assessment. The school accounted for nearly 21 per cent of the variation in the assessment of performance in the length tasks, whereas for attainment in both number and weighing the figure was 12 per cent. The school had less effect upon attainment in the sets and volume assessments. This may reflect variations in the extent to which children receive experience of different types of practical mathematics work. When we analysed attainment, at the individual pupil level, we found there was greater consistency over time in children's performance in length and number than in other areas of practical mathematics (see Chapter 6).

Turning to the effects of particular schools, the results indicated that for length, weight and number the differences between the most and the least effective schools could be substantial. For example, compared with an overall average of 3.7 points on the number assessment (which had a maximum score of 6), the most effective school improved attainments by 1.7 raw points, whereas the least effective school depressed scores by 0.7 of a raw point.

We found that there were fairly strong positive relationships between school effects upon attainment in the different areas of the practical mathematics assessment. These results show that schools which promoted attainment in one area also tended to promote attainment in other areas of practical mathematics. The relationships between school effects upon attainment in the different sub-tests of the practical mathematics test, oracy and progress in reading, mathematics and writing were also investigated.

We found there was a positive, though weak, relationship between school effects on the majority of the areas covered by the practical mathematics assessments and school effects on progress in mathematics and progress in reading. As might be expected, school effects on mathematics were more closely related to the practical assessments than were school effects on reading. The relationships were strongest between the effects on the number assessment and the effects on progress in the written mathematics assessment and effects on attainment in the assessment of length and the written mathematics test.

HOW MANY SCHOOLS WERE GENERALLY GOOD AT FOSTERING PUPILS' COGNITIVE DEVELOPMENT?

From our data we have shown that marked differences existed between schools in the extent to which they improved or depressed pupils progress in reading, mathematics and writing, and attainment in oracy.

(It was not possible to include the effects on practical mathematics attainment in these calculations because these data were not collected for all schools.) What we now wanted to establish was whether some schools were especially good at promoting not just one – but several of these cognitive areas.

We identified very clear differences between the sample schools in the number of cognitive areas on which they had a positive effect. Giving each school a score of one if it had a positive effect on any area and zero if it had a negative effect, a scale was constructed to record the total number of areas on which each school had a good effect. The maximum possible score was four (good effects on progress in reading, mathematics, writing quality, and on the general measure of oracy attainment) and the minimum was zero – poor effects on all areas. Figures in Table 9.8 show that in all, four schools scored zero. These schools had a negative impact on all four cognitive areas. Nine schools had a positive effect on only one of the four areas. In contrast, five schools had a positive effect on all areas and 15 had a positive effect on three of the four areas considered.

TABLE 9.8: Numbers of cognitive outcomes on which the schools had a positive effect

Numbers of cognitive outcomes on which school had a positive efffect	Number of schools
None	4
One	9
Two	16
Three	15
Four	5

N=49 (one of the 50 schools left the Project in the third year)

Some schools were remarkably effective in fostering children's learning and progress in the majority of cognitive areas. To demonstrate this we describe the effects of two schools. The first raised children's third year reading performance by an average of 24 per cent or 13 raw points (compared with an average score for all pupils of 54 raw points), mathematics performance by 21 per cent or six raw points (compared with an average for all pupils of 28 raw points), and writing quality by 15 per cent or nearly one raw point (compared with an average for all pupils of 6.2 raw points). In this school, therefore, even when we take into account initial attainment and background factors, children had made exceptionally good progress in reading, writing and mathematics during the years of junior education.

The second example of an effective school had the most positive effect on general performance in oracy (raising pupils' performances by 28 per cent or nearly six raw points above the average for all pupils of 21.5). It also had good effects on progress in reading and in mathematics, increasing performance over three years by 15 per cent or nearly eight raw points for reading and 21 per cent (six raw points) for mathematics, though effects on writing were only average, neither positive or negative.

In contrast to these more effective schools, a few were markedly ineffective. In one such school, effects on progress in reading, mathematics, writing quality and on oracy attainment were strongly negative. Children made less progress than predicted (given initial attainment and background factors) over the three years. In this school, reading scores were depressed by 19 per cent (10 raw points), mathematics scores by 21 per cent (six raw points), and writing quality by 15 per cent (nearly one raw point). For oracy, pupils' attainment was 14 per cent (three raw points) poorer than predicted. In all these cognitive areas, therefore, we found that the performance of children attending this school was poorer than expected over the junior years.

Our findings demonstrate that it is possible for schools to be very effective in several cognitive areas and, equally, that some schools are ineffective in the same areas. From our analyses it is clear that school membership over three years of junior education can make a very substantial difference to pupils' progress in different areas of learning.

THE IMPACT OF SCHOOL ON PUPILS' NON-COGNITIVE OUTCOMES

Behaviour

Information about each child's behaviour in school was collected from their class teachers, on a regular basis. Because of the difficulties involved in using teacher-based assessments, an overall measure of the child's behaviour was used. This overall measure helped to smooth out any aberrant ratings because, to score highly, a child would have to be rated by different class teachers as having difficulties in more than one year. To investigate the impact of school membership, we used similar methods to those we had employed in analysing the cognitive outcomes. Thus, the same range of background factors, pupil sex and age were taken into account. Our results indicate that school membership made a significant though not dominant contribution to the explanation of differences in behaviour over the junior years. Taking the overall measure of behaviour, it was found that background factors, sex and age, accounted for nearly 13 per cent of the variance, while school effects were responsible for only ten per cent of the variance. The amount of variation between children in their behaviour which can be accounted for, statistically, is lower than that achieved in the analyses of progress in cognitive areas, because no control was made for initial behaviour scores. As with the cognitive outcomes, we found that the size of the effects of some individual schools was substantial.

TABLE 9.9: The difference between the most and the least effective school in promoting pupils' behaviour

	Difference in raw score points*	% Difference from average
Most effective school	+19	+32
Least effective school	−9	−15
Overall average for sample	56.9	

* Maximum possible raw score on the third year behaviour assessment = 135

In the most effective school, good behaviour scores were increased considerably. In the least effective school, scores were also lowered.

Attendance

For most pupils, school attendance was very high during the junior years (as has been described in Chapters 6 and 7). Two measures were used to calculate the effects of school membership on this outcome. One was based on attendance in the third year, and one on change over the three years. Overall, children's background characteristics, sex and age accounted for only a small proportion of the variance in third year attendance (less than four per cent). These relationships are much weaker than those identified for the cognitive outcomes, even when no controls are included for initial attainment. The school made a slightly larger contribution than background factors, at 5.6 per cent. Even so, only a small proportion of the variation between children in their attendance was accounted for – less than ten per cent.

These results suggest that the school to which a child belonged did have some impact on attendance, even though the effect was small. In our sample the size of such effects ranged from a decrease in absence of nearly five per cent below that predicted in the most effective school, to an increase in absence of over four per cent above that predicted in the least effective school. For junior age pupils, therefore, there is some evidence that membership of particular schools may help to promote regular attendance whereas, in others, the reverse is the case.

When changes in attendance were examined, by taking into account the children's attendance in their first year, the size of the effects of particular schools were reduced to seven per cent.

TABLE 9.10: The difference between the most and the least effective school in promoting pupils' attendance

	Difference in % increase attendance*	% Difference from average
Most effective school	+4.9	+5
Least effective school	−4.3	−4
Overall average for sample	91.7	

---

* Maximum possible on the third year attendance assessment = 100%.

These results suggest that the impact of the school upon attendance during the junior years is of less importance than for behaviour and for the cognitive outcomes. This finding is in marked contrast to those reported in studies of secondary schools (see Reynolds & Murgatroyd, 1977; Rutter et al, 1979; Reynolds, 1982), and may reflect the fact that junior age children's attendance rates are usually very high, and that, because of their age and dependence on parents, they are able to exercise much less choice about attending school than are secondary school pupils.

Self-concept

The children's assessments of themselves in school (a measure of one aspect of self-concept) were obtained on only one occasion, at the end of the third year. Because of this, it was not possible to examine any changes in self-concept over the junior years. As with attendance, it was found that the background characteristics, sex and age of individual children did not account for much of the variance in children's ratings of themselves (a mere 3.2%). The school accounted for a higher percentage of the variance (8.4%), indicating that school membership can have an important impact upon the development of children's self-concepts in relation to school. The range between the school with the largest positive effect upon self-concept and that with the largest negative effect was over seven points.

TABLE 9.11: The difference between the most and the least effective school in promoting pupils' self-concepts

	Difference in raw score points*	% Difference from average
Most effective school	+3.9	+14
Least effective school	−3.3	−12
Overall average for sample	27.7	

* Maximum possible raw score on the third year self-concept assessment = 55

There was a range of possible scores from 11 to 55 points in self-concept. Nonetheless, under 12 per cent of the variance in self-concept scores was accounted for, suggesting that other factors must also have an important impact upon children's perceptions of themselves (peer groups and parental relationships may well be a major influence).

Attitudes

Information was collected, on a regular basis, about children's attitudes towards a variety of curriculum areas, and towards school. It was not appropriate to draw up a composite measure of attitudes because earlier analyses showed that children had very specific attitudes towards different activities, and that relationships between attitudes to school and to school activities were quite weak (see Chapter 6). The concept of progress or change in attitudes was also not considered appropriate in our study. Instead, school effects upon attitudes were examined for the third year assessment. This, it was hoped, would give the most accurate information about the cumulative effects of belonging to a particular school, because children had spent three years in its environment by this stage.

Information about the children's attitudes towards school and towards mathematics, reading and writing (the 3 curriculum areas for which we had information about both attainment and progress) was analysed. The results showed that, as with self-concept and attendance, the overall level of explanation of variance for the attitudes measures was low. Again, children's background characteristics, sex, and age made only a small contribution.

Interestingly, background factors, age and sex, were slightly more important in accounting for differences in general attitude to school, than in explaining attitudes towards specific curriculum areas. In all cases, however, school membership explained a larger proportion of the variation than background factors, sex and age (between 7.5% and 12.2%). School effects were considerable. They were largest for attitude to mathematics (12.2%) and smallest for attitude to reading (7.5%). It is possible that, as we have suggested earlier, pupils' attitudes to reading are more subject to influences from the home than are their attitudes towards mathematics.

TABLE 9.12: The difference between the most and the least effective school in promoting pupils' attitudes

	Difference in raw score points*	% Difference from average
Most effective school	+1.1	+38
Least effective school	−1.2	−41
Overall average for sample	2.9	

* Maximum possible raw score on the third year attitude assessment = 5.

Nonetheless, it seems that children's attitudes were affected by school membership and that the school was more important as an influence on such attitudes than were background factors. These results are in line with our findings about school as an influence on learning – especially upon progress in the cognitive areas.

In particular schools children's attitudes towards school and towards curriculum areas were more positive than in others, even when account is taken of the influence of age, sex and background factors. Thus, for example, looking at attitude to school – which was measured on a five point scale – in the school with the most positive impact, the average effect was an improvement of attitudes by over one raw point. In contrast, in the school with the least favourable impact, scores were depressed by over one raw point. This figure compares with an average raw score (in the third year assessment) of 2.9 on this measure. An indication of the range of responses to this attitude item is given by the following figures. In all, in the third year, 42.5 per cent of children's ratings of their attitude to school were positive (scores of 1 or 2) and 33.4 per cent negative (scores of 4 or 5).

We looked at the inter-relationships between schools' effects on the various non-cognitive measures. This was done to see whether there were any consistent patterns, such that schools which had a good effect on one area, also tended to have a good effect on other areas. The results revealed some statistically significant associations though, on the whole, correlations were not strong. Overall, schools which had a good effect upon pupils' attitudes to one area tended to have a good effect upon attitudes to other areas. In particular, attitude to school and attitude to mathematics were related. In addition, we found that school effects upon self-concept were also linked to effects on pupils' attitude to school and attitude to mathematics. There was, therefore, a general tendency for schools with a favourable impact upon pupils' attitude to school and to mathematics, to have a positive effect upon their self-concepts. Those with a negative impact upon attitude to school and to mathematics, tended also to have had a negative effect upon pupils' self-concepts. Our measure of behaviour was significantly, though weakly, related to two other measures of attitudes. It seems that schools with a positive effect upon behaviour tended to have a positive effect on attitude to school, and on attitude to mathematics. School effects upon attendance were generally uncorrelated with the other measures of non-cognitive outcomes.

HOW MANY SCHOOLS WERE GENERALLY GOOD AT FOSTERING PUPILS' NON-COGNITIVE DEVELOPMENT?

As with our analysis of the cognitive outcomes of education, we felt it was important to see whether some schools were especially effective at fostering children's non-cognitive development. To do this a total score was calculated for each school to record the number of non-cognitive outcomes on which it showed a positive effect. The maximum score possible was seven, representing positive effects on behaviour, self-concept, attendance, attitude to school, attitude to mathematics, attitude to reading and attitude to writing. The minimum score possible was zero – poor effects on all areas.

Our results show that five schools had a positive effect on only one of the seven non-cognitive areas considered, and a further eight a positive effect on only two (see Table 9.13).

In contrast, two schools recorded a positive effect on all seven areas, and five schools had a positive effect upon six outcomes. There is strong evidence from our data, therefore, of variation between schools in their effects upon pupils' non-cognitive outcomes. Some schools apparently paid more attention to promoting the social aspects of education than did others. Such differences could be striking. For example, in one school the effect on pupil behaviour over three years was markedly positive (scores were 32% or 19 raw points better than predicted – compared with an overall average for the pupil sample of 59.9 on this combined assessment). This school also had a positive effect on self-concept (5% or 1.4 raw points better than predicted – compared with an overall average for the pupil sample of 27.7), a substantial positive effect on attitude to school (improving attitudes by 41% or 1.2 raw points – compared with an overall average for all pupils of 2.9 on this five point scale) and moderately positive effects on attitudes to the curriculum areas of reading, mathematics and writing. In contrast to these effective schools, one school had a negative effect upon behaviour (children's scores were 13% or 8 raw points poorer than predicted), a poor effect on attitude to school (scores depressed by 24% or 0.7 of a raw point for this measure) and weak negative effects on self-concept and on attitudes to reading, mathematics and writing.

TABLE 9.13: Numbers of non-cognitive outcomes on which schools had a positive effect

Number of non-cognitive outcomes on which school had a positive effect	number of schools
None	0
One	5
Two	8
Three	9
Four	10
Five	8
Six	5
Seven	2
N=47*	

* One of the sample schools did not assess behaviour in the third year and attitudes were not assessed in another. These two schools, therefore, are not included in this table.

Particular schools thus seem to place a greater emphasis on the non-cognitive aspects of education than do others. In some of the sample schools, children's attitudes to school and to different curriculum areas, self-concepts and behaviour were improved. This suggests to us that their experience of school was positive and enjoyable. In other schools, however, attitudes, self-concepts and behaviour were depressed. For children in these schools, junior education was considerably less pleasant than it might have been.

THE LINKS BETWEEN SCHOOL EFFECTS ON COGNITIVE AND ON NON-COGNITITVE OUTCOMES

We used correlation techniques to examine the links between school effects upon cognitive and non-cognitive outcomes. The results show that effects on attitude to mathematics were weakly related to school effects on progress in mathematics over the junior years. Moreover, good effects upon progress in the quality of writing were associated with positive effects on attitude to reading. However, school effects on reading progress were not related to effects on attitude to reading. These results provide, therefore, only limited support for the view that schools which are effective in promoting pupils' progress in a particular area will tend to promote good attitudes towards that area.

There was some evidence that school effects upon progress in the quality of writing were related to attendance. In schools which had a positive effect on attendance, children tended to make more progress in writing during the junior years. Poor attendance was associated with poorer progress in writing. However, attendance was not related to school effects on progress in reading or in mathematics.

There was a strong and highly significant association between school effects upon self-concept and those on progress in mathematics. Schools with good effects on self-concept were very likely to have good effects on children's mathematics progress. Negative effects on mathematics progress were likely to be related to negative effects on children's self-concepts. The relationship between school effects upon self-concept and upon reading progress, although in the same direction as that identified for mathematics, was rather weaker.

For the sub-sample of schools which were involved in the practical mathematics assessment, it was possible for us to investigate the relationships between school effects on the various aspects of practical mathematics and those on children's non-cognitive outcomes. School effects on performance in volume tasks were significantly positively correlated with effects on attitude to mathematics and effects on self-concept.

School effects on tasks concerning length were also related to those on children's self-concepts. Positive effects on performance in number work, sets and volume were all positively correlated with school effects on pupils' attitudes to school – good attitudes and good effects on practical mathematics being related.

School effects on children's behaviour were positively related to all aspects of practical mathematics but especially to length and number work. Thus, schools which were effective in promoting practical aspects of the curriculum also had 'good' effects on children's behaviour during the junior years.

From our analyses we were able to establish whether, in general, school effects upon cognitive areas were independent of those upon non-cognitive areas. The results showed that these two dimensions were separate. Thus, positive school effects upon pupils' cognitive outcomes are not necessarily related to positive effects on the non-cognitive areas. Neither are negative effects upon one area necessarily related to negative effects on other areas, though, as will be discussed below, some schools do have good or poor effects on both of these areas.

One interpretation of the finding (that, in general, school effects upon pupils' cognitive and non-cognitive outcomes are independent) is that the sorts of processes which are responsible for schools exerting positive or negative effects upon these two dimensions may be different. We examine this possibility in Chapter Eleven. However, we found it encouraging to note that school effects upon cognitive outcomes are not negatively related to effects on non-cognitive outcomes. This shows that it is not necessary to sacrifice good effects on the non-cognitive or social aspects of junior education in order to promote pupils' progress in cognitive outcomes. Nor is it the case that, in promoting non-cognitive outcomes, progress in cognitive areas will be adversely affected.

Throughout this chapter we have presented data which illustrates the difference between the most and the least effective school in each of the cognitive and non-cognitive outcomes. Because the scales used for each of the outcomes is different, it is difficult to make valid comparisons between the outcomes. The following table is designed to overcome this difficulty. It uses the differences between the most and the least effective school expressed as a percentage of the overall mean.

TABLE 9.14 The most and the least effective schools

	% Difference from the overall average	
	Most effective	Least effective
Reading	+28	−19
Mathematics	+21	−21
Writing	+27	−21
Oracy	+27	−23
Self-concept	+14	−12
Behaviour	+32	−15
Attendance	+ 5	− 4
Attitude to school	+38	−41

HOW MANY SCHOOLS WERE GOOD AT PROMOTING BOTH COGNITIVE AND NON-COGNITIVE DEVELOPMENT?

Although the two dimensions of school effects on cognitive and non-cognitive outcomes were found to be independent, it is of importance to establish whether schools can be effective in promoting good outcomes for both cognitive and for non-cognitive areas. This is because the vast majority of teachers and parents are keen to promote children's progress and development in many different areas. Few would support a narrow focus on only one or other of the two dimensions, although, as Purkey and Smith (1983) have noted, most studies of school effectiveness have been limited to a consideration of only a small number of cognitive outcomes.

So that we could establish the extent to which schools were effective on a variety of the cognitive and non-cognitive outcomes, the total scores recorded on each area (ranging from 0 to 4 for the cognitive, and 0 to 7 for the non-cognitive) were cross-related. Figures in Table 9.15 show that a number of schools in the sample had positive effects on several cognitive and several non-cognitive areas. For example, 14 schools had positive effects on three or more of the cognitive and four or more of the non-cognitive outcomes. In contrast, five schools had positive effects on only one or none of the cognitive areas, and on only two or fewer of the non-cognitive areas.

TABLE 9.15: Relationship between schools' scores on the total of positive effects on cognitive and the total of positive effects on non-cognitive outcomes

Number of positive non-cognitive outcomes

		One	Two	Three	Four	Five	Six	Seven	Number of schools
Number	None		1		2			1	4
of positive	One	2	2	1	1	1	1		8
cognitive	Two	2	3	6		5			16
outcomes	Three	1		2	5	1	4	1	14
	Four		2		2	1			5
Number of Schools		5	8	9	10	8	5	2	47

We found that only a few schools scored highly on one dimension but not on the other. Thus, two schools recorded positive effects on all four of the cognitive areas but only two of the seven non-cognitive areas. Six schools, in contrast, had a poor effect on nearly all cognitive areas (one or none) but positive effects on four or more non-cognitive areas.

SUMMARY

In this chapter we have shown that school membership made a very important contribution to the explanation of variations in pupils' attainment and progress over three years in reading, writing and mathematics, to attainment in oracy and practical mathematics and also to the development of attitudes, self-concept and behaviour in school. The school for junior age pupils, had rather less effect upon attendance than upon other outcomes. Our results indicate that the school to which a child belongs during the junior years can have a beneficial or a negative effect on her or his progress and development. The importance of school in explaining variations in pupils' progress over the junior years is a major finding of this study. It is clear that the school makes a far larger contribution to the explanation of progress than is made by pupils' background characteristics, sex and age. This result is important for teachers, pupils and parents.

Some schools were particularly effective at promoting progress in specific areas of learning, and others were especially effective at promoting good behaviour, positive attitudes or self-concept. The relationships, though very complex, indicate that, on the whole, schools which promoted good progress in mathematics tended also to do so in reading. In addition, such schools helped to foster self-concept and, to a lesser extent, promoted a positive attitude to mathematics. There were weaker relationships between school effects on progress in writing and progress in other cognitive areas. However, schools with positive effects on writing progress, tended to have similar effects on attitude to reading, good progress in mathematics and good effects on attendance.

In general, we found that the effects of school membership on non-cognitive outcomes were not highly related to those on cognitive areas. It seems that the two dimensions were largely independent of each other. Nonetheless, amongst the sample of schools included in the study, there were striking differences in effectiveness. Some schools had positive effects on their pupils' progress and development in several areas. Others had a negative effect on several areas. From these results it can be seen that, for the pupil, the particular school she or he joins at age seven can have a highly significant impact upon future progress and development. The effects of junior schooling are likely to be carried forward with the child at secondary transfer and may have a long-term influence on later educational success and employment prospects.

One of the three major questions we have addressed is – do junior schools make a difference to pupils' educational outcomes? It is clear that schools do make a difference and that the difference is substantial. Some schools are effective in many different areas. These results confirm the value of including assessments of a variety of educational outcomes in a study of school effects. The use of only one or two outcomes might well provide a misleading picture of the general effectiveness of particular schools. By using information about a variety of cognitive and non-cognitive areas, this possibility is reduced.

In Chapter 11 we will investigate the factors responsible for differences between junior schools in their effectiveness. First, however, attention is paid to the question of whether schools differ in their effectiveness for particular groups of pupils.

10

Differences in Effectiveness

In the last chapter we showed that the school attended can have a major impact on the progress and development of pupils during the junior years. Individual schools were found to differ considerably in their effects. Some enhanced their pupils' progress and development in many areas. In others, however, pupils' progress and development was depressed. The second major question examined by the Project was 'Are some schools more effective for particular groups of children?' In this chapter, therefore, we will describe the results of our investigation of the impact of school on different groups. We have concentrated on differences according to social class, sex, and ethnic background because, as we have shown in Chapter 7, these factors were found to be related, significantly, to pupil progress in some of the cognitive outcomes. Age is not considered in this chapter, because there was no evidence that progress was influenced by pupils' age, nor that age-related differences increased over time.

We investigated the effects of school membership upon pupils of different groups (divided according to social class, sex, or ethnic background) using the same methods we had employed to investigate the effects of school membership upon all pupils, in the sample. (These methods are described in Chapter 9.) The results of our analyses are adjusted to take into account differences between schools in the numbers of pupils in the different groups which were the focus of interest.

We decided to limit our study to school effects on the progress of different groups of children in three cognitive areas – reading, writing and mathematics. This was because we could take into account pupils' initial attainment in estimating school effects for these three outcomes. For oracy, practical mathematics, and the various non-cognitive outcomes, this procedure was not possible, or not considered statistically appropriate. Because of the absence of adjustment for a pre-test, and the small numbers of pupils in some groups, it was thought that the calculation of school effects separately for these outcomes for different pupil groups might prove less reliable than the calculations of effects on progress in reading, writing and mathematics.

DIFFERENCES ACCORDING TO SOCIAL CLASS

It has already been noted (in Chapter 9) that there were striking differences between the Project schools in the social class backgrounds of their pupil intakes. Some schools had concentrations of pupils from more advantaged, non-manual backgrounds. Other schools received very high percentages of pupils whose parents were in semi- or unskilled-manual work. In the overall investigation of school effects described in the previous chapter, we took into account the background characteristics of the individual pupils in each school. However, it is possible that the overall school effect might mask differences within a school in its effectiveness in promoting the progress of children of different social class backgrounds. In order to investigate this possibility, we needed to calculate the effects of individual schools separately for children according to their social class backgrounds.

Because of the differential distribution of pupils from different social class groups, it was possible for us to calculate such effects in only 17 of the Project schools when effects on reading and mathematics progress were analysed. Only schools where progress data were available for five or more pupils in each of the two social class groups (non-manual and manual) were included in these analyses. It was not possible to use a more detailed social class classification, due to the small numbers of pupils which would result in such a school by school comparison.

Having obtained figures on the effects of individual schools for children of manual and of non-manual backgrounds, we compared the results. This was done to see whether schools had a similar sort of effect upon the progress of these two groups of children. Comparisons were made using correlation methods. These show whether, overall, schools which helped to promote the progress of pupils from non-manual origins, also helped to promote the progress of those from manual backgrounds. They also show whether schools which were ineffective for one group (depressing their progress below that expected on the basis of initial attainment) were also ineffective for the other.

Our results indicate that, for reading, the majority of schools which had a negative effect on children of non-manual origins also had a negative effect on those of manual origins. In contrast, schools which had a positive effect on one social class group usually had a positive effect on the other (see Table 10.1). Thus, the majority of schools which had a negative effect upon reading for the non-manual group also had a negative effect for those of manual origins, whereas those that had a positive effect for one group also had a positive effect on the other. The correlation was positive and strong ($r=0.75$). Of the 17 schools in which the number of pupils was sufficient for analysis, however, six were discrepant in their effects, having a positive effect for one group and a negative one for the other. For four of these, the school effect was in favour of the manual group.

TABLE 10.1 Correlations between the effects of individual schools on progress in reading, mathematics and writing for children of manual and of non-manual origins

	r	N of schools
Reading	0.75**	17
Mathematics	0.60**	17
Writing quality	0.43*	16

* p 0.05 (significant)
**p 0.01 (highly significant)

This finding, therefore, provides evidence that, in general, schools which promote the progress in reading of non-manual pupils, tend also to promote that of children from manual background. Moreover, those schools which are less effective (producing poorer progress than expected) are in general less effective for both groups. Nonetheless, a few schools appeared to favour one particular social class group rather than another. This indicates that it may be possible to help particular groups.

For mathematics a similar pattern emerged, though the correlation was not quite as strong as for reading (r=0.60). Here the effects on the two social class groups were discrepant in only four of the 17 schools, and the measure of association was fairly strong and positive. However, in contrast to reading, in three of the four schools where effects differed for the two social class groups, they favoured the non-manual group.

For writing quality the relationship between school effects on progress for non-manual and for manual children was rather weaker than that found for either reading or mathematics. Nonetheless, we found little evidence to suggest that in general schools were differentially effective or ineffective in promoting the progress of particular social class groups. Thus, the sign of school effects corresponded for ten of the 16 schools (either negative or positive for both groups). Of the six discrepant schools, three had a positive effect on the non-manual but a negative effect on the manual, and three a negative effect on non-manual and a positive effect on manual.

Overall, therefore, we found that there was little difference in the size of the effects of individual schools on the progress of children from different social class groups. Those schools which were effective for one group tended to be effective for the other. Conversely, those which were ineffective for one group were also usually ineffective for the other. Our results show, therefore, that effective schools tend to 'jack up' the progress of all pupils, irrespective of their social class background, while ineffective schools will usually depress the progress of all pupils. This means that in effective schools social class differences in attainment are not likely to be reversed, rather that all pupils will be performing at a higher level. These findings are in line with those reported by Rutter et al (1979) who found that their effective schools boosted the performance of all children. Rutter (1983) has also noted that if all schools became more effective, the result would be an improvement in overall standards for all children, rather than a removal of deeply rooted social class differences in educational achievement. Nonetheless, given the correspondence in school effects for different groups of pupils, it seems unlikely that the factors responsible for effectiveness would vary for children of different social class background.

DIFFERENCES ACCORDING TO SEX

In Chapter 7 we demonstrated that, as a group, girls had markedly higher attainments than boys in reading and writing in all years. Although differences in mathematics attainment were small, the girls had made slightly more progress than the boys in this area over a three year period. Adopting the same strategy employed in the investigation of school effects for pupils of different social class backgrounds, we also compared the impact of individual schools on the progress of boys and girls. Due to the larger numbers involved it was possible to calculate, separately for girls and boys, the size of the effects of individual schools for the majority of our sample schools (41 in reading and mathematics, 42 in writing). As can be seen in Table 10.2, the correlations between the size of the effects of individual schools on the two sexes were positive and significant. Nonetheless, they were rather weaker than those identified in the analysis of school effects according to social class.

10.2: Correlations between the effects of individual schools on progress in reading, mathematics and writing for girls and boys.

---

	r	N of schools
Reading	0.54*	41
Mathematics	0.57**	41
Writing quality	0.40*	42

** p 0.0001 (highly significant)
* p 0.01 (significant)

These results suggest that, in general, schools which had a positive effect in promoting reading progress for one sex also tended to have a positive effect for the other, whilst those which were ineffective for one sex were likely to be ineffective for the other. Nonetheless, there was some variability. Although for the majority of schools (29) effects for girls and for boys were in the same direction (positive for both or negative for both) the results were discrepant in 12 schools. In eight of these schools, effects on reading progress were positive for boys, but negative for girls.

Our data provide some suggestion that certain schools were more effective at promoting the reading progress of boys, rather than girls. Nonetheless, these findings should be treated with some caution since, overall, girls' attainment in reading was significantly higher than that of boys. It is possible that in some schools, where staff may have been especially aware of sex differences in attainment, particular attention was paid to boys' achievement in reading. Alternatively, staff may have paid attention to all those pupils with lower attainment, amongst whom boys were a majority.

School effects on mathematics were considered for individual schools separately for boys and for girls. We found that those which had positive effects for one sex tended to have a positive effect for the other. Similarly, schools which had a negative impact upon mathematics progress for one of the sexes, usually had a negative impact upon the other sex. Nonetheless, some discrepancies were also noted in this area. For 12 of the 41 schools the effects for one sex were positive and for the other negative. In contrast to findings for reading, however, in seven of these schools, effects on mathematics progress were positive for girls, though not for boys. It has already been noted that, over the junior years, girls made slightly more progress in mathematics than boys (there was no difference between the sexes in reading progress) and, in line with this result, the size of the school effect was slightly larger for girls. There is little evidence, therefore, to suggest that during the junior period girls were disadvantaged in comparison with boys in mathematics. If anything, it appears that, as a group, they were better able to benefit from the mathematical education they received.

For writing, the effects of individual schools on the two sexes were also found to be significantly positively correlated, though the relationship was weaker than that identified for either reading or mathematics. This indicates some variation according to pupil sex between schools in their effects on writing progress. Of the 42 schools involved in these analyses, ten recorded positive effects for one sex, but negative effects for the other. In eight of these schools the school effect on writing progress was in favour of boys. It also appears that, in terms of progress, the effect of some schools favoured boys in the sample. These differences were, however, generally small in size. Thus, although, overall, the girls attained more highly than the boys, in particular schools boys made more progress than girls during the junior years. Overall in the whole pupil sample neither sex was found to make significantly more progress than the other in this outcome.

Given the poorer attainment of boys in this area, it seems possible that particular attention may have been given in such schools to promoting the writing performance of low achievers. This might tend to benefit boys, because of their initially poorer writing performance.

The data suggest that a few schools may have been slightly more effective at promoting the progress of pupils of one sex rather than the other. Overall, however, there was little evidence to indicate that, in general, the relative progress of boys and girls depends on the particular school attended. Rather, it seems that some schools are effective in particular areas, whereas others are ineffective. Which school attended seems to make a difference to pupil progress, therefore, irrespective of a child's sex. Sometimes this effect is positive, in other cases negative. These results support the findings of our analysis for social class – that the more effective schools tend to 'jack up' the performance of all pupils. Given that schools which were effective for one group tended to be effective for others and that those which were ineffective for one group were also ineffective for others, the results suggests that the processes associated with school effectiveness are unlikely to differ for the two sexes.

DIFFERENCES ACCORDING TO RACE

The Project has provided evidence of a significant relationship between ethnic family background and attainment and progress in certain of the cognitive areas. Given this, it is important to establish whether schools were differentially effective for pupils of certain ethnic groups. Our analyses could only include schools where the number of pupils for whom data were available at entry and in the summer of the third year was greater than or equal to five, for each ethnic group. Unfortunately, due to the small numbers of pupils of particular ethnic groups at the school level, our analyses were limited to a consideration of effects for the Caribbean group compared with effects for children of all other ethnic backgrounds.

Caribbean pupils tended to be highly represented in only a few of the schools, reflecting geographical variations within inner London in the distribution of this group (see Chapter 7). Due to these differences in the distribution of pupils of different ethnic backgrounds, it was possible to calculate school effects separately for children of Caribbean and of 'other' ethnic backgrounds in only 12 of the sample schools, for reading and mathematics, and in 14 schools for writing. These school effects were then compared in order to establish whether there was evidence of any tendency for school effects to operate against the Caribbean group. The results of our comparisons of school effects for

Caribbean and for other pupils indicated that for reading and mathematics the effects for both groups tended to be strongly associated (see Table 10.3).

TABLE 10.3: Correlations between the effects of individual schools on progress in reading, mathematics and writing for children of different ethnic backgrounds.

	r	N of schools
Reading	0.73**	12
Mathematics	0.64**	12
Writing quality	0.18	14

** p 0.01 (highly significant)

Nonetheless, some discrepancies were apparent. When reading was considered it was found that, for three of the 12 schools (a quarter of those involved), the impact of school was positive for one ethnic group but negative for the other. However, there was no evidence of a consistent bias against Caribbean children, because in two of these three schools the impact was positive for Caribbean but not for 'other' children, and in one the effects were negative. What is clear, however, is that of the 12 schools considered in this analysis, only four had a positive effect on Caribbean children and only three a positive effect on the 'other' group. It is possible that one of the reasons which may account, in part, for the poorer progress of Caribbean children in reading was that they were more highly represented in schools which were generally ineffective in promoting reading progress for all children, than in schools which were especially effective for reading.

Turning attention to the effects of schools on pupils' mathematics progress, our results indicated that, in general, effects were closely associated for both ethnic groups. In two of the 12 schools considered, however, results were in a different direction. In these two cases, the effect for Caribbean children was negative, though positive for the 'other' group. Overall, only three of the 12 schools had a positive impact on mathematics progress for Caribbean children; the equivalent figure for the 'other' group was five. It seems that, as with reading, Caribbean children were over-represented in schools which were ineffective in promoting progress in mathematics.

For writing there was very little relationship between school effects for the two groups. Thus, the effects of individual schools were positive in seven of the 14 schools for Caribbean pupils and in eight for the 'other' group. Nonetheless, in six schools a positive effect was recorded for one but not for the second group. Three recorded a positive impact for Caribbean but not for the 'other' group, and in three the result was reversed. It does not appear, therefore, that these schools were generally less likely to promote the writing progress of Caribbean, than of 'other' pupils. It should also be remembered that there was no evidence that, at the individual pupil level, writing progress was related to ethnic background.

Overall, therefore, we did not find evidence of a systematic bias in the way schools affected children of different ethnic backgrounds. It does appear, however, that in this sample Caribbean pupils were over-represented in schools which were generally ineffective in promoting the progress of all pupils, irrespective of their ethnic background. This is a cause for considerable concern.

The analysis of school effects for different groups of pupils is highly complex. Furthermore, given the small numbers of certain groups of pupils in particular schools, the results of analyses according to race and social class should be treated with some caution. Having said this, however, the results of our investigations of the effects of individual schools on pupils' progress in cognitive areas indicate that, in general, there were few differences between groups in the effects of particular schools. Overall, schools which were effective in promoting progress for children of one group (whether pupils of a particular sex, social class or ethnic group) tended to be effective for children of other groups. Similarly, those which were ineffective for one group tended to be ineffective for other groups. Which school a pupil attends can thus have a significant impact upon her or his progress during the junior years. However, our data indicate that the nature of the school effect does not usually depend upon a child's background characteristics. Schools which are effective for girls, tend also to be effective for boys. Similarly, school effects for children of different social class or ethnic groups are quite closely related. Nonetheless, it is clear that the correlations between school effects for different groups, though all statistically significant and positive, do fall short of unity (agreement is by no means perfect). This may well be due to random fluctuations in school effects. Further work, using a larger sample of schools would be valuable to enable confirmation of the general conclusions presented here.

These findings are in line with those reported by Willms and Cuttance (1985) in their study of secondary schools. They examined individual school effects for groups of pupils classified as of different ability and concluded 'there are few schools that are particularly effective for low ability pupils but not high ability pupils and vice versa' (p.302). School effects for children of different sex, ethnic or social class groups were not examined by Willms and Cuttance in their study. It is not possible, therefore, to make a direct comparison between their results and those of the Project.

IS IT POSSIBLE TO OVERCOME DISADVANTAGE?

It is of considerable interest, and educational importance, to establish whether schools can help children to overcome the educational disadvantages related to background identified in this Project and in many previous studies. Overall, we have already shown that schools which were more effective for one group of children tended to be more effective for other groups. Thus, an effective school tends to raise the performance of all children, irrespective of their social class, sex or ethnic background, and an ineffective school tends to depress the performance of all pupils. Given this general trend, it is nevertheless worth focusing attention on the question of whether it is possible that, where schools were very different in their effectiveness in promoting reading and mathematics progress, social class differences in attainment could be reduced or eliminated. Social class has been selected for attention because social class differences in attainment were especially marked for junior age pupils, and there was some evidence of small but significant differences in progress in certain cognitive areas, and of teacher expectations, in favour of the non-manual group. The size of school effects for non-manual and for manual children were examined, therefore, for the 17 schools where the numbers of pupils in each of the two social class groups were sufficient for analysis. We compared school effects on reading progress for manual children in the most effective schools, with the effects on reading progress for non-manual children in the least effective schools. This was done to establish whether school attended could, in some instances, reverse the overall pattern of social class differences in attainment.

TABLE 10.4: Comparisons of individual school effects on pupils' reading progress for manual and non-manual groups

---

a) Most effective schools for pupils of manual backgrounds

School	Size of school effect on manual children*	Impact of school effect on reading attainment for average manual child
a	+14.6	66.1
b	+11.9	63.4
c	+ 6.6	58.1

Overall average raw reading score for manual group (summer year 3) = 51.5

* Expressed in raw score points

b) Least effective schools for pupils of non-manual backgrounds

School	Size of school effect on non-manual children*	Impact of school effect on reading attainment for average non-manual child
d	-11.8	53.1
e	−7.7	57.2
f	−7.6	57.3
g	−7.2	57.7

Overall average raw reading score for non-manual group (summer year 3) = 64.9

* Expressed in raw score points

Our results show that, in three schools which were particularly effective in promoting pupils' reading progress (out of the total of 17), the impact of the school raised the average reading attainment of manual children to a level above that achieved by non-manual children who had attended four schools which were particularly ineffective in promoting reading progress (see the figures shown in Table 10.4). Thus, social class differences were reversed in more than a third of the schools (7 in total) where we were able to conduct these analyses.

We made similar comparisons of school effects on pupils' mathematics progress. The results demonstrate that, as with reading, manual children who attended the most effective schools, attained more highly in mathematics by the end of their third year in junior school than did non-manual children who attended the least effective schools. In four of the 17 schools, the average child of a manual background had higher attainment in mathematics than non-manual children who attended four of the least effective schools (see Table 10.5).

It is clear, therefore, that although there is a general tendency for schools to be effective or to be ineffective for all groups of children, including those of different social class backgrounds, it is possible for schools to alter the overall patterns of social class differences in attainment. A child whose parents are in manual employment and who attends an effective junior school, is likely to attain more highly in reading and in mathematics than a child who has the advantage of a non-manual background, but who attends an ineffective school. Again, these results point to the importance of the school.

10.5: Comparisons of individual school effects on pupils' mathematics progress for manual and non-manual groups

a) Most effective schools for pupils of manual backgrounds

School	Size of school effect on manual children*	Impact of school effect on mathematics attainment for average manual child
s	+ 7.3	34.4
t	+ 5.9	33.0
u	+ 3.7	30.8
v	+ 3.3	30.4

Overall average raw mathematics score for manual group (summer year 3) = 27.1

* Expressed in raw score points.

b) Least effective schools for pupils of non-manual backgrounds

School	Size of school effect on non-manual children*	Impact of school effect on mathematics attainment for average non-manual child
w	−4.6	27.5
x	−3.9	28.2
y	−3.6	28.5
z	−2.4	29.7

Overall average raw mathematics score for non-manual group (summer year 3) = 32.1

* Expressed in raw score points.

SUMMARY

In this chapter we have shown that, in general, schools which were effective in promoting progress for one group of pupils (whether those of a particular social class, sex or ethnic group) were usually also effective for children of other groups. Similarly, those schools which were ineffective for one group tended to be ineffective for other groups. In terms of the second question posed at the beginning of this book, therefore, the answer is 'no' – school effectiveness does not seem to depend upon pupils' backgrounds. The implications of these findings are considerable. By attending a more effective school all pupils will benefit, even those who are at an initial educational disadvantage because of their particular background characteristics. Effective schools tend to be good for all their pupils. Even though overall differences in patterns of pupil attainment are not removed in the most effective schools, the performance of all children is raised and, as we have demonstrated, disadvantaged children in the most effective schools can end up with higher achievements than their advantaged peers in the less effective schools. In the next chapter we turn to the third major question addressed by the Project: what are the factors that make schools effective or ineffective?

11

Understanding Effectiveness

We have already demonstrated in Chapter 9 that the answer to our first question 'Are some schools more effective than others, when variations in the intakes of pupils are taken into account?' is 'yes'. Schools do make a difference. In the last chapter we examined school effects for different groups of pupils and were able to conclude that schools which are effective are effective for all pupils, irrespective of their backgrounds. The answer to our second question 'Are some schools or classes more effective for particular groups of children?'is, therefore, 'no'.

In this chapter our attention is focused upon the third question addressed by the Project. 'If some schools are more effective than others, what factors contribute to these positive effects?' In other words, our aim is to identify the ways in which the most effective schools differ from those which are least effective. Variations between schools in their resources, policies and in the strategies of their teachers will be related, therefore, to information about schools' effects on their pupils.

The chapter is divided into a number of sections. First, we provide a brief description of the types of information which were tested against school effects on the various pupil outcomes. We do not, however, give details of the statistical analyses which were conducted to examine the many and complex inter-relationships between all these different factors and schools' effects on each of the cognitive and the non-cognitive outcomes. (The interested reader is referred to Mortimore et al, 1986b for details of our strategy of analysis.) Rather we focus on our investigation of the way different factors found to have had a significant impact upon pupils' progress or development were, themselves, inter-related. From this investigation it has been possible to achieve a greater understanding of the mechanisms of effectiveness. In the final section, we will turn to the key factors which we have identified as playing a major role in effective junior education.

THE FACTORS TESTED

A great deal of information was collected about school and class policies during the four years of field work. Data were also collected about those aspects of school life over which the school and the class teacher can exercise little direct control. These latter aspects have been termed givens. The two sets of information, about policies and givens, include many factors which relate to the school as a whole and others which relate specifically to the classes within schools. Examples of some of the given factors are the status of schools (junior and infant or junior only; county or voluntary) and their staffing. Examples of policy variables at the school level (matters under the control of the school) are the methods of allocating pupils and teachers to classes, and the involvement of staff in decision-making. A few variables – pupil mobility, for example – do not fit easily into either category. Thus, mobility can be viewed as a given – schools have no control over pupils moving – but it may also be, in part, a function of either school or class reputations. Some parents, for example, may make an effort to send their children to a school with a 'good' reputation.

Certain factors may be under the control of the head or deputy at the school level (the way pupils are allocated to classes, for example) and thus are policy choices. However, at the class level, these may sometimes form given factors for teachers who have been assigned to work with particular classes. Despite these qualifications, however, the division of variables related to school and classroom processes and factors into the categories given and policy at the two levels – class and school – provides a useful framework for grouping the information about schools, teachers and classes. For the analyses of effectiveness these four broad categories have been further sub-divided as follows:-

1 School Level – 'Given' Variables
(i)   Building
(ii)   Status
(iii)   Resources
(iv)   Intake
(v)   Stability

2 School Level – Policy Variables
(i)   Head's style of leadership
(ii)   Type of organisation
(iii)   Staff – involvement and conditions
(iv)   Curriculum
(v)   Rewards and punishments used
(vi)   Relations with parents/parental involvement in school
(vii)   Equal opportunities
(viii) Atmosphere of school

3 Class Level – 'Given' Variables
(i)   Size
(ii) Class characteristics (age, social class, ability composition)
(iii) Classroom
(iv) Resources
(v)   Curriculum guidelines
(vi) Teacher characteristics
(vii) Change of teacher during the year

4 Class Level – Policy Variables
(i)   Aims of teacher
(ii)   Planning of teacher
(iii) Teacher strategies and organisation of the curriculum
(iv)   Management of classroom, including rewards and punishments
(v)   Atmosphere
(vi)   Level and type of communication between teacher and pupils
(vii) Parental involvement
(viii) Record keeping

METHODS

A large number of variables were derived from interviews, questionnaires, classroom observations, and from the ratings and notes collected by field officers during the study. These variables have been screened against the effects of school membership and of class membership on each of the cognitive and non-cognitive outcomes. In conducting such analyses, educational and research judgements have been used. For example, in investigating school effects upon reading progress, information relating specifically to another curriculum area was not used. Thus, teacher practices concerning mathematics work, such as the use of grouping for children for work in this curriculum area, or use of mathematics guidelines, were not included. However, variables relating to language guidelines and grouping for language work were included.

From our analyses we found that many of these given and policy factors were related significantly to pupils' progress and development in a variety of areas. The factors identified as important are discussed here, under the headings of the four broad categories noted earlier. (For details of the precise cognitive and non-cognitive outcomes to which they relate, grouped together as a table, see Mortimore et al 1986b). A more detailed examination of the way these factors may operate appears in the section entitled 'mechanisms of effectiveness'.

SCHOOL LEVEL 'GIVENS'

There was considerable evidence that a number of factors over which the school had little or no control were related significantly to schools' effects on their pupils.

School size

An important factor was the size of schools (as measured by the junior roll). Very small schools inevitably face a number of difficulties (see Luzio, 1983), but our data show support for middle to small sized schools with a junior roll of around 160 or fewer pupils. This range of school size was related positively to schools' effects on pupils' progress, particularly in cognitive areas. There is no evidence from the Project's findings that larger schools were associated with better progress in any area.

Voluntary status

There was a consistent pattern of associations between voluntary status and schools' effects upon a number of the cognitive and non-cognitive outcomes, although interestingly, it was negatively related to attainment in oracy, voluntary schools tending to depress pupils' skills in communicating effectively. The findings about the effects of voluntary schools will be discussed in more detail later in this chapter, but it is worth noting here that, in part, they seem to reflect the sorts of policy choices made in the classroom. In voluntary schools teachers seemed to be adopting more of the strategies which we found were generally associated with effectiveness in promoting pupil progress.

Distance travelled to school

Some variables seem to act as indicators of other factors. For example, the average distance travelled by pupils from home to school can be regarded as a partial and crude indication of parental choice. There is evidence that, in many cases where schools are particularly popular with parents, children may be drawn from far afield. Certainly, the distance factor was linked with voluntary status, and it is known that voluntary schools often have the advantage of community support.

We found that schools which drew pupils from further afield tended to have a positive impact upon several of the cognitive areas as well as attendance and attitude to reading. It is likely that schools which were chosen for very specific reasons may have had the advantages of greater parental support for their educational aims and, because of such support, were helped to be more effective. However, the average distance pupils travelled from home to school was rather weakly negatively related to school effects on behaviour.

Junior-only status

The type of school also appeared to matter. Schools that were composed only of junior-aged pupils (ages 7 to 11) were less likely to be associated with higher levels of progress than those that catered for pupils from five through to eleven. It appears that this factor was related primarily to pupils' progress in cognitive areas. However, it was also found to be important for one of the non-cognitive outcomes

– attitude to reading. Junior-only status, in contrast, was not found to be related positively to any of the outcomes considered. This finding may reflect different aspects of organisation in junior only, as opposed to junior and infant schools. It may also indicate the potentially disruptive effects on pupils of transfer to another school at age seven.

Headteacher's time in present post
The length of time which the headteacher had spent in her or his present post was another factor found to be important. Where the head was new (having been in post for less than three years) pupils' progress and development tended to be poorer than expected. In contrast, schools with mid-term heads (those who had been in post for between three and seven years) tended to have a positive impact upon their pupils' progress. The results suggest that, having established themselves, the mid-term heads may have been in a position to implement more effective management strategies. Additionally, the results of their earlier efforts may have been coming to fruition after several years in post. Where heads had been in their present post for eleven or more years, however, school effects on a number of areas, in particuar on non-cognitive ones, tended to be negative. There is evidence, therefore, that for headteachers, the time spent in their present post had a complex relationship with the school's effectiveness. The results suggest that both new and long-serving heads may need extra support.

Change in the management structure
We also found several indications that too much change and instability within the management structure of the schools was associated negatively with pupils' progress and development. This included changes of head and deputy headteachers and the frequent absence of either. It appeared that a change or frequent or prolonged absence of the deputy head was most closely linked with effects on pupils' educational outcomes.

Elsewhere it has been noted that the deputy provided an important link between the head and teaching staff in the school. It appears from our findings that the deputy has a key role to play in the effective functioning of the school. Where disruption of this role occurs, whether through a change or absence, the impact is negative.

Physical environment of the school
The quality of the physical environment provided for pupils in their school (in terms of the quality of the school and classroom decorations, provision of play areas etc.) was a factor which we found to be related to several educational outcomes. However, it appeared to be more closely related to the non-cognitive than the cognitive outcomes, although it was related, positively, to effects on pupils' progress in writing.

Pupil Composition

There was some indication that contextual effects related to certain aspects of the composition of pupil intakes to schools were associated with some of the educational outcomes considered in the Project. Thus there was a weak relationship between the educational priority status of schools and schools' effects on a number of areas. Those with more advantaged intakes tended to have a more positive effect. However, such schools were less likely to promote attainment in oracy. In addition, schools with first year pupil intakes who were attaining more highly in reading at entry, tended to have more positive impact on some of the non-cognitive outcomes. The academic composition of the pupils at entry, however, tended to be unrelated to cognitive outcomes, with the exception of writing progress. Here we found some suggestion that in schools where pupils scored more highly in reading at entry, their later progress in writing tended to be higher. Academic composition at entry, however, did not relate to pupils' progress in reading during the junior years, although there was some evidence that schools with a high proportion of pupils of non-manual origins tended to have a greater effect on pupils' attitudes to reading, their attendance and their reading progress. Though the relationships were fairly weak, they are, nonetheless, consistent with the finding that non-manual pupils made greater progress in reading than other social class groups and that teachers had higher expectations of them.

Factors related to pupil composition were more closely related overall to non-cognitive, than the cognitive outcomes and, in particular, they were associated with effects on attendance. Over and above the influence of the individual child's own background characteristics, therefore, it seems that the composition of pupils in the school was linked with patterns of attendance.

SCHOOL LEVEL POLICIES

Many more policy factors than givens were related significantly to schools' effects on pupils' educational outcomes.

Record keeping

We found that pupil progress and development tended to be promoted in those schools where the headteacher requested the staff to keep individual records of children's work, and where those records were discussed by the head and the class teachers concerned. In addition, the practice of class teachers passing on folders of children's work to their next teacher was also related to positive effects on progress. The keeping of individual records of pupil progress is just one indicator of the care and concern shown by many teachers over the development of each child within the class. It is a practice which is clearly likely to be helpful in identifying areas in which particular help is needed, and may enable early intervention to take place.

Forecasts, work-plans and the curriculum

Schools where the head requested teachers to provide forecasts of their work or work-plans were associated with a number of positive effects as was the head's involvement in influencing the school curriculum. Moreover, the head's involvement in curriculum planning, by establishing school-wide policies on subject guidelines, was also related to good effects in a number of areas. In particular, positive associations were found where guidelines, such as those produced by the Authority or by schools themselves, were used consistently by the staff. There was, however, a negative relationship where there was variation in the use of guidelines between individual teachers. The encouragement of staff involvement in the development of school guidelines was also beneficial and, as might be expected, such factors were most closely associated with effects on pupils' cognitive outcomes. These factors can all be seen as part of a strategy of positive leadership on the part of the headteacher in matters concerning the curriculum.

Course attendance and teaching strategies

Previous research has suggested that the relationship between the head and the rest of the teachers can be very important (see the review by Purkey and Smith, 1983). Leadership, however, was often exhibited in subtle ways. For example, constant attempts by the head to enforce certain teaching strategies failed to produce any positive effects, whereas those heads who only attempted to influence teachers when they felt it to be appropriate, did have a positive impact.

A similar subtle relationship was found with in-service training. Where heads stated that they encouraged and permitted class teachers to go on courses in school time as frequently as they wished, this was associated with poorer progress. In contrast, in schools where teachers were encouraged to go on particular courses for a 'good reason', there was a positive impact. This finding was supported by analysis of the class teacher interviews in that where teachers reported that they always received encouragement to attend any course, effects on pupils' progress were found to be negative. These results do not imply that teachers should not attend courses (the proportion of staff who had been on courses was related positively to writing progress, attendance, and attitudes to school and to mathematics), but rather that a school-based policy was beneficial.

Headteacher's emphasis on basic skills

In schools where the headteachers indicated that they laid a particular emphasis upon a basic skills approach, the impact upon pupils' progress in reading, mathematics and writing was negative. It appears, therefore, that this narrow approach did nothing to promote pupils' learning.

Moreover, such an emphasis was related to poorer effects in non-cognitive areas too.

Staff involvement in decision-making
The involvement of the deputy head and teaching staff in decision-making was another important characteristic of effective leadership by the head. Thus, where the deputy and/or teaching staff were involved in decisions about the allocation of pupils and of teachers to classes, the impact on pupils' progress and development tended to be positive. In addition, the staff's general involvement in decision-making and their involvement in decisions about spending the school's resources were associated with better effects in non-cognitive areas. The beneficial impact of staff involvement in the development of guidelines has already been remarked upon. An authoritarian style of leadership, where the head does not share responsibility for certain kinds of decision-making, therefore, was not related to effectiveness, in any of the areas under examination.

Non-teaching periods
In schools where teachers were allocated regular non-teaching periods as part of their timetables, the effects on a variety of educational outcomes were positive.

Rewards and Punishments
In schools where the headteachers emphasised punishments rather more than rewards pupils' progress tended to be inhibited; the greater the number of punishments listed, the more negative were the effects. In contrast, whenever the number of rewards exceeded the number of punishments, progress in reading was greater. Of the different methods of rewarding pupils adopted by the head, the use of stars and certificates in particular was associated with a beneficial effect on a number of non-cognitive areas.

We have taken the use of rewards and punishments to be a feature of the school climate. This, as we will show later, proved to be an important aspect of effective schooling. Other features of school life which we considered to be important contributors to the atmosphere also proved to be related positively to effects in a number of areas. For example the extent to which pupils were taken on trips and visits, whether staff ran clubs and activities for pupils at lunch time and after school, and the pupils' involvement in presenting assemblies. In addition, progress and development were promoted in those schools where the pupils tended to be happy and friendly – in schools where we found a 'fun factor' – and where they were generally well-behaved. Of course, these latter factors both contribute to, and are a reflection of, the school climate, just as effective learning can be as much the cause of a healthy atmosphere as it can be the product.

Parental involvement

It is clear that the involvement of parents in the school's life is related to greater effectiveness in promoting educational progress. Schools where parents helped in the classrooms, where they helped with visits and outings and provided other kinds of assistance tended to have a beneficial effect. Schools which provided regular progress meetings for parents to discuss their children's work, where they had facilities or a room for parents' use, and where it was the practice for parents to be allowed to call in at any time to see the head also were associated with progress.

The presence in schools of a Parent Teacher Association, however, had a negative association with progress in both cognitive and non-cognitive spheres. At first sight this finding is curious, but suggests perhaps that schools cannot simply assume that they are involving parents effectively merely by having such a body. Moreover, as will be shown later, this factor was related to some of the important given characteristics of schools.

CLASS LEVEL 'GIVENS'

We found consistent evidence that a change (or several changes) of class teacher during the school year could have a detrimental effect upon pupils' learning and upon their non-cognitive development. Thus, the experience of a change of class teacher during the school year was negatively related to effects in the cognitive areas. For those pupils who had experienced two or more changes in one year (or one change in each of two consecutive years) it appeared to be particularly damaging. Conversely, schools where few pupils had experienced such changes, were associated with positive effects in both attitudes and self-concept.

Class size

Amongst the given variables affecting classes, the average class size, which ranged from 15 to 34 in the first year, was related to mathematics progress. Pupils in schools with smaller classes made more progress though this only reached significance in the first year. Schools where classes had an average of 24 or fewer pupils generally made better progress than schools with larger classes, in particular, those with 27 or more pupils. This result is important because the majority of previous studies have generally found class size to be unimportant in explaining pupil achievement (see Simpson, 1982). It is likely to be due, in part, to the fact that this study examined progress rather than attainment. Also, most studies which have examined the impact of class size have examined the effects on achievement in language-based areas, rather than mathematics. When account is taken of other factors, the impact of class size increases. Thus, because mathematics progress was related to voluntary status, when this factor was controlled (by means of partial correlation analysis) the relationship between class size and mathematics progress was increased and was also significant in the third year (r=0.37 year 1 and r=0.21 year 3). In addition to a relationship with pupils' mathematics progress, we found that smaller class sizes were related to beneficial effects upon a number of other areas too, particularly the non-cognitive.

CLASS LEVEL POLICIES

Many variables connected with the way teachers taught were also related to pupils' progress and development during the junior years. The results of the Junior School Project show that the methods and strategies adopted by the teacher in the classroom and the nature of her or his communication with pupils can be of great importance in aiding effectiveness.

Communicating with pupils

There was strong evidence that those teachers who spent greater amounts of time communicating with pupils about the content of their work had a positive effect upon progress in all the cognitive areas. In addition, many of the non-cognitive areas benefited from this focus on work too. The amount of teacher time devoted to giving pupils feedback about their work also had a positive association with progress in a number of areas.

Conversely, where teachers spent a larger amount of their time not communicating with pupils or where they spent a higher percentage of their time communicating about routine (non-work) matters, the impact upon pupils' cognitive and non-cognitive development was negative. Progress was also improved in classes where pupils were involved in their work and where a high level of industry was observed. It appears, therefore, that high levels of teacher-pupil communication, a clear focus upon matters directly concerning work, and a high level of pupil industry all help to promote learning and non-cognitive development.

Pupil noise and movement

High levels of pupil noise and of pupil movement around the classroom were correlated negatively with progress and development. This is not to say that the absence of pupil talk and movement was necessarily beneficial. In fact none of the classes observed were completely quiet and all allowed freedom of pupil movement to some extent. It was clear, however, that high levels of noise and of movement were not associated with progress. These two factors were themselves related to less teacher time spent communicating about work, and with lower levels of pupil involvement with work.

Class interactions

The amount of teacher time spent interacting with the class (rather than with individuals or groups) had a significant positive relationship with progress in a wide range of areas. In contrast, where a very high proportion of the teachers' time was spent communicating with individual pupils, a negative impact was recorded. Two points, however, should be stressed. First, interacting with the class did not necessarily mean whole class teaching. In fact, measures of the extent to which a whole class teaching approach was adopted were very weakly and not significantly related to progress. Rather, it was the proportion of interactions involving the class, rather than any attempt to teach the whole class as one unit, that seems to have been associated with beneficial effects. Second, from analysis of the observational data, it was found that the majority of teachers' interactions were with individual pupils (over 60%, on average). However, some teachers more frequently introduced topics to the whole class, entered into discussions with them, and made teaching points to everyone. This was the case whether children were working individually, or in groups on different tasks, or on the same activity. Such class interactions appeared to be effective in promoting pupil progress. Effects tended to be positive where the teachers spent around a quarter or more of their time in communication with the class as a whole. This finding is in broad agreement with those reported by Galton & Simon (1980).

The association between the proportion of class interactions and pupils' progress may reflect the greater amount of attention received by members of the class through this mode of teaching. This is probably because, when all, or nearly all, of a teacher's time is spent communicating with individual children, each child can receive only a relatively infrequent number of such contacts in any school day, even though the teacher may be extemely busy. On average, pupils received only 11 individual contacts with the teacher in any one day. Given that those with poor behaviour or particular learning difficulties tended to receive a higher number of contacts, other children would tend to receive fewer than the average. The skill of the teacher, therefore, lies in achieving a balance of class, group, and individual communications which will maximise the amount of contact she or he has with each pupil without robbing those contacts of all individualised content.

Mix of Curriculum Activities

There was much variation between classes in the proportion of time during which all the pupils in a class were working on the same curriculum area in sessions, whether they worked alone, in groups, or as a class. A larger proportion of sessions spent on single activities (for example, everybody working on language, though sometimes on different language topics, or on the same topic but at different levels) was related positively to pupils' progress. For a few of the outcomes it was even beneficial for two curriculum activities to be running con-currently. In contrast, where teachers made more use of sessions de-voted to a mix of curriculum activities (working in three or more curriculum areas) at the same time, a significant negative impact on progress was found.

It is possible that the frequent use of mixed sessions may have an adverse impact because teacher attention and energy becomes divided between children working in a variety of curriculum areas. Alterna-tively, the organisation of mixed activities within one session may require higher levels of teacher organisation and management skill if it is to prove effective. These possibilities are discussed at greater length in the next section.

Our results suggest that it may be more effective for a teacher to keep a fairly narrow focus within individual sessions. However, an identical approach in all lessons is neither possible nor desirable. Therefore, it seems that teachers should maintain flexibility in their approach, adopting different forms of organisation, in response to the class and the curriculum area, but bearing in mind the difficulties inherent in using a high proportion of mixed-curriculum sessions.

Stimulating and well-organised teaching
There was evidence that the more time teachers spent asking questions the greater the positive effect upon progress. Furthermore the more teachers were able to make use of higher-order questions and statements (those designed to elicit problem solving, reasoning or imaginative responses from children) the better the progress made. This finding indicates clearly the beneficial effect of intellectually challeng-ing teaching, a feature which relates to teachers' expectations of their pupils. Not surprisingly, the efficient organisation of classroom work, so that there was always plenty for pupils to do (irrespective of the mode of organisation), tended to promote a number of favourable attitudes. In addition, when the work itself was interesting and the lessons bright and stimulating there were clear positive relationships within a wide range of outcomes. Telling or reading stories to children proved to be important too. The more time teachers were able to spend on this activity, the greater the effects upon a number of areas including, interestingly, oracy. Finally, when more time was spent by teachers listening to pupils read, individually, a link was evident with greater progress in writing, and better attitudes in a number of areas.

Pupil responsibility for managing their work
When the pupils' day was given a structure or framework by the teacher such that children were given single tasks to undertake over fairly short periods of time such as a lesson or an afternoon, and were encouraged to manage the completion of the tasks independently of the teacher, the impact was positive for a range of cognitive and

non-cognitive outcomes. However, when pupils were given a large measure of responsibility for managing a programme of work over a whole day, or over lengthy periods of time, the effect upon progress was found to be negative in a number of areas. It may be that such large responsibilities were too onerous for many children of the junior age range to undertake effectively without adequate support and guidance. It should be remembered that, even in the third year, nearly 40 per cent of the sample said that they tended to have difficulty in concentrating on their work. In addition, we found that when pupils were given a high degree of choice as to the content and nature of their work activities, the results tended to be poorer pupil progress. The level of inter-pupil co-operation encouraged was important too. Very high levels were associated with poorer effects in both cognitive and spheres. However, there was some indication that in these two areas – pupil choice and co-operation – the effects upon oracy were distinctly positive. This may perhaps be due to the need for a certain degree of communicative competence when negotiating with others and when making choices.

Pupil groupings
There was some evidence that where pupils worked on the same task as other pupils of roughly the same ability, or when all pupils worked within the same curriculum area but on different tasks at their own level, the effect upon progress was positive. In contrast, where all pupils worked on exactly the same task the effects were negative. This suggests the importance of teachers being sensitive to the varied abilities of pupils and of the need to provide work at appropriate levels of difficulty.

Textbooks
For mathematics there was evidence that, in the later junior years, when teachers followed textbooks closely the result was a positive effect upon progress, not only in mathematics itself, but also on pupils' attitudes to this curriculum area. Interestingly, no such relationships were identified for the use of language textbooks and progress in or attitudes towards language work.

Praise and criticism
There was a significant negative association between the amount of time teachers spent making critical comments and pupils' progress in a range of areas. Conversely, time spent on praise or neutral feedback about behaviour was related to positive effects. A positive attitude to

the class on the part of the teacher was important too. It related positively to progress in mathematics and to several of the non-cognitive outcomes. It seems, therefore, that positive reinforcement and firm but fair classroom management is more effective than a reliance on control through criticism. Furthermore, the positive climate created through the teachers' attitude and use of praise is also beneficial.

IDENTIFYING THE MECHANISMS OF EFFECTIVENESS

We showed above that a variety of factors and processes (both policy and givens) at the school and the class level were related significantly to effects on pupils' progress in cognitive areas, and on their non-cognitive development. Many factors and processes were found to be related to positive effects on more than one outcome, suggesting that the same factors and processes may help to increase the effectiveness of the school in promoting pupils' development in a range of areas. Furthermore, a number of the significant variables were themselves closely associated. By examining the ways in which these significant factors are interrelated, it is possible to gain a greater understanding of the mechanisms of effectiveness in junior education. Through this further analysis, key factors which prove important in the explanation of the differential effectiveness of schools, can be identified. We now, therefore, investigate the inter-relationships amongst significant variables at the school and class levels.

Relationships between school level given factors

Size and type of school
The size of the junior pupil roll and junior-only status were highly positively associated. On the whole junior and infant schools had smaller numbers of junior pupils than schools which catered just for junior-aged pupils. Both of these factors had a significant negative relationship with school effects on several outcomes. It may be that the impact of transfer (at age seven) to the generally larger junior-only schools was more disruptive to a pupil's progress and development than transfer into the smaller departments of JMIs. Junior-only status was also negatively correlated with the distance pupils travelled to school (a crude indicator of parental choice). They were thus less likely to draw pupils from further afield, despite their larger rolls.

Voluntary status
None of the voluntary schools in the sample was junior-only, so pupils attending voluntary schools, therefore, had not experienced the poten-

tially disruptive impact of transfer described above. Voluntary schools were also more likely to draw pupils from a greater distance than were county schools. This reflects differences in the entry criteria operated by voluntary schools. However, it also suggests that voluntary schools may have the advantage of greater parental support for their goals, because parents had chosen the school for specific reasons.

Voluntary schools were more likely to receive intakes containing a relatively high percentage of pupils from non-manual backgrounds. In addition, a higher percentage of the intakes to voluntary schools had obtained reading and mathematics scores in the top quarter of achievement at entry. Nonetheless, this factor, which is related to academic composition in terms of reading or mathematics achievement at entry, was not associated with school effects on pupils' progress in reading or mathematics. Thus, pupil academic composition in these areas did not determine the school's potential to be effective in promoting reading or mathematics progress. There was, however, some evidence that the measures of academic composition were associated with effects on pupils' attitudes to reading and writing, and to progress in writing. Moreover, voluntary schools in the sample tended to have the advantage of a better physical environment.

Educational priority (EP) status
The EP status of schools was related closely to voluntary status. Voluntary schools were more likely to draw pupils from socio-economically advantaged backgrounds. Nonetheless, EP status did not account for the positive impact of voluntary schools on cognitive development. EP status, generally was not found to be related to school effects on any cognitive area except oracy. Here, however, the more disadvantaged schools tended to have performed better than the more advantaged ones.

Change in management structure
Amongst our sample the voluntary schools were less likely to have had a change of headteacher. Where there had been a new head within the previous two years negative effects were found on a number of the outcomes. The voluntary schools, therefore, tended to experience a greater degree of stability than did county schools. Similarly, there was a weak positive relationship between new headteachers and junior-only schools, another factor which has been shown to be associated negatively with effects on pupils' educational outcomes. New heads also tended to be in post in the larger schools. There was, therefore, a three-way relationship between junior-only status, schools with large rolls, and new headteachers.

Schools which had experienced a change of headteacher were more likely to have experienced other disruptive occurrences, such as major building works, during the period of the research. In these schools, therefore, pupils had experienced a rather less stable working environment than had pupils in some other schools. It was also found that schools which had a new headteacher were less likely to have drawn pupil intakes from a distance. There is some suggestion that this indicator of parental choice was related to the years a headteacher had been in post. This association may well have been indirect; reflecting the links between voluntary status and the distance pupils travel to school (noted earlier).

Relationships between school level policy factors

Staff Involvement

The involvement of the deputy head had a positive impact on several educational outcomes. This supports Plowden's (1967) recommendation that heads should delegate more of their duties to their deputies. The extent of the deputy head's involvement in decision-making was related positively to the head's policy on obtaining forecasts from teachers about their work plans. It was also related positively to the use of a school system of language guidelines. As might be expected, in schools where the deputy was more involved in decision-making, staff involvement tended to be higher also. Thus, for example, there was a significant link between the measure of deputy head involvement, and the extent of staff involvement in decisions about priorities in resource allocation.

Teacher involvement in the development of school guidelines was found to be related positively to effects on a number of outcomes. This factor was also associated negatively with variations in guideline usage between teachers. This suggests that, where staff had been involved in the development of guidelines for their school, there was likely to be school-wide consistency in guideline usage. Where staff had not been involved, however, there was more likely to be variation, with teachers tending to adopt individual approaches to the use of guidelines for different curriculum areas. It appears, therefore, that staff involvement was related to a more consistent school-based approach to the curriculum. Involving staff in decisions about the allocation of classes was associated with the head's policy of asking teachers to keep individual records of pupil progress. In addition, where staff were involved in developing guidelines, it was found that they were more likely to be consulted about the allocation of classes. Analyses also reveal that in schools where staff had been involved in the development of guidelines heads tended to adopt a more cautious approach to in-service training. Conversely, where there was no school-based

approach to guideline usage (with variation occurring between individual class teachers), heads were more likely to have a laissez-faire
attitude to in-service course attendance, encouraging staff to go on
any course they wished to attend, irrespective of the school's
needs.

Headteacher's leadership

Various aspects of the head's management style were found to be
associated with effects on pupils' educational outcomes. The practice
of attempting selectively to influence teaching strategies, rather than
attempting to persuade all teachers to adopt a particular approach, or
making no attempt to influence, was associated with the policy of
having teachers maintain individual records of pupils' progress. Both
these aspects of the head's policy were related to positive effects. It
was also found that in schools where the head encouraged record
keeping, variation in guideline usage between teachers was less common. Moreover, where the head requested teachers to keep records
of pupil progress, teachers were more likely to be involved in decisions
about the allocation of classes.

In summary, our results point to some broad patterns in school
policies. It appears that where there is consistency within the school
in the use of guidelines, and where the deputy head and other teachers
are involved in decision-making, the impact can be positive. Where
heads encourage the keeping of individual records of pupil progress,
receive forecasts of teachers' work plans, adopt a selective influence
on teaching strategies, and consider the school's needs with regard to
teacher attendance on in-service training courses, the effects on pupils'
outcomes were found to be beneficial. These aspects, therefore, seem
integral to more effective leadership.

Parental involvement

Factors relating to parental involvement were found to be associated
with effects on some outcomes. In schools where parents were free
to call at any time to see the headteacher, parent helpers were more
likely to be used in the classrooms. Furthermore, in these schools,
pupils were more frequently taken on educational visits. Schools where
parents were free to call in at any time and where facilities were
provided for parents, also tended to be those where the head encouraged class teachers to keep individual records of pupil progress.
Moreover, in schools with an 'open-door' policy, teachers were less
likely to vary in their guideline usage. The provision of facilities for
parents was related positively to the involvement of staff in decision-
making, and with the frequency of progress meetings for parents. In
schools which held regular progress meetings, pupils were more likely

to be involved in presenting assemblies. These results are in broad agreement with those of other researchers who have investigated parental involvement and found that it tends to benefit schools as well as pupils (see, for example, the review by Mortimore and Mortimore, 1984).

Headteacher's emphasis on basic skills

Schools in which the headteacher placed a strong emphasis on basic skills were associated negatively with effects on pupils' progress in a number of areas. Such heads were also less likely to involve their deputies in decision-making and were less likely to require class teachers to provide forecasts of their proposed work.

School climate

Where pupils were happy, friendly and well behaved (all aspects of school climate) heads were less likely to have reported an emphasis on basic skills and in addition, pupils were given more opportunities to go on educational visits and trips in such schools. Fewer graffiti were seen in schools where pupils were observed to be happy, friendly and well behaved. Pupil demeanour and behaviour was also more positive in schools which had access to a grassy play area. Schools which ran clubs for pupils tended to have a greater number of different methods of rewarding pupils. These relationships suggest a generally positive ethos in such schools and the presence of the fun factor.

Relationships between school given and policy variables

There were also important connections between some of the given characteristics of schools and particular aspects of their policies. Analyses were undertaken to explore these possible links, to establish whether some of the given factors had constrained, in part, schools' policy choices.

Voluntary status and policies

We found that, as a whole, in our sample the heads of voluntary schools placed rather less emphasis on punishment than did those of county schools.

The relationship between voluntary status and the head's policy of asking teachers to produce regular forecasts of their work was weak but positive. Heads of voluntary schools were also more likely to have influenced the content of their school's curriculum and, in addition, their staff were more likely to have been involved in developing guidelines, and to use language guidelines.

There was a strong positive association between voluntary status and the measure of pupil demeanour and behaviour around the school. It is possible that such behaviour, in part, is related to some of the differences in the characteristics of the intakes to these schools, and to the quality of the physical environment (two given factors). However, it is likely also to reflect aspects of the policies adopted in schools and the staff-pupil relationships. It was also found that teachers in voluntary schools tended to receive more non-teaching periods than their peers in county schools. The heads of voluntary schools, however, were rather less likely to report that they gave parents the opportunity to attend progress meetings than were heads of county schools. In addition, the staff of voluntary schools were much less likely to organise lunchtime and after-school activities and clubs for pupils.

School size and policies
School size was related to a number of aspects of school policies. Thus, it was less common in larger schools for the heads to report that they asked teachers to provide regular forecasts of their proposed work, or to maintain individual records of children's progress. It was also found that such heads were less likely to have adopted a strategy of influencing teaching methods on a selective basis (only when judged 'necessary') and were more likely to have tried either to influence all teachers or, at the other extreme, to have made no attempt to exert any influence. They were also less likely to have influenced the curriculum of their school, or operated a school-based policy on in-service training. Moreover, in larger schools, staff were less likely to have been involved in the development of the school's guidelines, and there was a greater tendency for individual teachers to vary in the way they used such guidelines than was the case in smaller schools. It also appears that deputy headteachers were less involved in policy decisions in such schools, and that heads placed a greater emphasis on punishment, than did their counterparts in small schools.

It appears that the larger schools in the sample, in general, had developed practices and policies which were rather less effective in promoting pupil progress. It is possible that these findings reflect the greater difficulty of maintaining coherent school-wide policies on the curriculum in larger schools. In contrast, in smaller schools there may have been more chance for all staff to be aware of, and involved in, policy. Through closer staff contact, it may have been easier for the heads of smaller schools to implement effective school-wide policies, and to monitor the achievement of specific goals. Overall, these findings support the contention that effective schools have characteristics more suited to the management of small organisations than larger ones (see Rowan, 1983). Although school size has not always been found to be associated with school effectiveness, Rutter (1983) noted that a few studies have shown a minor advantage in outcomes for pupils in smaller schools.

Junior-only status and policies

The junior-only schools (which, as noted earlier were larger in size of roll than junior and infant schools and were all county schools) differed from the junior and infant schools in their approach to in-service training, in the head influences on teaching strategies and in the curriculum. Staff in junior-only schools were less likely to have been involved in developing any school guidelines, and there was more variation in the extent to which they used such guidelines. There was also less emphasis on record keeping and the discussion of records in junior-only schools. On the whole, heads of junior-only schools tended to place a greater emphasis on punishment than their counterparts in schools covering the entire primary age range.

In line with the findings on larger schools, our results show that junior-only schools differed from junior and infant schools in terms of a number of aspects of policy which were associated with effectiveness in promoting pupils' progress and development. These differences may help to explain the negative associations identified between junior-only status and school effectiveness.

Headteacher's time spent in post, and policies

Earlier in this Chapter we demonstrated that the headteacher's time in post was related to pupils' progress and development in a number of areas. In general, schools with new heads and long-serving heads were associated with negative effects, whilst schools where the head had been in post for three to seven years were associated with positive effects. We explored the links between aspects of policy and the head's length of time in post to establish whether there were any differences in the sorts of school policies they had adopted, and the results revealed that there were. Thus, long-serving heads were significantly more likely to emphasise basic skills than were other heads. Mid-term heads were the least likely to emphasise basic skills, and the same group were more likely to have involved their deputy in decision-making than were heads in the long-serving group. Both new and mid-term heads did not tend to make themselves available for parents to see at any time, but preferred a system of fixed appointments. In contrast, the long-serving heads tended to say they were available at any time. The long-serving group, however, were less likely to organise meetings for parents to discuss their children's progress. In addition, mid-term heads were significantly more likely, and new heads less likely, to have adopted a strategy of selective influence on teaching strategies, and to have operated a school policy on the use of guidelines. Whereas mid-term heads involved their teachers in the drawing up of school guidelines, this was not the case with new heads. In some cases, this may have been because new heads had not yet introduced changes to existing policy. Long-serving heads were less likely to ask teachers to produce forecasts of their work than were new heads.

In schools with mid-term heads, class teachers were more likely to report that they were allocated several non-teaching periods in their timetables than was the case in other schools. Pupils in these schools were also taken more frequently on trips and visits. In schools with long-serving heads, pupils were given fewer opportunities to be involved in presenting assemblies. In general, therefore, we found that, in schools with mid-term heads, the policies and practices associated with effectiveness in promoting educational outcomes were more common than in schools with a new or a long-serving head. Schools in the latter categories may benefit from forms of support which enable them to develop more effective practices.

Our data show that the given factors at the school level in many cases were related to the policies and strategies adopted. In some cases these relationships may reflect established policy traditions, perhaps related to the length of time spent by the head in her or his present post. In other cases, however, certain given factors may have constrained the policy choices possible. In particular, there is evidence that larger schools and junior-only schools differed from smaller schools and the junior and infant schools in terms of certain aspects of policy. It seems possible that the negative relationship between various outcomes and the factors of school size and junior-only status may be due, in part, to such policy differences. This suggests that in larger schools and junior-only schools, heads may have found it more difficult to implement effective school-wide policies. It is important that such inter-relationships between given characteristics and possible policy options are borne in mind when considering the ways in which junior schools might be able to improve their effectiveness.

Relationships between policy variables at the class level

Teacher-pupil communication
Sessions in which work covered only one curriculum area and the percentage of teacher time spent interacting with the class as a whole were strongly related. Thus, teachers who tended to organise pupils so that all worked within the same broad curriculum area, also communicated more with the whole class. Both these factors had a positive association with effects on pupils' progress and development. It was also found that the amount of teacher time spent on class interactions was consistently positively correlated with the amount of time teachers spent talking about pupils' work.

The use of sessions devoted to single, rather than mixed, curriculum activities was strongly negatively related to the extent of pupil responsibility for managing their work over a long period. As noted earlier, the encouragement of pupil responsibility over long periods was found to be correlated negatively with school effects on several outcomes. This suggests that in schools where teachers took responsibility for providing a structure which gave order and facilitated a balance and variety of work during the school day, and where there were clearly defined periods when all children worked broadly within one or two curriculum areas progress was likely to be promoted.

Higher-order communications

A factor which was of particular importance in promoting pupils' progress and development was the teacher's use of higher-order questions and statements (those which encourage responses by pupils which are imaginative or of a problem-solving kind). The percentage of teacher time spent on communicating with the whole class was correlated positively with the use of higher-order questions and statements and, to a lesser extent, with questions as a whole. In contrast, the amount of teacher time spent on contacts with individual pupils was weakly negatively associated with the use of higher-order questions and statements. Furthermore, in classes where the amount of teacher time spent communicating with individuals was very high, the time spent on routine (non-work) interactions also tended to be high. There was also a positive link between teachers' use of higher-order communications and the overall level of interest and challenge in their teaching sessions. Higher-order questions and statements were more frequently in evidence in sessions rated as being bright and interesting. Teachers who used class discussions as a teaching strategy also tended to make rather more use of higher-order communication.

Involvement with work

Pupils' involvement with their work was greater when there was plenty for them to do and when the teacher's approach was interesting and challenging. The following were also associated positively with high levels of pupil industry: teacher time giving work feedback; teacher time spent communicating with the whole class; a greater responsibility on the part of pupils for managing individual pieces of work; and positive reinforcement by the teacher of pupil behaviour and effort. Where teachers had a positive attitude to their class, pupils also showed more interest and involvement with work. Teachers who devoted more time to discussing work also ensured that pupils always had plenty to do, and offered more stimulating work for their classes. These teachers also promoted pupils' self-control and tended to encourage pupils to be responsible for managing designated tasks.

Organisation and planning of work

Where teachers provided plenty of work for pupils, progress was promoted. Provision of ample work by the teacher was related to a greater use of questions, less critical control, and more emphasis upon praise and positive reinforcement in the classroom. Well-organised teachers gave pupils more responsibility for managing their own pieces of work, and were also more likely to report that language work was planned to follow a particular sequence.

Where teachers sequentially planned language work, they were also more likely to keep written language records. These teachers also praised pupils' work more frequently, and showed a more positive attitude towards their class. Teaching sessions were more challenging where teachers had a long-term plan for language work, and pupils also appeared to be less noisy.

Pupil noise and movement

The extent of pupil noise and movement were associated negatively with most cognitive and some non-cognitive outcomes. Both these factors were themselves associated and were also related negatively to pupil involvement in work. Thus, where levels of pupil noise and movement were excessively high, pupils spent less time engaged in work. In addition, the level of pupil noise was correlated negatively with the amount of teacher time spent on work discussions. The amount of pupil and teacher time spent on work was higher in classrooms which were quieter. There was less noise in classrooms where the teacher had organised plenty for pupils to do, and where the pupils were obviously stimulated and challenged by the work. As might be expected, pupil involvement with work was related positively to the amount of the teacher's time spent actually discussing work.

There was also evidence that levels of pupil noise, pupil movement and the amount of teacher time spent on routine (non-work) contacts were higher where teachers tended to employ mixed-activity sessions (those where a class of pupils worked on three or more curriculum areas at the same time), and where teachers integrated curriculum areas in a topic-based approach. Conversely, where all pupils worked in a single curriculum area within a session, levels of pupil noise and movement tended to be lower. The amount of inter-pupil co-operation and the extent of pupil choice of work activities, in contrast, were higher in classes where the teacher made greater use of mixed-activity sessions. Not surprisingly, noise and movement were more marked when teachers were not communicating with the whole class. Noise levels were also found to be higher where the teacher did not have a positive attitude to her or his class. However, where teachers gave more emphasis to praising pupils, industry and involvement in work was higher.

Critical control
Teachers who placed a greater emphasis on critical control allowed pupils less responsibility for managing individual pieces of work. They also tended to express a more negative attitude towards teaching their classes. Furthermore, pupil industry was lower in classes where teachers frequently lost their temper with the children. Teachers who took pupils out to work in the local environment also tended to make less use of critical control in the classroom.

Structuring the pupils' day
The degree of pupil responsibility for managing a work programme over a long period was related negatively to several cognitive outcomes. This factor was also associated with the teacher's use of a mixed curriculum activities approach and, not surprisingly, was negatively related to the use of single activity sessions. It was also associated with lower levels of pupil industry and with less work-related talk between teachers and pupils.

It appears that the teacher's role in ordering activities during the school day is a crucial one, and is clearly linked to pupil progress and development. Nonetheless, there is evidence that pupil responsibility and independence within sessions, rather than for longer periods, was also beneficial. Thus, it should not be concluded that, overall, giving pupils responsibility for their work had an adverse impact. What appeared to be important was the encouragement of independence and responsibility within a well-defined framework.

Positive atmosphere within the classroom
The teacher's attitude towards the class appeared to be particularly important for pupils' non-cognitive outcomes. Enthusiastic teachers provided their pupils with more stimulating activities, and made more use of higher-order communication; their work was better organised and, in turn, pupils were more interested in work; they praised pupils' work more often and also reported being more satisfied with their job.

Relationships between given and policy variables at the class level

Teacher continuity and teachers' policies
A change of class teacher during the school year and a higher proportion of teacher time spent on routine (non-work) interactions with pupils were associated. In addition, the amount of teacher time spent not communicating with pupils was somewhat higher where a change of teacher had occurred. Conversely, the extent to which the teacher used higher-order questions and statements, and interactions related directly to the content of pupils' work was higher in schools where pupils had not experienced such a change. Levels of pupil noise and movement were observed to be higher, whilst the level of pupil industry

was lower, where pupils had experienced teacher change(s). This factor was also associated with a greater use of angry control comments and less use of neutral and positive feedback on behaviour. These results suggest that a change of class teacher during the school year can have a disruptive effect on pupil behaviour, which may lead to management difficulties for the new class teacher.

Class size and teachers' policies
The use of parental help in the classroom was more common in schools where classes were smaller. In addition, teachers of smaller classes tended to praise or make more neutral comments about pupils' behaviour, rather than becoming angry with children. However, in larger classes, teachers were more likely to talk to the whole class than in smaller classes.

These results appear to lead to a contradiction as a degree of communication with the whole class was associated with beneficial effects on several outcomes, whereas large class size in itself had a largely negative effect. Further investigation revealed that teachers of smaller classes tended to employ higher levels of interaction with individuals than teachers of larger classes. This greater reliance on contact with individuals may have diminished the beneficial effects of smaller class size because it was the use of a balance of class and individual contacts which was found to be more effective.

One of the reasons why the positive impact of smaller class size has not generally been found in past studies may be because the influences of teacher behaviour and practice were not taken into account, and, therefore, the impact of class size may have been masked. As Rutter (1983) has noted 'It makes little sense to examine class size without paying attention to the style of teaching' (p.16). The implication of the significant relationship between class size and type of audience addressed by the teacher is that, even in smaller classes, pupil progress is likely to be improved by ensuring that a certain proportion of teacher time is spent on communications with the whole class.

Relationships between school and class level given variables

It appears that voluntary schools had the advantage of more stable staffing during the period of the Project. Thus, analyses indicate that, in general, fewer children in voluntary schools had experienced more than one change of class teacher during a school year (or change in each of two separate years) than was the case in county schools.

The distance pupils travelled to school was also closely linked with the extent of teacher change. In schools where, on average, pupils travelled further (an indicator of parental choice), fewer children had experienced changes of class teacher during the school year than was the case in other schools. The incidence of class teacher change was lower in schools where a high percentage of the intake scored in the top quarter for reading at entry.

A higher proportion of pupils had experienced several changes of class teacher in schools where there was a new head. Conversely, in schools with a mid-term head, pupils were less likely to have had a change of class teacher during any year. In addition, in schools where a higher proportion of pupils had experienced changes of class teacher during a school year, disruptive occurrences, such as major building works, were more common.

Class size was strongly related to county/voluntary status. The voluntary schools generally had larger average class sizes than county schools, perhaps because of their popularity with some parents. Average class size was also significantly positively related to the percentage of pupils with a parent in non-manual work. This again reflects the close relationship between class size, voluntary status and the proportion of the intake of non-manual backgrounds.

To some extent teacher behaviour and practice varied between schools with different given characteristics. This is not altogether surprising, because the school can be viewed as an institution consisting of different spheres which influence each other, both directly and indirectly.

Voluntary status
In general, teachers in voluntary schools spent less time on routine (non-work) communications with pupils, and more time communicating directly about work. The levels of pupil noise and of pupil movement were lower, while pupil involvement in their work was observed to be higher. There was also some evidence that pupils in voluntary schools were less likely to be given responsibility for managing their work programme over a whole day, received less encouragement to work co-operatively with other children, and were given less choice of work activities.

Overall, it was also found that teaching sessions were organised around a single curriculum area more frequently in voluntary than in county schools. In addition, teachers in such schools tended to give pupils the same work as other pupils of similar ability in language and mathematics and followed mathematics textbooks more closely (especially in the later junior years). Thus in voluntary schools, teachers tended to adopt more of the strategies which were found to be associated with the development of a 'work-centred' classroom environment. There was also some indication that teachers in voluntary schools tended to provide pupils with more challenging teaching, when compared with those in county schools.

The broad pattern of differences in teaching strategies, identified between county and voluntary schools, help to explain why significant relationships were found between voluntary status and positive school effects on a number of outcomes, particularly those related to cognitive progress.

The distance pupils travelled to school
The average distance pupils travelled to school was associated with a similar pattern of differences in teacher behaviour and practice to that discovered for voluntary schools. In schools which drew pupils from further afield, teachers made greater use of higher-order communications with pupils, and made critical comments less frequently. In addition, teachers in these schools favoured working in a single curriculum area, made less use of mixed activity sessions, and spent more time communicating with pupils about their work. The distance factor was also associated with lower levels of pupil-responsibility for managing their work over long periods, and rather less encouragement of inter-pupil co-operation and choice of work activities.

Junior-only status
There was little evidence of systematic differences in aspects of teacher behaviour and practice between junior-only and junior and infant schools. There was a weak positive relationship between junior-only status and the amount of teacher time spent not interacting with pupils. Pupils in junior only schools also tended to be noisier in class and were allowed to be more mobile around their classrooms than their peers in junior and infant schools. Teacher time spent discussing pupils' work was also rather lower in junior-only schools, and there was some tendency for teachers to make greater use of mixed-activity sessions and to integrate the curriculum under topic work in such schools.

School size
Overall, few differences in teacher behaviour and practice were significantly related to school size. In larger schools, teachers tended to give pupils less feedback on their work, and lost their tempers over poor behaviour rather more than was the case in smaller schools. However, it also appeared that teachers interacted with the whole class rather more often in larger schools. As noted earlier, this form of communication was associated with beneficial effects on cognitive progress, and some aspects of non-cognitive development. Therefore, although larger schools were generally rather less effective, there was not a consistent trend for teachers in such schools to have adopted less effective teaching strategies.

Headteacher's time in present post
Some differences were identified between teachers in their behaviour when schools were classified according to the length of time the head had been in post. Where there was a new head, teachers tended to

make greater use of mixed-activity sessions. This may be a reflection of a preference on the part of new heads for a particular teaching approach. It was also found that where there was a new head, teachers tended to make fewer higher-order communications, spent less time discussing pupils' work, and gave pupils less feedback about their work. In the same schools teachers also spent less time on small talk and more time on routine (non-work) communication. Pupils' involvement with their work was lower, noise levels were higher and there was also some evidence that, in general, teaching was rather less exciting and less intellectually stimulating in these schools. In addition, pupils tended to be given greater responsibility for managing their work over long periods in these schools. It appeared that the teaching environment in schools with a new head was, in general, rather less work-centred, and intellectually stimulating, than in other schools. In contrast, in schools with a mid-term head, teachers tended to spend more time on feedback about work and on generally discussing work. They were also less likely to lose their tempers with the pupils than were their counterparts in other schools.

Where a long-serving head was in post, teachers generally spent a greater amount of time not interacting with pupils, and made less use of questioning as a teaching technique than in schools where heads had been in post for fewer than 11 years. There was also some evidence that, in schools with long-serving heads, teachers made less use of parental help in the classroom. This may be a reflection of more traditional views on the roles of parents and of schools.

Change of deputy head
There was some suggestion that parents helped less in the classrooms, and that teachers spent less time listening to pupils read where a change of deputy had occurred. Levels of noise in the classroom, the extent of pupil responsibility for managing their work over long periods, and of inter-pupil co-operation (factors generally associated with less positive school effects on pupils' educational outcomes) were all higher where a change of deputy had taken place. These results indicate that certain aspects of teacher behaviour and practice tended to differ between schools with specific given characteristics. Although these links are not necessarily causal, they help to explain why some of the given factors were associated with school effects on pupils' educational outcomes. In particular, differences in teacher behaviour and practice were found between voluntary and county schools; between those drawing pupils from further away; and between schools with a new, rather than a long-serving, or a mid-term headteacher.

Relationships between school and class policies
A number of relationships between various aspects of school policy and features of teacher behaviour and practice in the classroom were

identified providing some indication of two-way links between policy and practice at the school and the class level.

Headteacher's leadership
Indicators of the head's positive leadership, especially in connection with academic matters, were related significantly to particular aspects of teacher behaviour. Where heads asked teachers to provide forecasts of their work plans, teachers generally spent more time communicating with pupils, and, in particular, more time discussing pupils' work and telling stories, than was the case in schools where heads did not request forecasts. In addition, teachers were found to talk to the whole class more frequently in such schools. All these aspects of teacher behaviour were found to be associated with more effective teaching.

It also appeared that, in schools where forecasts were requested, teachers encouraged inter-pupil co-operation and kept records of pupils' work to a greater extent. In schools where the head asked teachers to keep individual records of pupils' progress, teachers tended to spend less time on non-work contacts with pupils, and more time giving feedback about work. Teachers in such schools were less likely to make use of critical comments, they tended to encourage pupils to manage particular pieces of work independently, and also encouraged some inter-pupil co-operation.

The head's strategy on the curriculum was also related to certain aspects of teacher behaviour. Where the head influenced the curriculum, teachers tended to spend less time talking to pupils about non-work matters, and allowed rather less pupil movement in class. Teachers in these schools also made fewer critical comments than did their counterparts in schools where the head was not involved in curriculum planning.

The head's attitude towards in-service training was found to be related to school effectiveness too. In schools where there was selective encouragement of in-service training, teachers made less use of criticism when controlling pupil behaviour, they tended to employ either positive or neutral varieties of feedback when dealing with pupil behaviour. The amount of teacher time spent on non-work communications and on critical comments was lower, and less frequent use was made of mixed-activity sessions, in schools where the head adopted a strategy of only selectively influencing the way teachers taught. Similarly, more teacher time was spent interacting with pupils in schools where the head selectively influenced teaching methods.

Teacher consistency
An agreed policy between teachers on the use of guidelines within the school was associated with more teaching time spent giving pupils feedback about work, higher levels of pupil involvement in their work, and also higher levels of inter-pupil co-operation in the classroom.

Furthermore, where there was such an agreed policy teachers generally spent less time on non-work interactions than was the case other schools. There was also some evidence that teachers made greater use of criticism in schools where there was no consistency between teachers in guideline usage.

School climate
One measure of school climate (pupil demeanour and behaviour around the school) was strongly positively related to the amount of class teacher-time spent in talking to pupils about work, making use of higher-order questions and statements, and in giving work feedback. It was also correlated positively with time spent by teachers talking to the class as a whole, and with a high level of pupil industry in the classroom. This measure of pupil demeanour and behaviour around the school was associated negatively with high levels of noise in the classroom and with a greater amount of teacher time devoted to non-work contacts with pupils. In schools where pupils helped to present assemblies, persuasion and reinforcement were the more dominant means of control used by teachers, rather than criticism or coercion.

A positive school climate, therefore, seems to be associated with those aspects of teacher behaviour related to more effective teaching, in particular the provision of a work-centred classroom environment. It is likely, however, that the relationship between school climate and teacher behaviour in the classroom operates in two directions. Effective teaching may well improve pupils' behaviour, attitudes and morale. However, it is also likely that effective teaching strategies are easier to adopt in schools where, in general, pupils are generally happy, interested, friendly and well-behaved around the school. An emphasis on punishment in the school (as measured by the variety of punishments used by the head) was associated with high levels of noise and inter-pupil co-operation in the classroom, and with less teacher time spent on intellectually challenging (higher-order) communication with pupils, and fewer teacher contacts with the class as a whole.

Involvement of the deputy and staff
In schools where the deputy participated in decision-making, higher levels of teacher communication about work, and fewer critical comments were recorded than was the case in schools where the deputy was less involved. The involvement of teachers in drawing up school guidelines was associated with exciting and stimulating teaching in classrooms, and greater pupil involvement with work. Another aspect of involvement – the participation of teachers in decisions about the allocation of classes – was associated with greater amounts of teacher time communicating about work generally, and, more specifically, giving pupils feedback about work. In such schools pupils were allowed less unrestricted movement in class and, in addition, greater use was made of parental help.

In schools where the head expressed general satisfaction with post-holders, pupils appeared to be more industrious and less noisy in class. It was also found that teachers in these schools devoted more time to contacts with the whole class and provided plenty of work for pupils to do.

We have shown that school policies associated with positive effects on pupils' educational outcomes were related to aspects of teacher behaviour and practices which were also themselves also linked with such positive effects. In particular, positive leadership by the head, and the involvement of staff in decision-making were associated with aspects of effective teaching. It seems likely, therefore, that effective policies at the school level and in the classroom are mutually reinforcing.

The Key Question

The third major question addressed by the Junior School Project concerned the factors which contributed to school effectiveness. We found that much of the variation between schools in their effects on pupils' progress and development was explained by differences in policies and practices, and by certain given characteristics. By investigating the inter-connections between the many factors linked with school effects on pupils' progress and development, we have been able to identify some of the mechanisms by which effective junior schooling is promoted. In particular, we have shown that the given features of schools and classes are closely related to many aspects of policy and practice. Moreover, effective school policies are associated with the adoption of more effective teaching strategies within the classroom.

The relationships described above under the heading 'mechanisms of effectiveness' have enabled us to draw together the many disparate findings reported at the beginning of this chapter into twelve key factors. However, it must be emphasised that these factors are not purely statistical constructs. They have not been obtained solely by means of quantitative analyses. Rather, they are derived from a combination of careful examination and discussion of the statistical findings, and the use of educational and research judgement. They represent the interpretation of the research results by an inter-disciplinary team of researchers and teachers.

KEY FACTORS FOR EFFECTIVE JUNIOR SCHOOLING

So far we have described the effects that a variety of factors and processes had upon pupils' educational outcomes. Many of these factors had an impact on a range of different outcomes. Similarly, features of the school and the classroom frequently were related to each other and, through a detailed investigation of these links, we have developed a framework of key factors that we believe contribute to effective junior schooling. This framework, however, is not intended to be a blueprint for success. Inevitably there were aspects of school life which we could not examine during the course of the Project. Furthermore, schools, like all institutions, are perpetually changing. Our survey was carried out between 1980 and 1984, and it was not possible to take full account of all the changes (particularly in approaches to the curriculum) that were evolving in schools and classrooms during that period. Nonetheless, a large number of factors were related consistently to effective junior schooling. Those factors which come under the control of the head, the staff or the class teacher we have grouped together under twelve headings. Before examining these factors over which schools and teachers can exercise control, we shall return briefly to less flexible characteristics of schools first discussed at the beginning of this chapter - the school and class givens. It is clear that certain of these given features make it easier to create an effective school.

Key given factors

Schools that cover the entire primary age range, where pupils do not have to transfer at age seven, appear to be at an advantage, as do voluntary-aided schools. Even though voluntary schools tend to have more socio-economically advantaged intakes than county schools, we still found that voluntary schools tended to be more effective. Smaller schools, with a junior roll of around 160 or fewer, also appear to benefit their pupils. Research by Galton at Leicester University has also suggested that smaller schools tend to be more effective. Class size is also relevant: smaller classes, (with fewer than 24 pupils) had a positive impact upon pupil progress and develpment, especially in the early years, whereas in clases with 27 or more pupils the effects were less positive.

Not surprisingly, a good physical environment, as reflected in the school's amenities, decorative order and immediate surroundings, was a positive advantage. Extended periods of disruption, due to building work and redecoration, can have a negative impact on pupils' progress. This was in line with Rutter's (1979) findings concerning the care of school buildings. The stability of the school's teaching force is also an important factor. Changes of head and deputy headteacher, though inevitable, have an unsettling effect upon the pupils. Every effort, therefore, should be made to reduce the potentially negative impact of such changes. Similarly, where there is an unavoidable change of class teacher during the school year, careful planning will be needed to ensure an easy transition, and to minimise disruption to the pupils. Where pupils experience continuity with one class teacher through the whole year, progress is more likely to occur. It is, however, not only continuity of staff that is important. Although major or frequent changes tend to have negative effects, schools were less effective where the headteacher had been in post for a long time. In the more effective schools, heads had usually been in post for between three and seven years.

It is clear, therefore, that some schools are more advantaged in terms of their size, status, environment and stability of teaching staff. Nonetheless, although these favourable given characteristics contribute to effectiveness, they do not, by themselves, ensure it. They provide a supporting framework within which the head and teachers can work to promote pupil progress and development. However, it is the factors within the control of the head and teachers that are crucial. These are the factors that can be changed and improved.

The 12 key factors described below are not arranged in any order of importance. However, we have grouped them into factors that concern school policy (1 to 4), those that relate to classroom policy (5 to 9), and, finally, aspects of relevance to school and class policy (10 to 12).

The twelve key factors

Purposeful leadership of the staff by the headteacher.
The involvement of the deputy head.
The involvement of teachers.
Consistency amongst teachers.
Structured sessions.
Intellectually challenging teaching.
The work-centred environment.
Limited focus within sessions.
Maximum communication between teachers and pupils.
Record keeping.
Parental involvement.
Positive climate.

1. Purposeful leadership of the staff by the headteacher
Purposeful leadership occurred where the headteacher understood the needs of the school and was involved actively in the school's work, without exerting total control over the rest of the staff. In effective schools, headteachers were involved in curriculum discussions and influenced the content of guidelines drawn up within the school, without taking complete control. They also influenced the teaching strategies of teachers, but only selectively, where they judged it necessary. This leadership was demonstrated by an emphasis on the monitoring of pupils' progress, through teachers keeping individual records. Approaches varied – some schools kept written records; others passed on folders of pupils' work to their next teacher; some did both – but a systematic policy of record keeping was important. With regard to in-service training, those heads exhibiting purposeful leadership did

not allow teachers total freedom to attend any course: attendance was encouraged for a good reason. Nonetheless, most teachers in these schools had attended in-service courses.

Thus, effective headteachers were sufficiently involved in, and knowledgeable about, what went on in the classrooms and about the progress of individual pupils. They were more able to feel confident about their teaching staff and did not need to intervene constantly. At the same time, however, they were not afraid to assert their leadership where appropriate.

2. The involvement of the deputy head

Our findings indicate that the deputy head can have a major role to play in promoting the effectiveness of junior schools. Where the deputy was frequently absent, or absent for a prolonged period (due to illness, attendance on long courses, or other commitments), this was detrimental to pupils' progress and development. Moreover, a change of deputy head tended to have negative effects. The responsibilities undertaken by deputy heads also seemed to be significant. Where the head generally involved the deputy in policy decisions, it was beneficial to the pupils. This was particularly true in terms of allocating teachers to classes. Thus, it appears that a certain amount of delegation by the headteacher, and the sharing of responsibilities, promoted effectiveness.

3. The involvement of teachers

In successful schools, the teachers were involved in curriculum planning and played a major role in developing their own curriculum guidelines. As with the deputy head, teacher involvement in decisions concerning which classes they were to teach, was important. Similarly, we found that consultation with teachers about decisions on spending was associated with greater effectiveness. It appears that schools in which teachers were consulted on issues affecting school policy, as well as those affecting them directly, were more likely to be successful. We found a link between schools where the deputy was involved in policy decisions and schools where teachers were involved. Thus, effective primary schools did not operate a small management team – everyone had their say.

4. Consistency amongst teachers

We have already shown that continuity of staffing had positive effects. Not only, however, do pupils benefit from teacher continuity, but it also appears that consistency in teacher approach is important. For example, in schools where all teachers followed guidelines in the same way (whether closely or selectively), the impact on progress was positive. Where there was variation between teachers in their usage of guidelines, this had a negative effect.

5. Structured sessions

The Project findings indicate that pupils benefitted when their school day was given some structure. In effective classes, pupils' work was organised in broad outline by the teacher, who ensured that there was always plenty of work to do. We also found that the progress of pupils benefitted when they were not given unlimited responsibility for planning their own daily programme of work, or for choosing work activities, but were guided into areas of study or exploration and taught the skills necessary for independently managing that work. In general, therefore, teachers who organised a framework within which pupils could work, and yet encouraged them to exercise a degree of independence, and allowed some freedom and choice within this structure, were more successful. Children developed and made progress particularly in classrooms where most pupils were able to work in the absence of constant support from their teachers. Clearly, when pupils can work autonomously in this way the teacher is freed to spend time in areas she or he considers a high priority.

6. Intellectually challenging teaching

Not surprisingly, the quality of teaching was very important in promoting pupil progress and development. Our findings show clearly that, in those classes where pupils were stimulated and challenged, progress was greatest. The content of teacher-pupil classroom talk was vitally important. Progress was encouraged where teachers used more higher-order questions and statements, when they encouraged pupils to use their creative imagination and powers of problem-solving. Additionally, in classrooms which were bright and interesting, where the context created by the teacher was stimulating, and where teachers communicated their own interest and enthusiasm to the children, greater pupil progress occurred. In contrast, teachers who frequently directed pupils' work without discussing it, or explaining its purpose, were less effective.

A further important feature was the expectation in the more effective classrooms that pupils could manage independently the tasks they were engaged upon. In such classes teachers only rarely intervened with instructions and directives, yet everyone in the class knew what to do and could work without close supervision.

7. Work-centred environment

In schools where teachers spent more of their time discussing the content of work with pupils, and less time on routine matters and the maintenance of work activity, the effect was positive. Time devoted to giving pupils feedback about their work also appeared to be very beneficial.

The work-centred environment was characterised by a high level of pupil industry in the classroom. Pupils appeared to enjoy their work and were eager to commence new tasks. The noise level was low, although this is not to say that there was silence in the classroom. In fact, none of the classes we visited were completely silent. Furthermore, pupil movement around the classroom, was not excessive, and was generally work-related. These results receive support from the views of pupils. Even in the third year over 40 per cent of pupils reported that they had difficulty in concentrating on their work most of the time. Where levels of noise and movement were high, concentration seems to be more difficult to maintain. Work-centred classrooms, therefore, had a business-like and purposeful air, with pupils obviously enjoying the work they were doing. Furthermore, where classrooms were work-centred, lessons were found to be more challenging.

8. Limited focus within sessions
It appears that pupils made greater progress when teachers tended to organise lessons around one particular curriculum area. At times, work could be undertaken in two areas and also produce positive effects, but, where the tendency was for the teacher regularly to organise classroom work such that three or more curriculum areas were running concurrently, then pupils' progress was marred. This finding is related to a number of other factors. For example, pupil industry was lower in classrooms where mixed-activities occurred, noise and pupil movement were greater, and teachers spent less time discussing work and more time on routine issues and behaviour control. Thus, such classrooms were less likely to be work-centred. More importantly, in mixed-activity sessions the opportunities for communication between teachers and pupils were reduced (see key factor 9 below).

A focus upon one curriculum area does not imply that all the pupils should do exactly the same work. On the contrary, effects were most positive when the teacher geared the level of work to pupils' needs, but not where all pupils worked individually on exactly the same piece of work. It seems likely that, in mixed-curriculum sessions, the demands made upon the teachers' time, attention and energy can become too great for them to ensure effective learning with all groups. Furthermore, it becomes more difficult in such sessions for the teacher to call the class together should the opportunity arise to share an interesting point that may emerge from the work of a particular group or pupil. We recognise that there are many occasions when teachers may wish to diversify the work in the classroom, and beyond, into more than one curriculum area. Sometimes such diversification is unavoidable, perhaps through the constraints of timetabling or, because of the nature of the work in progress, but, for the reasons cited above, we would urge the utmost caution over the adoption of a mixed-curriculum methodology as a basis for teaching and learning.

9. Maximum communication between teachers and pupils

We found evidence that pupils gained from having lots of communication with the teacher. Thus, those teachers who spent higher proportions of their time not interacting with the children were less successful in promoting progress and development. The time teachers spent on communications with the whole class was also important. Most teachers devoted most of their attention to speaking with individuals. Each child, therefore, could only expect to receive a fairly small number of individual contacts with their teacher. In fact, as we described earlier, for each pupil the average number of such contacts over a day was only eleven. Given that some children demand, and receive, more attention than the average from their teachers, this means that others have very few individual contacts per day. By speaking to the whole class, teachers increased the overall number of contacts with children, as pupils become part of the teacher's audience more often in such circumstances. Most importantly higher-order communications occurred more frequently when the teacher talked to the whole class.

We are not, however, advocating traditional class teaching. Our findings did not show any such approach to be beneficial for pupils and, in fact, we found no evidence of readily identifiable teaching styles at all. We feel that teaching is far too complex an activity for it to be categorised in this way. On the contrary, our results indicate the value of a flexible approch, that can blend individual, class and group interaction as appropriate. Furthermore, where children worked in a single curriculum area within sessions, (even if they were engaged on individual or group tasks) it was easier for teachers to raise an intellectually challenging point with all pupils. Such exchanges tended to occur when teachers were introducing a topic to the class before pupils were sent off to work individually or in groups. Class discussions were also a popular forum for gathering all pupils together, as was storytelling. These activities offered teachers a particular opportunity to challenge and stimulate their pupils.

10. Record keeping

We have already commented upon the value of record keeping in relation to the purposeful leadership of the headteacher. In addition, it was also an important aspect of teachers' planning and assessment. Where teachers reported that they kept written records of pupils' work progress, in addition to the Authority's Primary Yearly Record Summary, the effect on the pupils was positive. The keeping of records concerning pupils' personal and social development was also found to be generally beneficial. Furthermore, in many effective schools, teachers kept samples of pupils' work in folders to be passed on to their next teacher.

11. Parental involvement

Our findings show parental involvement in the life of the school to be a positive influence upon pupils' progress and development. This included help in classrooms and on educational visits, and attendance at meetings to discuss children's progress. The headteacher's accessibility to parents was also important; schools operating an informal, open-door policy being more effective. Parental involvement in pupils' educational development within the home was also clearly beneficial. Parents who read to their children, heard them read, and provided them with access to books at home, had a positive effect upon their children's learning. Curiously, however, formal Parent-Teacher Associations were not found to be related to effective schooling. Although the reasons for this are not clear it could be that some parents find the formal structure of such bodies to be intimidating and are thus deterred from involvement, rather than encouraged. We also found that some parents feel that PTAs tend to be run by small cliques of parents. We would not wish to advocate, of course, that schools disband their PTAs, but if a school has an Association and is not involving parents in other ways it would perhaps be worth considering how parent-school relationships could be opened up.

12. Positive climate

The Junior School Project provides confirmation that an effective school has a positive ethos. Overall, we found the atmosphere to be more pleasant in the effective schools, for a variety of reasons. Both around the school and within the classroom, less emphasis on punishment and critical control, and a greater emphasis on praise and reward was beneficial. Where teachers actively encouraged self-control on the part of pupils, rather than emphasising the negative aspects of their behaviour, progress and development were enhanced. What appeared to be important was firm but fair classroom management. The class teachers' attitude to pupils was also important. Positive effects resulted where teachers obviously enjoyed teaching their classes, valued the fun factor, and communicated their enthusiasm to the children. Their interest in the children as individuals, and not just as learners, also fostered progress. Those who devoted more time to non-school chat or small talk increased pupils' progress and development. Outside the classroom, evidence of a positive climate included: the organisation of lunchtime and after-school clubs for pupils; involvement of pupils in the presentation of assemblies; teachers eating their lunch at the same tables as the children; organisation of trips and visits; and the use of the local environment as a learning resource.

It is important to note that the climate in effective schools was not only positive for the pupils. The teachers' working conditions also contributed to the creation of a positive climate. Where teachers had non-teaching periods, the impact on pupil progress and development was positive. Thus, the climate created by the teachers for the pupils, and by the head for the teachers, was an important aspect of school effectiveness. This further appeared to be reflected in effective schools by happy, well-behaved pupils who were friendly towards each other and outsiders, and by the absence of graffiti around the school.

LINKS WITH OTHER STUDIES

Many of these key factors have been identified in the results of other studies or reports and we will describe some of the links between our study and the findings of other research here. However, it must be stressed that the selection of studies is not intended to be exhaustive. A more detailed and thorough discussion of the results of many of the major studies of school effectiveness, particularly those undertaken in the United States, has been provided by Purkey and Smith (1983). Reviews by Cuttance (1980a, 1980b, 1986), Rutter (1983), Grosin (1985) and Reynolds (1985), and the contributions of Rowan et al (1983) and Taylor (1985), provide further information about school effectiveness research. A summary of major findings on effective learning and teaching is given by the United States Department of Education (1986).

Positive leadership
A number of other studies have pointed to the importance of the headteacher's leadership in promoting school effectiveness. For example, Weber (1971), in an American study of four inner-city schools recognised as 'exemplary', identified 'strong leadership' as one of eight school-wide characteristics that influenced pupils' reading achievement. Trisman et al (1976), likewise, noted the importance of strong 'instructional leadership' in their study of schools which were unusually effective in promoting reading progress. Work by Armor et al (1976) examined schools which had been especially successful in promoting the reading achievement of minority children. They concluded that schools where the principal achieved a balance between a strong leadership role for themselves and maximum autonomy for teachers were more effective.

Brookover et al (1979) compared matched pairs (in terms of intakes) of elementary schools which were differentiated by the achievement of their pupils, and concluded that one of seven important factors which led to higher pupil achievement was the leadership role of the principal. Similarly, the Californian State Department of Education (1980) compared schools where pupils' reading scores were improving with those where reading scores were decreasing. This study also confirmed the value of positive leadership, and noted that such leadership was more effective when it included the sharing of responsibility for decision-making and planning. Our results support this conclusion.

Tomlinson (1980) and Levine and Stark (1981) have also drawn attention to the importance of the principal's leadership in effective schools. In the British context, Rutter et al (1979), in a major study of secondary schools in inner London, noted the importance of the headteacher's leadership in the promotion of school effectiveness. More recently, the Thomas Report (1985) which examined ways of improving primary schools in the Inner London Education Authority, commented on the necessity for clear and sensitive leadership by the headteacher.

The involvement of the deputy head
This finding is in accordance with the suggestions of Plowden (1967) and Coulson and Cox (1975) that deputies should be more involved in decision making. As we saw in Chapter 4, it was often the duty of the deputy head to take charge of the day-to-day organisation of schools and to ensure that everything ran smoothly. Furthermore, many deputy heads had a particular pastoral role in the school, relating both to pupils and other teachers. Finally, they placed great emphasis on their role as a link between the head and the rest of the staff, a role of which many headteachers were also aware.

Far less attention has been paid to the role of the deputy head in previous studies of school effects. There is evidence, however, that the sharing of responsibility for decision-making and planning is an important aspect of effective leadership by the head (see the study by the California State Department of Education, 1980). Our findings indicate clearly the value of involving the deputy head in such decision-making and planning. Similarly, in the Thomas Report (1985) it is stated 'we believe that many primary schools would benefit from increased delegation of responsibilites to members of staff' (p.66). This report also argued that the deputy should be involved in staff leadership and the formulation of school policies.

The involvement of teachers
Staff involvement is, therefore, related to the first factor, the headteacher's purposeful leadership. An authoritarian style of leadership will not encourage staff participation and involvement in decision-making. The study by the California State Department of Education (1980) pointed to the importance of sharing the responsibility for decision-making and planning with other staff. Glenn (1981) conducted case studies of four urban elementary schools. Amongst other factors, she suggested that school effectiveness was enhanced where there was joint planning by the staff. Levine and Stark (1981) also emphasised the importance of 'grade-level decision making' which encouraged collaborative planning amongst teachers. Moreover, the conclusions of the Thomas Report (1985) noted the value of staff involvement in decision-making in primary schools. The authors state '... it is a matter of high priority that each school should have a sense of wholeness.

That can be achieved ... after the adjustments that inevitably follow staff discussions arranged to consider proposals' (p. 66).

Consistency amongst teachers

Glenn's study (1981) also pointed to the benefits of consistency amongst teaching staff, particularly in the use of through-the-grades reading and mathematics programs. Edmonds (1979a, 1979b) emphasised the importance of school-wide policies and agreement among teachers in their aims. Similarly, Levine and Stark (1981) found that coordination of curriculum, instruction and testing to focus on specified objectives achieved through careful planning and staff development, was of value. Tomlinson (1980) also suggested that it was important for teachers to have a common purpose and clearly agreed goals. In the secondary sector, Rutter et al (1979) found that consistency amongst teachers promoted effectiveness, and noted that staff consensus on the value and aims of the school as a whole was related to greater success in promoting pupils' educational outcomes.

Structured sessions

Structure was also shown to be important by Traub et al (1976) who found that higher pupil performance in basic skills occurred, where there was an emphasis on a more structured approach to learning in which students did not have complete freedom to decide their programme of activities. Similarly, Stallings (1976), in a study of pupils' progress in reading and mathematics in elementary classrooms, found that one of the factors related to higher achievement was the teachers' use of 'systematic instructional patterns'. In a review, Rosenshine and Stevens (1981) also noted the importance of order, structure and purposefulness in the classroom, in promoting pupils' progress. Similarly, Solomon and Kendall (1976) found that excessive pupil choice and responsibility for planning their own work was disadvantageous for pupil achievement and self-esteem. These authors argued it was not a choice between teacher control and pupil control, rather a question of teacher control versus lack of control of learning activities.

Intellectually challenging teaching

Many studies we have already noted in this chapter have indicated that high expectations of pupils are beneficial (see research by Weber, 1971; Armor et al, 1976; Trisman et al, 1976; Rutter et al, 1979, California State Department of Education, 1980; Glenn, 1981; and reviews by Brophy, 1983 and Pilling and Kellmer Pringle, 1978). Evidence of the value of intellectually challenging teaching is also provided in the study of junior pupils conducted by Galton and Simon (1980). In addition, Levine and Stark (1981) have noted that effective elementary schools emphasised the development of higher-order cognitive skills such as reading comprehension, and problem solving in mathematics.

Work-centred environment

Weber's (1971) study also emphasised the importance of an atmosphere of order, purposefulness, and pleasure in learning. Work by Rosenshine and Berliner (1978) has indicated that, where academic engaged time was higher, pupil progress in basic skills was promoted. Brookover and Lezotte (1979), in an analysis of factors which differentiated schools in which pupils' reading scores increased from those where scores were decreased, found that a greater amount of teacher time spent on direct instruction was a characteristic of improving schools. Brookover et al (1979) also noted that more time spent on instruction was related to effectiveness.

Work in junior schools in Britain has also shown that the amount of teacher time spent communicating with pupils about their work was related positively to pupil progress. Galton and Simon (1980) noted 'all three groups of successful teachers had more task interactions than the typical teacher in the sample' (p. 196). In addition, Tomlinson (1980) stressed the importance of the efficient use of classroom time. Fisher et al (1980), in a study which examined the characteristics of good schools, found that academic learning time was increased, while Glenn's (1981) work has noted the importance of efficient, coordinated scheduling and planning of activities.

Our findings also support those of Armor et al (1976), which demonstrated that an orderly atmosphere in schools was associated with greater effectiveness. Rutter et al (1979) also indicated that strategies of classroom management which kept students actively engaged in learning activities had a beneficial effect on pupils' educational outcomes.

Limited focus within sessions

We have found no references in published studies of school effectiveness to the identification of a limited focus as defined in our research being an important aspect of effectiveness. This is likely to reflect the absence in past studies of data about the way teachers mix different curriculum activities.

Maximum communication

Work by Galton and Simon (1980) similarly found that the amount of teacher-pupil contact was important. They noted for all three groups of successful teachers 'the most striking and perhaps the most important feature was that the teachers all achieved above-average levels of interactions with their pupils' (p. 186). Our results demonstrate that one of the ways teachers were able to increase the level of communication with pupils was by the use of a balance of class and individual contacts. Galton and Simon (1980) also found that one of their groups of more successful teachers were the 'class enquirers', who combined whole-class teaching with individual work. As with our Project, these authors also found a positive link between the use of higher-order questions and statements and maximum communication.

The Thomas Report (1985) also noted that teacher communication with the whole class could be valuable. Thus, the authors commented 'Here and there our visits to classrooms coincided with an intensive piece of work by a teacher using exposition and discussion with a group of children or the whole class. Almost always this teaching brought a sense of eagerness and involvement to the work that was less often apparent when children were working on their own' (p. 32). They also noted that arrangements for individual work on any large scale frequently break down 'because teachers find it impossible to give sufficient individual attention to children and have to engage children too much in work that is simply time-filling'. Galton and Simon (1980) similarly found that where teachers devoted most of their time to communicating with individuals, the children of necessity spent most of their time working on their own.

Record keeping
A number of previous studies of effectiveness have also noted the importance of school-wide systems for the monitoring and evaluation of pupil progress. Thus, Weber's (1971) work noted the value of careful evaluation of student progress. Edmonds (1979a, 1979b, 1981) found that the frequent monitoring of pupil progress was related positively to effectiveness. Levine and Stark (1981) also emphasised the need for schools to adopt simple procedures for tracking student and class progress and achievement. The California State Department of Education study (1980) noted the necessity for teacher accountability for pupil performance, and the provision of accurate information on that performance. Dean (1980) also reported that 'record-keeping is an essential ingredient in making education continuous' (p.14).

Parental involvement
Studies conducted in the United States have also suggested that parental involvement is an influential aspect of school effectiveness. Thus, Armor et al (1976) noted the value of high levels of parent-teacher and parent-headteacher contact. In Britain, work by Hewison and Tizard (1980) has demonstrated a link between parental involvement and reading attainment for junior pupils. Mortimore and Mortimore (1984) provide a review of research which has examined the impact of parental involvement. Hargreaves (1984) and Thomas (1985) have also noted the value of increasing parental involvement in secondary and in primary schools. Thus, the Hargreaves report notes 'For very many years we have known, both from well established research findings as well as from common sense, that parental commitment is a cornerstone of the school's success. If parents are interested in their children's schooling, if they are supportive of the school's endeavours,

if they act in partnership with teachers, then the children will achieve more in school'(p.14).

Positive climate
Other studies have reached similar conclusions concerning a positive climate. As Purkey and Smith (1983) noted, the literature indicates that a student's chance of success in learning cognitive skills is heavily influenced by the climate of the school. Trisman et al (1976) found that more effective schools tended to have a good school atmosphere including student-teacher rapport. Work by Moos (1978) noted the importance of a positive classroom climate. Brookover et al (1979) found the quality of the school's social climate was related positively to the promotion of pupil achievement. Edmonds (1979a, 1979b) and Edmonds and Frederiksen (1979) have also reported that a school climate conducive to learning was necessary to promote achievement. In Britain, Rutter et al's (1979) work provides evidence of the significance of the characteristics of schools as social institutions. The Rutter study indicated that the school ethos was influential in determining effectiveness. It also noted the importance of praise and of the emphasis on rewards rather than punishments.

SUMMARY

It is clear, therefore, that there are many links between the factors identified as important in the Junior School Project, and those found to contribute to school effectiveness in previous research. Nonetheless, some factors have received less attention in past studies; in particular, the key role of the deputy head, and the value of a limited focus in the classroom. Although a few studies have noted the value of maximising communication between teachers and pupils, in general, this aspect has received only limited attention in most analyses of school effectiveness.

The 12 key factors point to effective schools as being friendly, supportive environments, led by heads who are not afraid to assert their views and yet are able to share management and decision-making with the staff. Class teachers within effective schools provide a structured learning situation for their pupils but give them freedom within this framework. By being flexible in their use of whole class, group and individual contacts, they maximise communications with each pupil. Furthermore, through limiting their focus within sessions, their attention is less fragmented. Hence, the opportunities for developing a work-centred environment and for presenting challenging work to pupils are increased.

Whilst the 12 key factors we have outlined may not constitute a recipe for effective junior schooling, they can provide a framework within which the various partners in the life of the school – headteacher and staff, parents and pupils, and governors – can operate. Each of these partners has some role to play in fostering the overall success of the school, and when each makes a positive contribution, the result can be an increase in the school's effectiveness. In the final chapter, we move on to consider the implications of our findings for the varied groups of people responsible for the education of children in primary schools today.

12

Towards More Effective Schooling

In this final chapter we shall discuss some of the implications of the study for the various partners involved in the resourcing and management of schools. Our discussion is unlikely to be exhaustive – no doubt as we discuss further the results of our research with teachers and parents, other implications will occur, but we hope it will point to some of the ways in which schools can be made more effective.

Our research, with the exception of the home interviews which were supported by a grant from the Leverhulme Trust, was funded by a Local Education Authority. This Authority is considering how best the research findings can be used to support the quality of education on offer in its schools. In this chapter, however, we shall be considering the implications for all authorities. We believe the findings are applicable to schools in other parts of the United Kingdom, although we acknowledge that their relevance might be greatest for inner urban areas. Furthermore, through our contact with educationalists abroad, we are hopeful that the study will be seen as having relevance in many different education systems. Our previous experience suggests that many school boards in Canada and the United States will be eager to examine the findings in order to find out if they can assist their work towards more effective schooling.

In order to avoid repetition, the chapter is organised so that implications affecting particular partners in the education service are grouped together. We deal, for instance, with those findings which have a clear message for government at a national level separately from those which apply to the jurisdiction of a Local Education Authority. Similarly, we attempt to tease out those which apply to headteachers from those that apply, more generally, to classroom teachers. We recognise, however, that some overlap is inevitable.

We consider, in turn, the possible implications of our study for the following groups: central government; teacher-trainers; Local Education Authorities; the teachers' professional associations; school governors; headteachers; teachers; and, finally, parents and pupils. However, before beginning this exploration of possible implications, we wish to draw attention to three findings which have an importance for all involved in education.

Investment in Education

We believe our data illustrate the importance of the adequate funding
of the education service. The Inner London Education Authority is a
generous LEA. All the schools in the sample were well equipped and
had sufficient resources to support the pupils' learning. Because all
the schools were well funded, we did not find resourcing to be a key
factor. Had our sample been drawn, however, from a range of LEAs
– with both high and low-spending traditions – it is unlikely this would
have been the case.

We were also fortunate in that we completed the fieldwork before
the 1985/87 teachers' dispute got under way. The dispute would undoubtedly have inhibited the excellent co-operation with teachers that
we enjoyed. It would also have illustrated the need for teachers to be
reasonably paid. Effective schools need effective teachers. Teachers
are more likely to be effective if they feel that their contribution to
society is valued.

Views of intelligence

The second implication of our work that applies to everybody involved
in education, concerns common views of intelligence. This is not an
appropriate place to discuss theories of intelligence, yet it would be
unfortunate if we failed to draw attention to the implications of our
findings for the ways that teachers and parents view ability. What our
data illustrate is that children's performance changes over time. Given
an effective school, children make greater progress. Greater progress
leads to greater capability and, if handled sensitively, to greater confidence. In this way children's ability grows. Thus effective schools
can change pupils.

We believe the years between 7 and 11 to be particularly important
since children are still able to change their view of themselves as good
or poor learners. We know from our other work on transition that,
as children move into secondary schools, this flexibility diminishes
(see the ILEA Secondary Transfer Bulletins, listed in Appendix 1).
The responsibility of teachers is to ensure that their pupils do not
adopt fixed views of their own abilities but, rather, come to realise
that they have considerable potential which, given motivation and
good teaching in an effective school, can be realised.

It is also important that the other partner in the child's education,
the parents, should regard ability in the same way. Despite the recent
revelations about the work of Sir Cyril Burt – a psychologist devoted
to the study of intelligence, who towards the end of his career fabricated
much of his data – many parents still view their children's ability as
fixed. We hope our data will persuade both teachers and parents that
this is not so and that change is possible. We believe that, in the right
circumstances, children can become more intelligent.

Schools matter

The third – and the most important – implication that stems from our study is that schools matter. They matter in two senses: because, as we have just argued, they can help pupils change and develop; and also, because their effects are not uniform. Individual schools matter a great deal to the pupils that attend them.

The extent to which individual schools vary has been illustrated vividly by our data. This message will be welcomed by those parents who have always known this but is also likely to cause some consternation. Clearly, not all parents can choose the most effective schools. There are no simple answers to this problem. We do not believe open enrolment or a voucher scheme could work. An application of market forces which expanded the most effective schools and allowed the least effective to wither away would do more harm than good. The effective schools would lose some of the very qualities – including smaller size – that distinguished them, whilst the pupils in the less effective schools would be likely to obtain a very poor education as the withering took place.

In our view the answer must be to use the principles of effective schooling that the study has identified to develop a framework of effective education for all schools. Thus parents, rather than removing their children and going in search of a more effective alternative, should work with their fellow parents, the school governors and the headteacher to make their child's school effective. For some schools with given characteristics less favourable than others (see Chapter 11), the task may be daunting but, with goodwill and the enthusiastic support of the Local Education Authorities, we believe it to be possible. There are numerous examples of schools in this country and, especially, in Canada that have worked to this end and, as a result, have experienced positive change.

These three implications are of overriding importance. They underlie many of the specific actions that can be undertaken by individual partners in the life of each school. We turn now to a discussion of the part each partner can play in the creation of effective schools.

IMPLICATIONS FOR CENTRAL GOVERNMENT

Under the 1944 Education Act, responsiblity for education is divided between central government, in the form of the Secretary of State and the Department of Education and Science, the Local Education Authorities and individual headteachers. The role of central government, until fairly recently, was limited to providing resources through a rate support grant mechanism, guiding national negotiations with teachers associations, overseeing, in very general terms, the curriculum, and acting as an arbiter in disputes between the other partners or those involving parental complaints.

During recent periods of administration, however, the role of central government has been increased considerably and the Education Reform Bill seeks to increase the powers of the Secretary of State still further. These changes have been documented fully elsewhere and we will draw attention only to a few of the most relevant here. Among these are: an increased control of resources, with new powers to allocate specific educational support grants for particular projects and, in the case of some Authorities, power to set a limit on the amount of money levied through the rates; a proposed national curriculum; a more dominant role in secondary school examinations, with the abolition of the Schools Council and the establishment of two new bodies made up of appointees of the Secretary of State. In addition, an enhanced role in teacher training, with members of Her Majesty's Inspectors monitoring the work of University Departments of Education; and the creation of policies sympathetic to greater parent-power.

Whilst we were writing this book government intentions to introduce testing for seven and eleven year olds have been announced. In our research we have made full use of tests. We have also commended the use of diagnostic testing by sensitive class teachers. We view with some alarm the blanket testing of whole age-groups of children.

Our data have drawn attention to the relationship of smaller schools and smaller classes to effective practice. These options are usually more expensive than larger schools and larger classes. We hope central government will see the need for adequate resources to be made available for schools. In part this will mean providing more for some LEAs, through the distribution of the rate support grant, but it could also mean using government influence to persuade certain LEAs to spend more, and by ensuring that they would not be penalised for doing so.

In the case of both schools and classes we wish to be cautious in our recommendations. We appreciate that there must be a trade-off between the benefits we have identified for smaller schools, and the difficulties of providing an adequate educational experience for pupils. We consider that schools that have at least one and no more than two forms of entry (between 30 and 60 pupils) each year are well placed to provide an adequate range of experiences. Where schools are bigger, we consider extra steps will have to be taken to ensure that the benefits conferred by a small roll can be compensated for in other ways.

The question of class size is especially interesting since, as many readers will know, the weight of the research evidence has supported the opposite view: that larger classes are more effective. In our view this evidence is defective since it is based on surveys that have usually contained two flaws. They frequently have been unable to take account of teachers' decisions to place children with learning difficulties in very small classes, and they have usually not addressed questions to do with the nature of the classroom activities. They thus have failed to recognise that in teaching based on whole-class methods where the teacher spends a high proportion of time lecturing, the number of pupils is less important than where she or he works with individuals or where much individual work has to be marked. Furthermore, because they have usually related class size to attainment on any one occasion they have been unable to consider progress. In contrast, our data relate to progress rather than attainment (although, as we have already demonstrated, we can look at that too). The finding that better progress in both cognitive and non-cognitive areas is associated with smaller classes, particularily for younger children, was no surprise. Like many parents and teachers we had recognised that the opposite view was likely to be based on misunderstandings and a lack of adequate measures. That said, we wish to avoid arguing that small classes must always be appropriate. In our view, the head and teachers should exercise their discretion to distribute the precious resource of teacher time in the most economic way and use the opportunity of bigger classes to pay for smaller ones elsewhere.

In our schools the average class size was 25, compared with a range of 15 to 34 in the first year. In some Authorities the average is considerably larger. It is also true that, in general, younger pupils are grouped in larger classes than older ones. Given our findings, this possesses a curious logic and we will be delighted if our study is used to argue for a reduction in the class size of younger pupils, even if this has to be paid for by an increase in the class size of older children.

One other aspect of our findings that has a bearing on resources concerns the appearance of classrooms. Whilst we realise that this is the responsibility of the LEA, it is clear that some LEAs are having to cut back on programmes of maintenance and decoration because, when pressed, it is easier for them to stop such programmes than to make other savings. The poor decorative order of many classrooms has also been commented upon by HMIs in their annual reports on the provision of education. In our experience the state of decoration does matter - for both pupils and teachers, and for parents visiting the school – and central government should ensure that adequate resources for both capital and revenue are available. Central government could also exercise its role in bringing pressure to bear on those LEAs who claim to under-spend on education. Whilst, in recent years there have been a number of directives from central government applying pressure to curtail the spending of LEAs – most notably with rate-capping – there have been no instances of under-spending Authorities being similarly pressured. We hope our data will convince government that, whilst resources are not a guarantee of effectiveness, good schooling is easier to achieve when givens such as well-maintained classrooms are attended to.

IMPLICATIONS FOR TEACHER-TRAINERS

Apart from the general implications that have already been discussed, we hope teacher-trainers – whether in colleges of education or university departments of education – will see specific implications in our data. Each of the 12 key factors that we have identified should be of interest to teacher-trainers and should help them develop an understanding of effective schools in their students, but some factors – especially those concerned with classroom teaching skills – will have special relevance. At a time when there is a trend towards making student teachers more aware of practical skills, and indeed in some courses increasing the proportion of time devoted to school-based activities, it is appropriate that attention should be focused on classroom processes. Thus five of the twelve key factors identified – structured sessions, intellectually challenging teaching, a work-centred environment, a limited focus and the importance of maximum communication – have a direct bearing on how student teachers will approach their task. Further factors such as record keeping and parental involvement, expectations and the use of praise in feedback will also affect the way student teachers carry out their role.

Structured sessions
Theories of learning and teaching differ about the amount of direction teachers should provide for young children. At one extreme it could be argued that self-direction is the best way to facilitate learning. At the other extreme, it is often claimed that direct instruction is best. Interestingly, our data support neither of these extreme positions. In the structured sessions that we observed, teachers sought to provide a considerable degree of freedom for pupils, but did so within a well-defined framework. In this way those pupils who were highly motivated, and who became engaged in learning could pursue their work with enthusiasm, whilst those who were less well motivated were not left to flounder on alone. In those classrooms where there was less structure, all too often motivated pupils lost their enthusiasm and the less motivated became even more bored and distracted without the teacher – who was often engaged with individual pupils – realising what was happening.

The implication for the student teacher is that the provision of structure and support for children in their learning is essential. She or he must be aware that children will vary in their motivation and will require differing degrees of support and must learn to look out for the signs of increasing disaffection. She or he should encourage children to plan their own learning and should include some time for an audit of which tasks have been achieved and of what has been learned.

Intellectually challenging teaching

It must surely be of the utmost importance for those coming to teaching for the first time to appreciate that a major task must be to provide pupils with teaching which challenges and stimulates. Other aspects of classroom practice – the maintenance of order, the organisation of books and learning activities, the sensible use of time – provide the teacher with opportunities to challenge and develop the minds of pupils. The skilled practitioner, as we so often observed, had developed ways to provide this kind of teaching by asking thought-provoking questions at the right moment, posing problems or challenging preconceptions. Of course this has to be done sensitively, as some pupils are better able to rise to the challenge than others and skilled teachers avoid situations in which pupils are humiliated by failure. But there is no doubt that the quality of the discourse in the classroom is one of the most important distinguishing features of effective teaching.

Work-centred environment

For student teachers one of the most difficult tasks is to learn how to create within the classroom the kind of environment which supports and fosters purposeful activity. A number of writers – most notably Kounin (1970) in the United States and Marland (1975) in the United Kingdom – have described ways in which skilled teachers manage the classroom so as to avoid disruption and encourage an atmosphere that leads to effective learning. In our schools the most effective teachers did this by planning learning tasks appropriate to the level of their pupils, ensuring there was plenty of work for children to pursue and focusing as much of their classroom talk as possible upon work related matters. Effective classrooms were free of distracting noise and movement and were, on the whole, places where children were not only working, but happy to work. Such a work-centred environment may appear, to a casual observer, to be the natural order maintained, seemingly, very easily by the teacher. As we know, this inference would be quite wrong. In order for the environment to be ordered in the manner described, the teacher, by virtue of skilful management and personal example will have trained the class to work in this way.

Limited focus

In recent years primary teacher trainers have encouraged their students to organise classes so that groups of pupils can work at different areas of the curriculum simultaneously. This trend away from whole class-teaching, in large measure, represents a turning away from the somewhat stultifying approach evident in so many junior classes and encouraged by the 11+ examination that existed in British schools from 1944 until the mid 1970s. In addition, many contemporary approaches to teaching require the relative intimacy of the small group for their success.

Our findings, however, point to the problems inherent in the attempt to organise too many different learning experiences within any one classroom. We believe that, in those classrooms where this was the dominant organisational mode, teachers were too often unable to cope with the myriad demands made upon them and consequently could rarely ensure that learning in each separate area was progressing satisfactorily. In addition, because pupils were engaged in such different tasks the teacher's attention tended to be upon management rather than teaching, so opportunities for the kind of intellectually challenging teaching discussed earlier arose too rarely. The results, as our data illustrate, are poorer teaching and learning. Interestingly, in discussing this finding with heads and teachers, we have been surprised at how welcomed it has been. It appears that many experienced and extremely skilful teachers, whose normal practice has been to limit the curriculum focus of their lessons, have been led to feel guilty about their failure to manage more diverse activities. We believe, therefore, that teacher-trainers and others responsible for disseminating innovatory practice should ensure that the advice they give to teachers and student teachers does not, albeit unintentionally, generate needless feelings of guilt and inadequacy.

Maximum communication

The final finding that we have singled out for the attention of teacher-trainers concerns the importance of exploiting to the full opportunities within the classroom to communicate with pupils. As with the limited focus discussed above, this finding illustrates the importance of teachers sharing out their time and attention effectively. The least effective teachers waste these vital resources or allow them to be used up in unplanned, unproductive ways. Our most effective teachers demonstrated that they were in control of these resources and that they could use them to the maximum benefit of the class. They had at their disposal a repertoire of approaches which ranged from interactions with individuals, through groups to the whole class. The task which student teachers face is to develop such a repertoire, and to learn when and how to implement different approaches. All teachers need to have the ability to reflect upon and evaluate how effectively they are communicating with pupils, but it is of particular significance to those approaching the task for the first time. In giving their students this insight into their classroom practice, through observation and feedback, the study of video-taped lessons or the critical appraisal of teaching practices, teacher-trainers can help their students enormously.

Record keeping

Our data show quite clearly the need for the careful recording of pupil progress. We are not advocating a dull chore. We believe the individual record should be one of the main working tools of the classroom. We have been much impressed by the developments in secondary schools of records of achievement and other forms of profiling in which the pupil and teacher use the record to review progress and to plan new tasks. The way such profiles in secondary schools are becoming the basis for reports to parents, and the channel by which the headteacher can monitor progress, illustrates a very useful method by which record keeping can be built into the life of the school.

Parental involvement
In Chapter 3 we described the various kinds of parental involvement taking place in our schools. In Chapter 11 we revealed that parental involvement – or at least some forms of it – was one of our key factors. It is clear, however, from our earlier comments that some teachers are unsure of themselves in such activities. The implication for teacher trainers is that they need to prepare their students for this aspect of classroom life. Our data show that there were three times as many teachers who were positive about the idea of parental involvement as were negative. This attitude needs to be coupled with the appropriate skills to utilise such an untapped resource.

Expectations
As we have commented in earlier chapters, expectations are complex phenomena. Though they are abstract, they appear to be far from ephemeral, affecting, as they seem to do, the performance of pupils in such positive or negative ways. Our data are also complex and not likely to reveal easy answers. As we have shown, special attention given to particular pupils on the basis of their race, class or sex – and designed to help such pupils – can, in effect, become a message of lower expectation and lead to a depressed performance. What, in our judgment, is critical is that teacher-trainers impress on their students the need to lift and to sustain expectations. Academic study of the power of expectations is clearly important, but so also is the commitment to action.

The use of praise
Notwithstanding the need for careful judgment in the differential actions of a teacher implied by the previous paragraph, we feel bound to point out that the amount of criticism we observed exceeded the amount of praise. Furthermore, as we noted in Chapter 4, praise gets less as pupils grow older. We encountered a few teachers who thought that the giving of praise too generously may lead to 'inflation' and a consequent devaluation. Whilst there may be a strong element of truth in this idea, and whilst indiscriminate praise is obviously highly confusing to pupils, it remains our view – as a result of many hours classroom observation – that the system can take much more praise before infla-

tion becomes a real possibility. The implication for teacher-trainers is clear – impress upon students the value of praise and the limitations of negative criticism.

The implications of the study for LEAs are many and varied. It is they who are charged with administering the education service and who thus have an overarching interest in effective education. We think it is most appropriate that the study itself should have been carried out by an LEA research department. It is important that LEA members and officers understand the implications of our data so that they can encourage heads and teachers to consider the application of our findings to their own schools. Many of the implications are important because they increase the understanding of what happens in schools. We hope, for instance, that LEA inspectorate and advisory services will use our results to assist them in their tasks of ensuring and maintaining quality in the education service.

We believe, however, that the study can also be used as a framework for improvement and we have been encouraged in this view by the early reactions of many inspectors and advisers from a number of different LEAs and, indeed, by educators in the United States and Canada. In identifying many of the dimensions on which schools and classes vary, and in describing aspects of good practice, we have provided guidelines for the elaboration of action plans, so that aspects of school life can be appraised critically, and programmes of improvement implemented. In reaction to the *Fifteen Thousand Hours* study (Rutter et al, 1979) many schools drew up action plans and sought to improve the areas of school life identified by the study as important and which, in their own judgement, were in need of improvement. The results, in some cases were startling. (See, for instance, Toews and Murray Barker, 1985 for an account of the change achieved by a Canadian junior high school.)

We hope the Junior School Project will stimulate similar exercises in school improvement. There are a number of implications, however, where the LEA has a more direct responsibility than just acting as an intermediary between the data and the practitioners. We refer here to the given factors described in Chapter 11. The factors to be discussed concern the status and size of schools, their decorative order and their stability in terms of head and teacher turnover. Other findings concerning the selection and the level of support offered to headteachers, the vulnerability of pupils who are the youngest in their year, and the importance of parental involvement, will also be discussed since these are areas in which policy decisions by the LEA may make an immediate impact on the schools.

School status

There are two ways in which a junior school's status can vary: one concerns the age range of its pupils; the other, its legal standing. In inner London, schools for junior-aged pupils can either cater for pupils from 5 to 11 (junior mixed and infants, sometimes with nursery classes) or for pupils in a more restricted age span (from 7 to 11). In other parts of the country the issue is complicated by the existence of middle schools with different ages of entry and exit.

Our data show that those schools taking the wider age group were advantaged. This was probably because of the absence of a move between schools at age 7 with all its attendant disruption and strains. Our parallel study of transition from primary to secondary schools has illustrated just how traumatic a move between schools can be for pupils aged 11. It is unlikely that younger children will be better able to manage such a change. Inner London in recent years has seen a trend towards amalgamations between separate junior and infant schools. Our finding support the wisdom of this trend.

The legal standing of schools also varies. Although there are a number of different ways in which schools may be established, the essential difference is between those that are designated as county schools – falling completely under the administration of the Local Education Authority – and those that have voluntary status and, although funded almost entirely by the LEA and subject to their policy guidelines, retain an element of independence. Most but not all voluntary schools are denominational.

Our data show that voluntary schools, in general, received more advantaged pupils than did county schools, attracted pupils from a much wider catchment area but, additionally, tended to be more effective. Voluntary status was one of the given factors that, we argued, helped – but did not ensure – schools to become effective. We think there are three main reasons why this happens. First, we consider that our measures of pupil background – though accurate – are necessarily crude and may underestimate the difference between pupils attending each type of school. Thus, even with exactly the same social class and racial background, it is quite possible that two pupils might have very different family styles. One style might place a much greater emphasis on the value of learning and the support that should be given to the school than the other. Second, voluntary schools, based on denominational membership, may also elicit a greater commitment from both parents and pupils, which may act as a strong cohesive force. The third reason, however, is simply that the voluntary schools in our sample tended to be more in tune with the 12 key factors of effectiveness that we identified. In this, of course, they are no different from the best of the county schools.

The implication for LEAs, therefore, can only be general since the status of schools is fixed in law. Some may argue that consideration should be given to allowing county schools some of the freedom that is enjoyed by the voluntary schools. Such an idea would be in tune with the recommendations of the 1986 Audit Commission report. It would also build on the existing practice in inner London which allows local discretion over a substantial proportion of school resources. None of this, however, is to support the proposal for grant-maintained schools outside of the jurisdiction of the LEA. Such schools would make coherent planning impossible and would depend entirely on the market force of parental choice.

School and class size
The optimum size of schools is a much debated topic. Those who argue for large primary schools draw attention to the economy of scale, the richness of pooled resources, the availability of specialist staff, the existence of postholders with curriculum responsibilities, and the availability of teaching support staff in the office, library and media resources areas of school life. Against these arguments the small school lobby claim the benefit of greater teacher continuity, more detailed knowledge of pupils, closer co-operation and involvement with parents, and the positive ethos that can only be captured in a small family setting. Interestingly, our data support neither view. As we noted in Chapter 11, it was the schools with between one and two form entry which were likely to be the most effective. Compared to village schools with just one or two teachers, these are large, yet compared to primary schools with three or four forms of entry, they are clearly small.

Individual Local Education Authorities will have quite different needs and will have to make their decisions on efficient school-provision according to a variety of principles and pressures. Our data will allow them to justify keeping schools open that, perhaps, they might have thought too small to be effective. Our data, however, do not justify very small schools.

The question of class size is also contentious. In England and Wales, traditionally, primary classes have been bigger than secondary. Nursery class size is frequently the biggest overall whilst sixth forms are usually the smallest. This pattern has developed historically but is frequently justified in terms of the developmental nature of learning: as learning supposedly becomes more rigorous, so classes need to become smaller in order to allow students to have individual attention. A different view suggests that, as students grow older they become more independent and have greater access to information and, therefore, could progress quite adequately in bigger rather than smaller classes. But this latter view carries little weight in comparison to the traditional pattern.

Within each phase of schooling (nursery, primary and secondary) there are also considerable variations between Local Education Authorities. Thus the overall average pupil teacher ratio (PTR) for primary schools in England in 1986 is 21.8. The least generous LEA has an overall primary average PTR of 23.8; whereas 17.1 is the figure for the most generous.

As we have earlier noted, however, a number of research studies have claimed that larger, rather than smaller, classes have been associated with better attainment. Our data, which was able to examine the progress of individual pupils, refutes these views. We found smaller classes led to greater progress, especially for young pupils and, interestingly, especially in the area of mathematics. The implication of this finding for LEAs is clear: wherever possible, moves to shift the extra resources needed to finance small classes from older to younger pupils should be supported. Even within tight financial controls imposed by central Government, it may be possible to shift resources whilst remaining within an overall budget. Much will depend, however, on the attitudes of the teacher associations towards this idea.

Maintenance and decoration of school buildings

Primary school buildings range from gloomy Victorian 'three deckers' to purpose-built, light and airy modern constructions. In inner London, as we have described earlier, a high proportion of buildings are of the Victorian kind. As we have also noted, the type of building did not appear to make a difference to the effectiveness of the school. In contrast the maintenance and decoration of the building did. The implication for Local Education Authorities, therefore, is that they should do all they can to maintain the decoration of primary schools. The problem is that in a time of financial stringencies, the painting cycle, which ensures that each school gets decorated every few years, becomes an easy target. At such times the number of years between each re-decoration increases.

There is a further point. In Chapter 3 we drew attention to the amount of necessary building work that took place in the schools over the four years of the research. For each school the start of a major building contract – even if planned well in advance, rather than being the result of an asbestos crisis - will come as a shock. It would undoubtedly be very helpful if LEAs drew up guidelines based on experience and the good practice that had emerged from similar situations. In addition to the guidelines it may be useful for LEAs to have in store spare stationary, equipment and common books for those schools where emergency work necessitates an unplanned evacuation and subsequent decanting to another site.

Stability of staffing

Our data show quite clearly that serious or frequent change can have negative effects on a school. The change of head or deputy frequently had an unsettling effect on pupils which was reflected in their progress. Similarly, changes of class teacher during a school year also led to poorer progress. At the same time, we also show that heads who had been in post for a long time (over 11 years) were generally associated with less effective schools. Local education authorities, therefore, through their inspectorate, advisory services and officers, have the difficult task of attempting to maintain stability or, at least, of trying to mitigate the negative effects of sudden and unplanned change. With long-serving headteachers the task is different and the implication for LEAs is that they need to find ways of supporting those heads and, if possible, of rekindling their energy and enthusiasm. In this situation, in many school boards in the United States or in Canada, heads would be transferred from one school to another. In England, where heads have tenure within their schools, this is not possible. One way of helping would be for LEAs to provide sabbaticals of a term, or even a year, to headteachers. Whilst out of their schools they could visit other schools, follow academic courses, or use the time to reflect on their aims and on the changes that have taken place in education, and in society, since they first become a head. When they returned to their school it is hoped that they would have developed new ideas and enthusiasm.

As regards changes of classroom teachers, scope for LEAs is less clear. One way in which the effects of such change on the pupils involved could be mitigated, however, is by the vigorous implementation of school-wide curriculum plans. Whilst the main thrust for such plans to be developed will naturally fall to the head, the LEA advisory service should do all in its power to encourage heads and post-holders to do this. Given the pattern of teacher change due to illness, maternity leave and the natural comings and goings of employees, the importance of guidelines that can provide a continuity beyond the actual person in the teacher's role is very clear. If such guidelines were to be achieved, in the detailed form that is needed, then the casual illness or even the prolonged absence of a teacher on maternity leave would be less likely to have such a negative impact on the learning of the class.

Support to new headteachers
Although not a direct finding of our study, the need for support for new headteachers follows from our data that show that new heads (less than two years in post) are generally associated with less effective schools. Although most Local Education Authorities have schemes for the induction of new teachers, few have such schemes for new heads, yet the challenge they face is considerable. They have to create their leadership role at the time when they are least familiar with the school. In some cases the deputy head is their only ally, yet this person may have been a competitor for the post. In other cases, staff will resist change and hanker after the style of a former headteacher. Support for the head during the initial period of their headship is vital

yet, frequently, because inspectorate and advisory services are hard pressed, it cannot be delivered adequately.

Two ways in which this problem could be addressed are through development of headteachers' centres, based on the successful model of teachers' centres, and through the establishment of a support network. Headteachers' centres could provide a meeting place for heads, a library and resource centre, and a place for in-service training sessions. A support network could link up a new head with an experienced one or with an appropriate ex-head or ex-advisor. The benefits of this link would be that the new head had access to someone who could advise, or just act as a sounding board, yet who was not involved either in a supervisory or, indeed, in a rival capacity. Care, however, would need to be taken that the advice from such a person was not contrary to that being given by the local inspector or adviser. Provided this was avoided the link could play a vital part in the induction over the first two years of headship. Local Education Authorities will need to consider, most carefully, the cost implications of either of these suggestions. In the case of headteachers' centres, there will be the costs of premises and support staff. In the case of the support network, the only costs will be in the form of a consultancy fee for time given to the new head, and this may prove to be a useful investment.

For heads who have survived their first two years, there is also an ongoing need for support. As society changes so the need for adaptable headteachers increases. We are not arguing that basic philosophies will need to be overhauled – indeed the list of headteachers' aims that we included in Chapter 3 remains impressive – but rather that the challenges facing heads change, and that suitable training and support may enable them to meet them successfully. There are, of course, implications in what we are arguing for LEAs' selection processes. Our advice would be that investment in reviews of headship appointments drawing on all the available research evidence would be repaid. Here, however, we wish simply to suggest that the traditional models of management training for heads be widened to reflect the tasks faced in many schools. The evidence we cite in Chapter 3 suggests that headteachers do intervene more in the classroom practice of their colleagues and it is essential that those interventions are carried out in ways that ensure the results are positive. Management courses should also include components based on industrial relations and, in the light of current interest, appraisal techniques. Both of these aspects of management have frequently been ignored in training for headteachers, even though they play such a large part in the training of managers in business or industry.

A further idea for the training of heads concerns children with special needs. An increasing number of pupils with special needs are being educated alongside other children in primary schools and heads need training in how best to support this development. As we noted in Chapter 4, in some schools there was little communication between postholders and teachers with special needs responsibilities. We also noted that many of the teachers with special needs training felt they were considered poor relations by their colleagues and, as a result, reported their frustrations. Heads, therefore, need help to ensure that an integrated school also has an integrated staff.

Support for children who are young in their years
Our data have illustrated, in a number of different ways, the difficulties facing children whose birthdays fall towards the end of the school year. As we noted in Chapter 7, these children can be up to 11 months younger than other pupils in the class groups. Moreover, we found that, for some of them, their immaturity is compounded by a reduced length of time that they spend in infant schooling. Where a Local Education Authority has a policy of admitting all these children who will reach the age of five during the school year, at the start of the autumn term, the situation may be eased. But great care needs to be taken to ensure that they are provided with appropriate educational experiences rather than just being thrown in with the other children. The LEA may, anyway, decide that this is insufficient to ensure that this group of pupils have an equal opportunity to achieve. Other ways of supporting these pupils may need to be considered. Such ways could include the delegating of a special responsibility to one of the advisory staff; the grouping of such children so as to allow a more favourable pupil-teacher ratio; extra support through the use of ancilliary staff; a parental involvement programme (in any case this was identified as a key factor associated with effectiveness); and such minor, but important, recommendations as the special monitoring of progress. In our view it is important that this last measure be sustained into the junior years where many teachers are less concerned with the age difference within the year than are their colleagues in the infant departments. Part of the problem appears to be that teachers can forget the age difference and assume that, in comparison with other pupils, such children are simply less able. One easy way of reminding teachers of pupils' younger age would be to group the names of pupils on the attendance registers in birth order. In this way, teachers would be reminded constantly of the special characteristics of this group. It would clearly be important that, if adopted, this device was used positively in order to raise expectations rather than, inadvertently, to lower them.

Involving the parents
A parental involvement programme, as noted in the last paragraph, brings a number of advantages to the school. Its likelihood of success, however, depends on the quality of its base within the LEA. We have already discussed the arguments for such involvement in earlier chap-

ters and in the section dealing with implications for teacher trainers. Here we wish to make two suggestions. The first is that all LEAs should develop a clear policy on parental involvement. Such a policy should obviously be formulated in co-operation with parents' groups. Its benefits would be that many of the problems that can arise would be predicted and avoided and that the work would be given status. The second suggestion flows on from the policy; we believe a code of practice specifying the roles and conduct of teachers and parents and laying down procedures to be followed in the event of any disagreement would be enormously useful. This emphasis on policies and Codes of Practice may appear somewhat legalistic and may give the impression that we forsee many problems in parent involvement. This is not our view. We believe it is one of the most exciting developments in education but we think that the more secure the foundations of parental involvement the more it is likely to be successful.

In this section we have discussed some of the possible implications for Local Education Authorities stemming from our data. We have focused on those aspects of school life in which the LEA has a direct influence. Quite clearly, there are also many areas of school life where the influence of the LEA is indirect. Some of these will be discussed in connection with the influence of other groups.

IMPLICATIONS FOR THE TEACHERS' PROFESSIONAL ASSOCIATIONS

We have included a discussion of the implications of the findings for the teachers' professional associations because we view their influence as extremely important and because we appreciate that, without their support, initiatives to improve schools may be hindered. In England and Wales the teachers' associations are sometimes represented as giving less attention to educational than to salary matters. In our view this is not always an accurate view though we understand how, during an extended dispute over salary and conditions of service, this impression is gained. In other countries where pay and conditions are more satisfactory to members of teachers' professional associations, a greater emphasis is often placed on educational developments. In some provinces in Canada and in some of the States in the USA, for instance, the Teachers' Federation is a keen supporter of curriculum development and innovation. It has also to be noted that one forum for the involvement of the British associations in curriculum matters – the Schools Council – was abolished in 1983.

In our view there are implications for the teachers' associations in all of our findings. That some schools are more effective than others is not likely to surprise many practitioners, but the size of the differences in progress between the most and least effective schools will be of interest. Our finding, showing that schools, rather than background, have the greatest influence on levels of pupil progress, should be welcomed since this illustrates the central role that school plays in young peoples' lives. The importance of the given factors – discussed at length in the previous section – should also be of interest to the teachers' associations. Especially interesting will be the finding about class size. Teachers' associations have traditionally questioned the research on class size; our data supplies the much needed empirical proof that they were right to do so.

We hope the teachers' associations will support our choice of implications for the teacher trainers that have been discussed in an earlier section. We hope too that they will see as a positive contribution the development of measures for monitoring pupils' progress. We hope that if ever a Teachers' Council - based on models from other professions – is established, it will play a major part in the search for effective schools.

IMPLICATIONS FOR SCHOOL GOVERNORS

We hope governors, like other groups concerned with schools, will be interested in our findings and that they will see a number of implications in our data for how they should carry out their task of overseeing the life of schools. We believe that making schools as effective as possible is important. One of the ways of doing this is by having effective governors. Effective governors, in our view, are those who, whilst supporting the school in every possible way, exercise their responsibility by visiting the school, communicating with parents, and questioning, constructively and positively, the management of the head and the performance of the staff. We think it important that the lay nature of the governing body is seen as positive; its role is not the same as that of the LEA advisory service.

We have, of course, seen the research findings of the study on governing bodies carried out at Brunel University and have noted the somewhat disappointing conclusions about the impact of parent governors reached by the research team, but we have also seen school communities where parent governors and the governing body play a key role in the life of the school. The 1986 Education Act increases the power of individual governing bodies at the expense of the Local Education Authorities. It is even more important for governors to understand how effective schools work. We hope our study will provide a framework in which governors can examine the way in which their own schools perform. We hope, too, that our list of twelve key factors will provide a checklist of good practice for governors to consider in relation to their own schools.

IMPLICATIONS FOR HEADTEACHERS

There are a great many implications for headteachers in the findings of our study. In a sense, almost all the implications that arise affect, directly or indirectly, the management of the school and, hence, the role of the head. In order to avoid repetition, however, only those that have an immediate, and direct, significance for heads will be discussed here. These are: class size; the role of leadership in the school; the need to involve the deputy head and staff; consistency; parental involvement; record keeping in the school and the importance of high expectations and a positive school climate.

Class size
The arguments concerning class size have already been stated. The implication for headteachers of our findings is that school organisation needs to provide smaller classes for young pupils. In some cases this may mean creating the extra resources for these smaller classes by running larger classes for the older pupils. Any change in the established order of resourcing is difficult but we think this issue needs to be considered very carefully by heads and their colleagues.

Leadership
The type of purposeful leadership that we found to be most effective has been described earlier. Here it may be helpful to focus on the implication of this finding for a headteacher. How should she or he respond? In our view, heads need to have a very clear view of their leadership role. They need to be able to divide the decisions they are required to make into two groups: those which it is quite properly their responsibility to take and for which any attempt at delegation to a staff decision would be seen as a dereliction of duty, and those which, equally properly, belong to the staff as a whole. In some cases it will be perfectly clear to which group a certain decision belongs; in others, it will be extremely difficult to decide. Mistakes will be made and the consequences – as when the staff discover that a decision affecting their way of working has been taken with no opportunity for them to voice an opinion on the matter, or where there is a conflict of interests between individual teachers on the staff – will have to be suffered. However, if the head is perceptive and sensitive she or he will soon learn to distinguish which decisions are which. The 1987 Education Act has given heads new powers. Forthcoming legislation may increase these further. The skills of leadership are essential if these powers are not to be misused.

The involvement of the deputy and the staff
Our data illustrate that deputies have a key role in the management of the school and that, if this role is not properly carried out, the

school is likely to be less than effective. The implication of this finding for the head is that she or he needs to allow the deputy their own role. This should not just be an imitation of the role of the head, although of course, it will include standing in when the head is elsewhere.

Some heads find it difficult to delegate tasks and feel a powerful deputy to be a threat. This situation is not good for a school as staff will tend to take sides and be either for or against one or the other. Pupils, too, will notice the tension and the school community will be divided. Heads, therefore, need to delegate with some care. They need to recognise that they have the natural authority within the school and that their deputy does not. If deputies are too dominant and take to themselves too many powers, then heads should intervene to reassert their own authority. It must be recognised, however, that knowing when and how best to do this is difficult and requires fine judgement. For inexperienced heads, the challenge is considerable. Hence the need for the special support we recommended in an earlier section. However, the issue must be faced if we are to get away from the situation reported in Chapter 3 where a number of deputies expressed their frustration at not having their skills used sufficiently.

Our data also illustrate the importance of allowing and encouraging all the staff to play a full part in the life of the school. The examples we chose to use, in order to illustrate this finding, were concerned with the allocation of pupils to classes, and the tailoring of curriculum guidelines to the individual school. The principle, however, is clear: the headteacher cannot think of the school as her or his school, but must recognise that all who are involved share some ownership in its well being. In this way the head can operate the leadship we described in an earlier section without exerting total control over the staff. This is the sort of leadership which does not seek to enhance the status of the head but, rather, to benefit the whole institution.

Consistency

In an earlier section we illustrated consistency by reference to the use of curriculum guidelines. Some heads were able to ensure a common approach to the curriculum; others were not. The implication for the head is that she or he has to create enthusiasm amongst the staff so that colleagues are willing to sacrifice some of their own individuality in favour of a common approach. This will not apply simply to the curriculum but will include the manner in which pupils are related to and dealt with. The benefits for the pupils are likely to be considerable: there will be clear indications of what is, and is not, acceptable behaviour; individual teachers will not have to be tested out; there will be a sense of security within the school. The benefits for the teachers are that they will feel part of a team rather than being just an individual. For heads to achieve consistency in such a pluralistic society is not easy. Teachers are as divided as any other groups over political views, attitudes and even over trade union rivalry. However, where a school can achieve a consistency the benefit to all members is enormous.

Parental involvement
As we have noted in earlier sections, one of our findings with the biggest implications for the way in which a headteacher organises the school is that parental involvement is related to effectiveness. This did not apply to parent-teacher associations which were found to be related negatively to progress, but did apply to parents helping in school and in working with their children at home.

Parents can help in schools in many different ways. In some schools they are, in effect, used as unpaid assistants to wash paint brushes and clean up after practical activities. In other schools, they are encouraged to bring whatever talents and experience they have into the school and they work with individuals or groups of children. The management of parental involvement can be a challenge for the head. On the one hand, she or he will wish to use whatever talents are available for the good of the school. On the other hand, parents are not trained teachers (and if they happen to be they are not usually under contract to the LEA) and cannot simply be treated as if they are. When things go wrong, as, for instance, when a parent and a teacher disagree about a particular incident in a classroom, it may be difficult for the head to rectify the situation. Hopefully, with goodwill such situations will not occur frequently, but there will be occasions on which the head will need to act diplomatically, yet firmly, in order to avoid an unhelpful clash.

Although a first national study of parental involvement has only just been commissioned, the experience of those who have worked with parents in classrooms is that the most usual problem is the reluctance of parents to play as full a part as the teacher would like, rather than the parent taking over. There may be occasions, however, in which a parent exhibits an attitude to an individual or group of pupils which is contrary to the spirit of the school through, for instance, making a racist remark. Dealing with this will take the head into the area of parent training and she or he may resent the time and energy needed for such a task. This will have to be set against the benefits of the resource that parents bring into schools and classes. We hope that the policy and Code of Practice recommended in the section dealing with the LEA, will prove useful in such cases.

The second type of parental involvement – encouraging parents to work with their own children in the home – avoids the potential difficulties that we have been describing. It also is of proven benefit as has been illustrated not only by our study, but by the work of Tizard and colleagues (1982). For many parents, of course, helping with their children's learning will be nothing new, the novelty will be in the encouragement given by the head and the staff to this – previously so often discouraged – activity. For other parents, however, the situation may be quite different and the production of guidelines or a parent handbook drawn up by the schools' teachers and parents may prove very helpful.

The implication for the headteacher of a policy of encouraging parents to help with their children's learning is that she or he will need to monitor whether this happens. If it is realised that some parents can – or will – not do so, then some extra help will have to be provided otherwise the children of those parents will be disadvantaged in comparison to their peers.

These two types of parental involvement need careful management, but offer practical ways of increasing the effectiveness of the school. Headteachers and their colleagues cannot afford not to give them serious consideration. Similarly, in relation to our finding on the negative value of the parent teacher association, heads need to consider how to turn the PTA into a more positive aspect of school life. In our experience, PTAs too frequently become the exclusive province of a small group of committed enthusiasts. Those who do not form part of such a group – because they feel less comfortable in the group, do not have fluent English, have less time to give, or are less committed – can easily feel they are being excluded. The answer cannot be to close down the PTA, but rather to open it up so that other parents feel more welcome within it. One way of doing this is to alter its focus away from – what for some associations is their only activity – fund raising, to include other educational activities.

Record keeping

Not only do our data provide strong support for the practice of record keeping, but they underline the importance of the head being involved in the process. Records can be a time-consuming chore, or they can be an essential part of the learning and teaching of the school. In effective schools records were the latter. If heads involve themselves in the regular review of the pupils in the school, then the message to the staff is that the records matter. If records are kept up to date and used to monitor the progress of pupils then they provide a sound basis for reports, parents evenings and other ways of providing feedback to parents and pupils. In this role they are similar to the records of achievement and other kinds of profiles being used increasingly in secondary schools, as we noted in the section dealing with implications for teacher-trainers.

Positive climate

Our final key factor – the need for a positive climate in the school – has direct implications for the role of the head. As with so many of the other factors, the style of leadership exercised is important. Where the head, by example, has high expectations and sets a tone which is positive about learning and positive about pupils, it is much more likely that teachers and, indeed, pupils will also exhibit such traits. If the school is positive, and has an atmosphere in which it is expected that all pupils will succeed (even if not to the same level or at the same time) then pupils will feel valued; so will staff. Interestingly, our data show that teachers, like pupils, need to be considered. Where there was some time set aside for preparation and marking, the climate was more positive.

The role of a modern headteacher is not easy, nevertheless we were very impressed with the majority of the heads in our sample. Those in the more effective schools managed to integrate their roles as curriculum leader, resource and personnel manager, link with parents and LEA agent so that each role was carried out efficiently, and yet a high proportion of their time could be spent creating a positive climate. Clearly those that had developed leadership styles which allowed them to draw on the strengths of their colleagues without diminishing their own authority, and who enabled others to feel some ownership of the school, had enormous advantages over those who had different styles. Some even managed to create an institution in which the 'fun factor' – noted in Chapter 4 - was very obvious and provided a school in marked contrast to those in which the dominant influence was the weariness of the staff – also noted in Chapter Four. The challenge for the headteacher in seeking to create an institution with a positive climate is enormous. It is, however, extremely rewarding when it is achieved.

IMPLICATIONS FOR TEACHERS

As with heads, we believe that there are a great many implications, stemming from our data that affect teachers. In general we found the aims of teachers (as expressed in Chapter 4) worthwhile. From our observations we conclude, however, that the way these aims are implemented is very variable. Some teachers were unaware, for instance, of the power of their own actions and of how these served as a model – for good or bad – to be emulated by their pupils. Others lacked the insight to see that their expectations were lower for some pupils than for others. The area of expectations is extremely complex, and we have already drawn attention (in the implications for teacher trainers) to strategies to raise and then to sustain higher expectations: yet it is crucially important. Teachers' expectations are transmitted in both direct and subtle ways, as we have described in earlier chapters. Where they differ for groups of pupils – girls rather than boys; children from middle-class families rather than from working class; black rather than white – they are perpetuating differences in achievement that are deeply unjust.

Thus, the first implication for all classroom teachers must be the need to focus carefully on classroom practice and to challenge the existence of such differential expectations. This is, of course, related to the views of ability that we discussed at the beginning of this chapter. If teachers believe that pupils can change and that learning can become easier in the right climate, then they will transmit that positive view to their pupils. They will need to bear in mind, however, the important findings, discussed in Chapter 6, that teachers take much more note of pupils' written work than of their spoken skills in estimating their ability. Interestingly, this finding may explain why, in so many cases, the judgment of an educational psychologist (using an oral assessment) is so often more favourable than that of the class teacher who is familiar with the written work of the child. A positive view of children's development will also allow teachers to take account of the differences between those young for their year (as discussed in Chapter 7) and their peers without allowing them to lower their expectations.

We now turn to a consideration of five of the key factors concerning classroom strategies – structured sessions; intellectually challenging teaching; work centred environment; limited focus; and maximum communications. Others are important, however, and we hope teachers will take note of them and, indeed, of those we have spelled out for heads, governors and others. We will not deal in detail with the need for praise – a point we have laboured elsewhere – but we hope teachers will be assured of its importance.

Structured sessions

As noted earlier, structured sessions allow pupils freedom to manage their own work within a framework which ensures that important aspects are not omitted, and that time is not wasted. In our view it is what effective teachers have always done. The message of our study for such teachers, therefore, is to keep up the good work since such a strategy is closely related to school effectiveness. To those teachers who try to follow patterns which either allow pupils complete freedom in the classroom or no freedom at all, we would urge caution and point to our data for empirical support.

Intellectually challenging teaching

It is most unlikely that any teachers will be surprised by our finding on the efficacy of teaching which challenges pupils and, by this challenge, causes them to question their own knowledge, skills and assumptions. The only surprise might be expressed regarding the methods we identified as to how this tends to happen. As we argued earlier, some teachers see the opportunity to challenge pupils as lying in some form of individual work rather than in group or class sessions. Our data show that, in its extreme form, this is mistaken and that challenging questions were much more likely to arise from group or class sessions than from individual interactions, which tended to be preoccupied with classroom management issues. There is a simple explanation for this finding. Most individual interactions were isolated – there was seldom time for a teacher to have an extended conversation with an individual pupil – and challenging questions can seldom be put without an appropriate building up or focusing of ideas. The implication for some classroom teachers of this finding is that they may need to reconsider their classroom practice and to seek to use the opportunity of group and class sessions to promote, systematically, the sort of higher-order questions that challenge pupils. For many teachers this will be an extension of their ordinary practice; for others, we hope our data will provide evidence for a change.

Work-centred environment
This factor is also likely to surprise few teachers. Children cannot work when surrounded by distractions, where the noise level is high and movement excessive and disruptive. This is not to say that the most effective classes were silent or that pupils were kept on their chairs. Where talk was about work it was encouraged; where the learning task required movement, it was permitted but the atmosphere was first and foremost work-centred. Moreover, teachers spent more time themselves talking to pupils about the content of their work and giving work feedback. The implication of this finding, therefore, is essentially for those class teachers who have not given sufficient emphasis to the creation of such an environment.

Limited focus within sessions
This finding is related to our discussions of the need for a structure and the importance of challenging questions. In the most effective schools teachers did not usually attempt to teach in more than one or two curriculum areas simultaneously. In less effective schools, where this happened it was unusual for the teacher – even if very talented – to be able to satisfy the numerous demands made by pupils and, at the same time, to be in a position to provide intellectually – challenging teaching. Whilst recognising that, for all sorts of good reasons, teachers often wish to diversify the work in the classroom, it is important that they do not repeatedly overreach themselves. In addition, as we noted earlier, many teachers have felt that they ought to be able to handle a variety of topics at the same time. The implication of our data is that they should think again. For some teachers this will be a relief; for others, a challenge both to the preconceptions and to their ingenuity. We hope our data will provide them with sufficient reasons for re-examining their practice.

Maximum communication between teachers and pupils
The main implication for classroom teachers of this finding is that, whilst organisation before the pupils arrive is very important, once they are in the classroom, the emphasis should be on communication and interaction. We were surprised at how, in a few classrooms, the amount of communication was very limited with teachers busying themselves with administration and pupils being expected to work by themselves. This tended not to be the pattern in the most effective schools where much teacher-pupil communication took place. As noted earlier, whenever teachers engaged the attention of the whole class, they increased, vastly, the number of opportunities for communication and especially for higher-order questions to be posed or statements to be made.

This section has attempted to focus on particular implications for class teachers. We have, therefore, concentrated on the factors affecting the classroom but we hope teachers will not restrict their attention and interest to those alone, but rather that they will recognise the need to study the school as a whole. Although at the time of writing the working of the teachers' contract has only just begun, we hope teachers will use their 1265 hours to increase still further their influence on pupils.

IMPLICATIONS FOR PARENTS

We believe there are many implications for parents in our study. Some are to do with choice: schools matter; individual schools make a great deal of difference to the chances of progress for an individual pupil; the choice of which junior school to send your child to is important. Others are concerned with helping schools become more effective: the twelve key factors; the importance of parent involvement; the role of parents and governors in the life of the school. In this section we shall discuss, briefly, some of each type of implication though, as with other groups, we hope parents will find the whole of the book to be of interest and will see the interconnections of so many of the ideas drawn out in this chapter.

Parental choice
Our study provides justification for parental choice and also proves a problem to parents who wish to exercise that choice. The justification is provided by the data that demonstrate, conclusively, that whether a child attends one school or another – regardless of natural talents and family background – it is likely to make a major difference to how much progress the child makes on a variety of measures. The problem is twofold: first, it is sometimes difficult to recognise the truly effective school since its effectiveness can only be judged in relation to detailed knowledge of the characteristics of its intake; and second, that not everybody's children can fit in to the most effective schools.

The first part of the problem could be solved if all Local Education Authorities had the data and the measures to analyse it. But the second part could not. We have considered the current ideas of open enrolment and vouchers and have rejected them on the grounds that schools cannot be stretched like elastic to make room for more pupils and that, as we have described earlier, the smaller schools were, on average, more likely to be effective than were the larger ones. Whilst, therefore, choice as a principle remains important, as far as the majority of school pupils are concerned, it is more important to focus on ways to improve all schools.

Making schools more effective

We believe parents have a role to play in improving schools. One of the key factors associated with effective schools, as we have discussed earlier, is parental involvement. This enables parents to play a direct role in the life of the school which is independent from supporting the learning of their own children. There is much more, however, that parents can do to help their school. In the most effective schools, parents are deeply involved in the life of the school. Through the work of the parent governor, parents have access to a considerable amount of information about the school and about the policy choices open to its governing body. Parents bring commitment, energy, expertise and knowledge to a school and a sensitive head is able to find ways of exploiting these qualities. In some Local Education Authorities there is a tradition of consulting parents on major issues; some schools follow a similar policy and ensure that parents understand their aims and the implications of any significant changes that are being considered. In many cases consideration of those changes have been initiated by the parents themselves.

We have observed how in some schools an evening is set aside each month to allow an 'open door' meeting to take place in which parents can raise any matter of concern with the head and staff. Such meetings were affected by the prolonged teachers' action on their pay claim but are now possible within the directed time of teachers. They offer an excellent means of communication between parents and the parent governor and between parents and the staff. We recommend that they be considered by parent governors who can only benefit from the increased contact with groups of fellow parents. We hope that parents will use opportunities like the 'open door' meetings to become more involved with schools. We hope they will use this study to increase their understanding of how schools work and of how they can be improved.

SUMMARY

This chapter has been concerned with the implications of our study for the various groups involved in education: central government;

teacher-trainers; the Local Education Authorities; the teachers' professional associations; school governors; headteachers, teachers; and finally, parents. Findings with particular relevance for each of these groups have been discussed and possible implications drawn out. Finally, however, it must not be forgotten that the group for whom the implications of our study are the most serious are those who have the most to gain or lose: the pupils themselves. We have not spelled out a list of implications for pupils for, in a sense, everything we have written carries implications for their future. We hope some of the two thousand or so pupils that made up our sample – and who are now in their secondary schools – will read this book. We hope they find acceptable our interpretation of what they said and did. We thank them for their co-operation and, since any changes that are made as a result of our work to junior schools cannot now benefit them, we hope that they will be satisfied with the results and with our discussions of the implications arising from the study for all who are involved with junior education.

References

AITKIN, M., BENNETT, N. & HESKETH, J. (1981a) Teaching Styles and Pupil Progress: A Re-Analysis. British Journal of Educational Psychology. Vol. 51, Part 2, pp 170-186.

AITKIN, M., ANDERSON, D. & HINDE, J. (1981b) Statistical Modelling of Data on Teaching Styles. Journal of the Royal Statistical Society. A, Vol. 144, Part 4, pp 419-461.

ALPERT, J (1974) Teacher Behaviour Across Ability Groups: A Consideration of the Mediation of Pygmalion Effects. Journal of Educational Psychology. Vol. 66, No.3, pp 348-53.

ANDERSON, C. S. (1982) The Search for School Climate: A Review of the Research. Review of Educational Research. Vol. 52, No.3, pp 368-420.

ARMOR, D., CONRY-OSEGUERA, P., COX, M., KING, N., MCCONNELL, L., PASCAL, A., PAULY, E., & ZELLMAN, G. (1976) Analysis of the School Preferred Reading Program in selected Los Angeles Minority Schools. (Report No. R-2007- CAUSD), Santa Monica FA, The Rand Corporation.

ARMSTRONG, M. (1980) Closely Observed Children. London, Writers and Readers.

ASHTON,P., KNEEN, P., DAVIES, F. & HOLLEY, B. (1975) The Aims of Primary Education: A Study of Teachers' Opinions. Schools' Council Research Studies, London, Macmillan.

ASSESSMENT OF PERFORMANCE UNIT (APU), (1981) Language Performance in Schools. Primary Survey Report, No. 1, London, HMSO.

ASSESSMENT OF PERFORMANCE UNIT (APU), (1982) Language Performance in Schools. Primary Survey Report No. 2, London, HMSO.

BARKER LUNN, J. (1970) Streaming in the Primary School. Slough, NFER.

BARKER LUNN, J. (1971) Social Class, Attitudes and Achievement. Slough, NFER.

BARKER LUNN, J. (1982) Junior Schools and their Organizational Policies. Educational Research. Vol. 24, No. 4, pp 259-60.

BARNES, D. (1976) From Communication to Curriculum. Harmondsworth, Penguin.

BENNETT, N. (1976) Teaching Styles and Pupil Progress. London, Open Books.

BENNETT, N. (1978) Recent Research on Teaching: A Dream, a Belief, and a Model. British Journal of Educational Psychology. Vol. 48, Part 2, pp 127-147.

BLACK REPORT (1980) Inequalities in Health: Report of a Research Working Group. London, DHSS.

BLAND, R. (1979) Measuring 'Social Class': Discussion of the Registrar General's Classification. Sociology. Vol. 13, No.2, pp 283-29.

BLATCHFORD, P., BURKE, J., FARQUHAR, C., PLEWIS, I. & TIZARD, B. (1985) Educational Achievement in the Infant School: the Influence of Ethnic Origin, Gender and Home on Entry Skills. Educational Research. Vol. 27, No. 1, pp 52-60.

BOYDELL, D. (1974a) The Teacher Record: A Technique for Observing the Activities of Junior School Teachers in Informal Classrooms. University of Leicester, School of Education.

BOYDELL, D. (1974b) The Pupil Record: A Technique for Observing the Activities of Junior School Pupils in Informal Classrooms. University of Leicester, School of Education.

BOYDELL, D. (1974c) Teacher-Pupil Contact in Junior Classrooms. British Journal of Educational Psychology. Vol. 44, Part 3, pp 313-318.

BOYDELL, D. (1975) Pupil Behaviour in Junior Classrooms, British Journal of Educational Psychology. Vol. 45, Part 2, pp 122-129.

BROOKOVER, W.B., SCHWEITZER, J.H., SCHNEIDER, J.M., BEADY, C.H., FLOOD, P.K., & WISENBAKER, J.M. (1978) Elementary School Social Climate and School Achievement. American Educational Research Journal. Vol. 15, No. 2, pp 301-318.

BROOKOVER, W.B., BEADY, C., FLOOD, P., SCHWEITZER, J. (1979) School Systems and Student Achievement: Schools Make a Difference. New York, Praeger.

BROOKOVER, W.B. and LEZOTTE, L.W. (1979) Changes in School Characteristics Coincident with Changes in Student Achievement. East Langing, Institute for Research on Teaching, Michigan State University.

BROPHY, J. (1979) Teacher Behaviour and its Effects. Journal of Educational Psychology. Vol. 71, No. 6, pp 733-759.

BROPHY, J (1983) Research on the Self Fulfilling Prophecy and Teacher Expectations. Journal of Educational Psychology. Vol. 75, No. 5, pp 631-661.

BROPHY, J. & GOOD, T. (1974) Teacher Student Relationships: Causes and Consequences. New York, Holt, Rinehart & Winston.

BUNCH, C. (1984) Attitudes Revealed in Children's Stories. Research and Statistics Branch, London, ILEA.

BURSTALL, C (1968) French from Eight: A National Experiment. Occasional Publication Series, No. 18, Slough, NFER.

CALIFORNIA STATE DEPARTMENT OF EDUCATION (1980) Report on the Special Studies of Selected ECE Schools with Increasing and Decreasing Reading Scores. Sacramento, California, Office of Program Evaluation and Research.

CHATFIELD, C. (1985) The Initial Examination of Data. Journal of the Royal Statistical Society. A. Vol. 148, Part 3, pp 214-253.

CHAZAN, M. & JACKSON, S. (1974) Behaviour Problems in the Infant School: Changes over Two Years. Journal of Child Psychology and Psychiatry. Vol. 15, No. 1, pp 33-46.

COLEMAN, J.S., CAMPBELL, E., HOBSON, C., MCPART-LAND, J., MOOD, A., WEINFELD, F. & YORK, R. (1966) Equality of Educational Opportunity. Washington, National Center for Educational Statistics.

COOK, A. & MACK, H (1971) The Headteacher's Role. Schools' Council, London, Macmillan.

COULSON, A. & COX, M. (1975) What do Deputies do? Education 3-13. Vol. 3, No. 2, pp 100-103.

CROLL, P (1981) Social Class, Pupil Achievement and Classroom Interaction. In B. Simon, & J. Willcocks (Eds.) Research and Practice in the Primary Classroom. London, Routledge & Kegan Paul.

CUTTANCE, P.F. (1980a) Coleman, Plowden, Jencks and now, Rutter: An Assessment of a Recent Contribution to the Debate on School Effects. Scandinavian Journal of Educational Research. Vol. 3, pp 191-205.

CUTTANCE, P.F. (1980b) Do Schools Consistently Influence the Performance of their Students? Educational Review. Vol.32, No.3, pp.267-280.

CUTTANCE, P. (1986) Effective Schooling: A Report to the Scottish Educational Department. Centre for Educational Sociology, University of Edinburgh.

DAVIE R., BUTLER, N. & GOLDSTEIN, H. (1972) From Birth to Seven. London, Longman.

DEAN, J. (1980) Continuity. In C. Richards (Ed.) Primary Education: Issues for the Eighties. London, A & C Black.

DOUGLAS, J.W.B. (1964), The Home and the School. London, MacGibbon & Kee.

DUSEK, J. & JOSEPH, G. (1983) The Bases of Teacher Expectancies: A Meta-Analysis. Journal of Educational Psychology. Vol.75, No.3, pp 327-346.

DWECK, C.W. & REPUCCI, N.D. (1973) Learned Helplessness and Reinforcement Responsibility in Children. Journal of Personality and Social Psychology. Vol.25, pp 109-116.

ECOB, R. & SAMMONS, P. (1985) Oracy and its Relation to Other Cognitive Attainments and Socio-economic Characteristics of Pupils: Some Results from the ILEA Junior School Study.

Paper presented to the British Educational Research Association Conference, University of Sheffield, August 1985.

EDMONDS, R.R. (1979a) Effective Schools for the Urban Poor. Educational Leadership. Vol.37, No.1, pp 15-27.

EDMONDS, R.R. (1979b) Some Schools Work and More Can. Social Policy, Vol.12, No.2, pp 56-60.

EDMONDS, R.R. (1981) Making Public Schools Effective. Social Policy. Vol 12, pp 56-60.

EDMONDS, R.R., & FREDERIKSEN, J.R. (1979) Search for Effective Schools: The Identification and Analysis of City Schools that are Instructionally Effective for Poor Children. (ERIC Document Reproduction Service No. ED 170 396).

EGGLESTON, S.J., DUNN, D.K., & AJJALI, M. (1985) The Educational and Vocational Experiences of 15-18 Year Old Young People of Ethnic Minority Groups. Department of Education, University of Keele.

ESSEN, J. & GHODSIAN, M. (1979) The Children of Immigrants: School Performance. New Community, Vol. 7, No.3, pp 422-429.

ESSEN, J. & WEDGE, P. (1982) Continuities in Childhood Disadvantage. London, Heinemann.

FINDLAYSON, D.S. (1973) Measuring 'School Climate'. Trends in Education. Vol.30, No.1, pp 19-37.

FISHER, C.W., BERLINER, D.C., FILBY, N.N., MARLIAVE, R., CAHEN, L.S.& DISHAW, M.M. (1980) Teaching Behaviours, Academic Learning Time, and Student Achievement: An Overview. In C. Denham & A. Lieberman (Eds.) Time to Learn. Washington D.C., Department of Education.

FREYMAN, R. (1965) Further Evidence on the Effect of Date of Birth on Subsequent Performance. Educational Research. Vol.8, No.1, pp 58-64.

GALTON, M. & DELAFIELD, A (1981) Expectancy Effects in Primary Classrooms. In B. Simon & J. Willcocks (Eds.) Research and Practice in the Primary Classroom. London, Routledge & Kegan Paul.

GALTON, M., SIMON, B. & CROLL, P. (1980) Inside the Primary Classroom. London, Routledge & Kegan Paul.

GALTON, M. & SIMON, B. (1980) Progress and Performance in the Primary Classroom. London, Routledge & Kegan Paul.

GLENN, B.C. (1981) What Works? An Examination of Effective Schools for Poor Black Children. Cambridge Mass. Center for Law and Education, Harvard University.

GOLDSTEIN, H. (1980) Fifteen Thousand Hours: A Review of the Statistical Procedures. Journal of Child Psychology and Psychiatry. Vol.21, No.4, pp 363-366.

GOLDSTEIN, H. (1984) The Methodology of School Comparisons. Oxford Review of Education. Vol. 10, No.1, pp 69-74.

GOLDSTEIN, H. (1986) Multilevel Mixed Linear Model Analysis Using Iterative Generalised Least Squared. Biometrika. Vol. 73, pp.43-56.

GOOD, T. (1979) Teacher Effectiveness in the Elementary School: What Do we Know About it Now? Journal of Teacher Education. Vol.30, Part 2, pp 52-64.

GOOD, T. & BROPHY, J. (1971) Questioned Equality for Grade One Boys and Girls. Reading Teacher, Vol.25, No.3, pp 247-252.

GOODACRE, E. (1968) Teachers and Their Pupils' Home Background. Slough, NFER.

GOODLAD, J.I. and Others (1979) A Study of Schooling. Indiana, Phi Delta Kappa, Inc.

GORMAN, T.P., WHITE, J., HARGREAVES, M., MACLURE, M. & TATE, A. (1984) Language Performance in Schools: 1982 Primary Survey Report. Assessment of Performance Unit DES, London, HMSO.

GORMAN, T. & HARGREAVES, M. (1985) Talking Together: NFER/ILEA Oracy Survey. Slough, Department of Language, NFER

GRAY, J. (1981a) A Competitive Edge: Examination Results and the Probable Limits of Secondary School Effectiveness. Educational Review. Vol.33, No.1, pp 25-35.

GRAY, J. (1981b) Towards Effective Schools: Problems and Progress in British Research. British Educational Research Journal. Vol.7, No.1, pp 59-69.

GRAY, J. (1983) Questions of Background. Times Educational Supplement. 8th July, p 4.

GRAY, J. & HANNON, V. (1985) HMI's Interpretation of School Examination Results, Division of Education, University of Sheffield, April, 1985.

GRAY, J. & JONES, B. (1983) Disappearing Data. Times Educational Supplement, 15th July, p 4.

GRAY, J. & JONES, B. (1985) Combining Quantitative and Qualitative Approaches to Studies of School and Teacher Effectiveness. In D. Reynolds (Ed.) Studying School Effectiveness. Basingstoke, Falmer.

GROSIN, L. (1985) Theoretical Considerations and Strategy for Investigations of School Process and Pupil Outcome in the Swedish Comprehensive School. Paper presented to the British Educational Research Association Conference at the University of Sheffield, August 1985.

HARGREAVES, D. (1984) Improving Secondary Schools. London, ILEA.

HEWISON, J. & TIZARD, J. (1980) Parental Involvement and Reading Attainment. British Journal of Educational Psychology. Vol.50, Part 3, pp 209-215.

HILSUM, S. & CANE, B. (1971) The Teacher's Day. Slough, NFER.

HMI Survey (1978) Primary Education in England. London, HMSO.

HMI/DES (1985) The Curriculum from 5 to 16 (Curriculum Matters 2), London, HMSO.

HUNTER, J., KYSEL, F. & MORTIMORE, P. (1985) Children in Need: The Growing Needs of Inner London Schoolchildren. Research and Statistics Branch, RS 994/85, London, ILEA.

HUTCHISON, D., PROSSER, H. & WEDGE, P. (1979) The Prediction of Educational Failure. Educational Studies. Vol. 5, No.1, pp 73-82.

JENCKS, C.S., SMITH, M., ACKLAND, H., BANE, M.J., COHEN, D., GINTIS, H., HEYNS, B. & MICHOLSON, S. (1972) Inequality: A Reassessment of the Effect of Family and Schooling in America. New York, Basic Books.

KOUNIN, J.S. (1970) Discipline and Group Management in Classrooms. New York, Holt, Rinehart & Winston.

KYSEL, F. (1982) Language Census 1981. Research and Statistics Branch, RS 838/82, London, ILEA.

KYSEL, F., VARLAAM, A., STOLL, L. & SAMMONS, P. (1983) The Child at School – A New Behaviour Schedule. Research and Statistics Branch, RS 907/83, London, ILEA.

LEVINE, D.U. & STARK, J. (1981) Extended Summary and Conclusions: Institutional and Organizational Arrangements and Processes for Improving Academic Achievement at Inner City Elementary Schools. Kansas City, Center for the Study of Metropolitan Problems in Education, University of Missouri-Kansas City.

LITTLE, A. & MABEY, C. (1972) An Index for Designation of Educational Priority Areas. In A. Shonfield & S. Shaw (Eds.) Social Indicators and Social Policy. London, Heinemann.

LITTLE, A. & MABEY, C (1973) Reading Attainment and Social and Ethnic Mix of London Primary Schools. In D. Donnison & D. Eversley (Eds.) London: Urban Patterns, Problems, and Policies. London, Heinemann.

LUZIO, J. (1983) A Study of Some Small Schools in Hackney 1982-1983. Research & Statistics Branch, London, ILEA.

MABEY, C. (1981) Black British Literacy: A Study of Reading Attainment of London Black Children from 8 to 15 years. Educational Research. Vol.23, Part 2, pp 83-95.

MABEY, C. (1985) Achievement of Black Pupils: Reading Competence as a Predictor of Exam Success among Afro-Caribbean Pupils in London. Ph.D thesis, University of London.

MACCOBY, E. & JACKLIN, C. (1980) Psychological Sex Differences, In M. Rutter (Ed.) Scientific Foundations of Developmental Psychiatry. London, Heinemann.

MADAUS, G.F., KELLAGHAN, T., RAKOW, E.A. & KING, D.J. (1979) The Sensitivity of Measures of School Effectiveness. Harvard Educational Review. Vol.49, No.2, pp 207-230.

MARJORIBANKS, K. (1979) Families and their Learning Environments: An Empirical Analysis. London, Routledge & Kegan Paul.

MARKS, J., COX, C. & POMIAN-SRZEDNICKI, M. (1983) Standards in English Schools. London, National Council for Educational Standards.

MARKS, J., COX, C. & POMIAN-SRZEDNICKI, M. (1986) ILEA Examination Performance in Secondary Schools. London, National Council for Educational Standards.

MARLAND, M. (1975) The Craft of the Classroom: A Survival Guide. London, Heinemann.

MAUGHAN, B., MORTIMORE, P., OUSTON, J. & RUTTER, M. (1980) Fifteen Thousand Hours: A Reply to Heath and Clifford. Oxford Review of Education. Vol.6, No. 3, pp 289-303.

MEYER, W.U. (1982) Indirect Communications about Perceived Ability Estimates. Journal of Educational Psychology. Vol.74, No.6, pp 888-897.

MOOS, R.H. (1978) A Typology of Junior High and High School Classrooms. American Educational Research Journal. Vol. 15, pp 53-66.

MORTIMORE, J. & BLACKSTONE, T. (1982) Disadvantage in Education. London, Heinemann.

MORTIMORE, P. (1979) The Study of Secondary Schools: A Researcher's Reply, in The Rutter Research: Perspectives 1. School of Education, University of Exeter

MORTIMORE, P. (1983) Achievement in Schools. Research and Statistics Branch, RS 829/82, London, ILEA.

MORTIMORE, P. & MORTIMORE, J. (1984) Parents and School, Education Special Report. Education 5th October.

MORTIMORE, P., SAMMONS, P., STOLL, L., LEWIS, D., & ECOB, R. (1986a) The Junior School Project: A Summary of the Main Report, Research & Statistics Branch, London, ILEA.

MORTIMORE, P., SAMMONS, P. STOLL, L., LEWIS, D. & ECOB, R. (1986b) The Junior School Project: Main Report Parts A, B, C & Technical Appendices, Research & Statistics Branch, London, ILEA.

MURPHY, J. (1974) Teacher Expectations and Working-Class Underachievement. British Journal of Sociology. Vol.25, No.3, pp 326-44.

NASH, R. (1973) Classrooms Observed: The Teacher's Perception and Pupil's Performance. London, Routledge & Kegan Paul.

O'SHEA, A.T. (1984) Management in Primary Education – An Evaluation of the Department of Education's Programme of Training in Education Management for Principals of Primary Schools in Northern Ireland. Northern Ireland Council for Educational Research.

PALARDY, J. (1969) What Teachers Believe – What Children Achieve. Elementary School Journal. Vol.69, pp 370-374.

PIDGEON, D. (1970) Expectation and Pupil Performance. Slough, NFER.

PILLING, D. & KELLMER PRINGLE, M. (1978) Controversial Issues in Child Development. National Children's Bureau. London, Paul Elek.

PLEWIS, I. (1985) Progress in Language and Mathematics in the Reception Year of Infant School: A Preliminary Analysis. London, Thomas Coram Research Unit.

PLOWDEN REPORT (1967) Children and their Primary Schools. London, HMSO.

POWELL, J. & SCRIMGEOUR, M. (1977) System for Classroom Observation of Teaching Strategies. Edinburgh, Scottish Council for Research in Education.

PRAIS, S.J. (1983) Formal and Informal Teaching: a Further Reconsideration of Professor Bennett's Statistics. Journal of the Royal Statistical Society. A. Vol. 146, Part 2, pp 163-169.

PRIMARY MANAGEMENT STUDIES (1978) So Now You Are a Deputy Head. Primary Management Report PM4/78, London, ILEA.

PROSHANSKY, H. & NEWTON, P. (1968) The Nature and Meaning of Negro Self-Identity, In M. Deutsch, I. Katz & A. Jensen (Eds.) Social Class, Race and Psychological Development. New York, Holt.

PURKEY, S.C. & SMITH, M.S. (1983) Effective Schools: A Review. Elementary School Journal. Vol.83, No.4, pp 427-452.

RADICAL STATISTICS EDUCATION GROUP (1982) Reading Between the Numbers: A Critical Guide to Educational Research. London, BSSRS, 9, Poland Street, London W1V 3DG.

RALPH, J.H. & FENNESSEY, J. (1983) Science or Reform: Some Questions about the Effective Schools Model. Phi Delta Kappan. Vol.64, Part 10, pp 689-694.

RAMPTON REPORT (1981) West Indian Children in Our Schools: Interim Report of the Committee from Ethnic Minority Groups. London, HMSO.

RATHBONE, M. & GRAHAM N.C. (1981) Parent Participation in the Primary School. Educational Studies. Vol.7, No.2, pp.145-150.

REYNOLDS, D. (1982) The Search for Effective Schools. School Organisation. Vol. 2, No.3, pp 215-237.

REYNOLDS, D. (Ed.) (1985) Studying School Effectiveness. London, Falmer.

REYNOLDS, D. & MURGATROYD, S. (1977) The Sociology of Schooling and the Absent Pupil: The School as a Factor in the Generation of Truancy. In H.C.M. CARROLL (Ed.) Absenteeism in South Wales: Studies of Pupils, their Homes and their Secondary Schools, University College of Swansea, Faculty of Education.

ROSENSHINE, B. & BERLINER, D.C. (1978) Academic Engaged Time. British Journal of Teacher Education, Vol.4, Part 1, pp 3-16.

ROSENSHINE, B. & STEVENS, R. (1981) Advances in Research on Teaching. Unpublished manuscript, University of Illinois, May 1981.

ROSENTHAL, R. & JACOBSON, L. (1968) Pygmalion in the Classroom: Teacher Expectation and Pupils' Intellectual Development. Holt, Rinehart and Winston, New York.

ROWAN, B., BOSSERT, S.T. & DWYER, D.C. (1983) Research on Effective Schools: A Cautionary Note. Educational Researcher. Vol.12, No.4, pp 24-31.

RUNHAM, J. (1985) Secondary Transfer Project: Bulletin 6 – Pupils' Early Experiences of Secondary School. Research and Statistics Branch, RS 1003/85, London, ILEA.

RUSSELL, R. & STARTUP, M. (1986) Month of Birth and Academic Achievement. Personality and Individual Differences. Vol.7, No. 6, pp 839-846.

RUTTER, M. (1983) School Effects on Pupil Progress: Research Findings and Policy Implications. Child Development. Vol.54, No.1, pp 1-29.

RUTTER, M. & MADGE, N. (1976) Cycles of Disadvantage. London, Heinemann.

RUTTER, M., MAUGHAN, B., MORTIMORE, P. & OUSTON, J. (1979) Fifteen Thousand Hours. London, Open Books.

RUTTER, M., MAUGHAN, B., MORTIMORE, P. & OUSTON, J. (1980) Educational Criteria of Success; A Reply to Action. Educational Research., Vol.22, No.3, pp.170-174.

SAMMONS, P., KYSEL, F. & MORTIMORE, P. (1983) Educational Priority Indices: A New Perspective. British Educational Research Journal. Vol.9, No.1, pp. 27-40.

SAMMONS, P., MORTIMORE, P., & VARLAAM, A. (1985) Socio-economic Background, Parental Involvement and Attitudes, and Children's Achievements in Junior Schools. Research and Statistics Branch, RS 982/85, London, ILEA.

SAMMONS, P. & STOLL, L. (1988) Me at School – A Measure of Primary Pupils' Self-Concepts. Research and Statistics Branch, London, ILEA (forthcoming).

SERBIN, L. A. (1983) The Hidden Curriculum: Academic Consequences of Teacher Expectations, In M. Marland (Ed.) Sex Differentiation and Schooling. London, Heinemann.

SHARP, R. & GREEN, A. (1975) Education and Social Control – A Study in Progressive Primary Education. London, Routledge & Regan Paul

SHORT, G. (1985) Teacher Expectation and West Indian Underachievement. Educational Research. Vol.27, No.2, pp 95-101.

SIMON, B. (1980) Inside the Primary Classroom. Forum, Vol.22, No.3, pp 68-70.

SIMPSON, S.N. (1982) Statistical Assessment of School Effects Using Educational Survey Data. Ph.D. thesis, University of London.

SOLOMON, D. & KENDALL, A.J. (1976) Final Report: Individual Characteristics and Children's Performance in Varied Educational Settings. Chicago, Spencer Foundation Project.

STALLINGS, J.A. (1976) How Instructional Processes Relate to Child Outcomes in a National Study of Follow Through. Journal of Teacher Education. Vol.27, Part 1, pp 43-47.

STOLL, L. & SAMMONS, P. (1988) Smiley – A Scale for Measuring Primary Pupils' Attitudes. Research and Statistics Branch, London, ILEA (forthcoming).

STONE, M. (1981) The Education of the Black Child in Britain: The Myth of Multiracial Education. Glasgow, Fontana.

STRACHAN, V. & SAMMONS, P. (1986) ILEA Junior School Project: The Assessment of Creative Writing. Research and Statistics Branch, London, ILEA.

STRIVENS, J. (1985) School Climate: A Review of a Problematic Concept, In D. Reynolds (Ed.) Studying School Effectiveness. London, Falmer.

SUMMERS, A.A. & WOLFE, B.L. (1977) Do Schools Make a Difference? American Economic Review. Vol.64, pp 639-652.

SWANN REPORT (1985) Education for All: The Report of the Committee of Inquiry into the Education of Children from Ethnic Minority Groups. London, HMSO.

TAYLOR, W. (1985) The Task of the School and the Task of the Teacher. Paper presented to the DES conference on Better School Evaluation and Appraisal for Both Schools and Teachers, University of Birmingham, November 1985.

THOMAS, N. (1985) Improving Primary Schools: Report of the Committee on Primary Education (The Thomas Report). London, ILEA.

THOMPSON, D. (1971) Season of Birth and Success in the Secondary School. Educational Research. Vol.14, No.1, pp 56-60.

TIZARD, B., BURGESS, T., FRANCIS, H., GOLDSTEIN, H., YOUNG, M., HEWISON, J. & PLEWIS, P. (1980) Fifteen Thousand Hours: A Discussion. Bedford Way Papers 1. University of London, Institute of Education

TIZARD, J. SCHOFIELD, W. & HEWISON, J. (1982) Collaboration between Teachers and Parents in Assisting Children's Reading. British Journal of Educational Psychology, Vol.52, Part 1, pp 1-15.

TOEWS, J. & MURRAY BARKER, D. (1985) The Baz Attack: A School Improvement Experience Utilizing Effective Schools Research. Calgary, Calgary Board of Education.

TOMLINSON, T.M. (1980) Student Ability, Student Background and Student Achievement: Another Look at Life in Effective Schools. Paper presented at the Educational Testing Service Conference on Effective Schools. New York, May 1980.

TRAUB, R., WEISS, J. & FISHER, C. (1976) Openness in Schools: An Evaluation, Research in Education: Series 5, Toronto, OISE.

TRISMAN, D.A., WALLER, M.I. & WILDER, C.A. (1976) A Descriptive and Analytic Study of Compensatory Reading Programs: Final report. Princeton, N.J., Educational Testing Service.

UNITED STATES DEPARTMENT OF EDUCATION (1986) What Works Research About Teaching and Learning. Washington, United States Department of Education.

VARLAAM, A. (1974) Educational Attainment and Behaviour. Greater London Intelligence Quarterly. No.29, pp 29-37.

VARLAAM, A., WOODS, J., MORTIMORE, P., & SAMMONS, P. (1985) Parents and Primary Schools. Research and Statistics Branch, RS 987/85, London, ILEA.

WEBER, G. (1971) Inner-City Children can be Taught to Read: Four Successful Schools. Washington, D.C., Council for Basic Education.

WHYTE, J. (1983) Beyond the Wendy House: Sex Role Stereotyping in Primary Schools. York, Longman Schools Council Resources Unit.

WIDLAKE, P. (1980) Primary-School Practice and Pupil Success, Ch. 7 In M. Marland (Ed.) Education for the Inner City, London, Heinemann.

WILLIAMS, P. (1964) Date of Birth, Backwardness and Educational Organisation. British Journal of Educational Psychology. Vol. 34, Part 3, pp 247-255.

WILLMS J.D. & CUTTANCE, P. (1985) School Effects in Scottish Secondary Schools. British Journal of the Sociology of Education. Vol.6, No.3, pp 289-306.

WYLIE, R. C. (1963) Children's Estimates of their Schoolwork Ability as a Function of Sex, Race, and Socio-Economic Level. Journal of Personality. Vol. 31, pp 203-24.

APPENDIX 1:
The Secondary Transfer Project

Introduction

In a four year longitudinal study carried out by Research and Statistics Branch, the ILEA has been following the progress and development of a cohort of children in 50 junior schools. These children transferred to secondary school in September 1984. At this date 49 of the schools remained in the study.

The Secondary Transfer Project has studied the transition to secondary school of approximately 1600 pupils from these primary schools. The children's attitudes, attainments, behaviour and attendance have been examined before transfer and during their first two terms at secondary school. The transfer practices of primary and secondary schools have also been investigated. In addition, the views of parents have been sought, before and after transfer. Finally, primary and secondary teachers have been asked to comment on ways of making transfer at age 11 easier. The aim of the project has been to investigate ways in which transition could be improved, for pupils, parents and teachers. A more detailed explanation of the methods of study is given in Bulletin 1. The following bulletins are available

Bulletin 1	An introduction
Bulletin 2	The views of primary school pupils
Bulletin 3	The views of parents before transfer
Bulletin 4	The views of primary teachers and headteachers
Bulletin 5	'My first day at school' – pupils' first impressions
Bulletin 6	Pupils' early experiences of secondary school
Bulletin 7	The views of secondary school teachers
Bulletin 8	Pupils' views of secondary school – a follow up
Bulletin 9	The views of parents after transfer
Bulletin 10	Primary/secondary liaison
Bulletin 11	The first year at secondary school: general, curricular and pastoral organisation
Bulletin 12	Equal opportunities
Bulletin 13	Special needs
Bulletin 14	Reading attainment and progress
Bulletin 15	Attendance – before and after transfer
Bulletin 16	Pupils' adjustment to secondary school
Bulletin 17	The Secondary Transfer Project – an overview

Index

ability: flexible views on, 264; and teacher expectations, 169–71:- behaviour and, 172–5
absences, teacher, 72; *see also* attendance
accommodation difficulties, 10
activities, management of children's, 64–9
aesthetic curriculum, 18
age differences: in cognitive and non-cognitive attainment, 118–29, 278; and teacher expectations, 163–4
age of entry, of sample pupils, 94–5
aims, headteachers; see headteachers
aims, teachers', 52–5, 285
Aitkin, M., 2, 7
Alpert, J., 170
amalgamations, school, 38
Anderson, C. S., 60
APU, *see* Assessment of Performance Unit
Armor, D., 256, 258, 259, 260
Armstrong, M., 2
art, teaching of, 89–90
Ashton, P., 52
Asian children: attainment, 152–62; intake, 92, 177–8; and teacher expectations, 168–9
assemblies, 20
assessment, teachers' of pupils' ability; see teachers, assessment
Assessment of Performance Unit (APU), Language Survey (1981, 1982), 5, 117, 143, 145, 146; see also Gorman
atmosphere; see classroom; school climate
attainment: at entry, 96–8; impact of school on, 185–92; relationship with attendance, 116; relationship with attitudes, 115; relationship with behaviour, 114–15
attainment level, differences between schools, and school intakes, 181–2
attendance: age factor in, 126–7; development during junior years, 104; impact of schools on, 195–6; and race factor, 159; relationship with attainment, 116; sex difference factor,

150; and social class factor, 139–40
attitudes: age factor in, 127; development during junior years, 104–8; impact of schools on, 197–9; and race factor, 159; relationship with attainment, 115; sex difference factor, 149–50; and social class factor, 140; to curriculum, by teachers, 79–80; see also "Smiley" attitude assessment
audio-visual departments, 10
Audit Commission report (1986), 274
autonomy, pupil, 54

background, impact of differences on cognitive attainment, 117–62
Barker Lunn, J., 13, 15, 34, 164, 169
Barnes, D., 78
behaviour: at entry, 97–8; control of, 67–9; development during junior years, 102–4; impact of schools on, 194–5; relationship with attainment, 114–15; and teacher expectations, 171–5; see also "Child at School" behaviour schedule
behaviour difficulties, 20: age factor in, 125–6; and race factor, 158–9; in school intakes, 182–3; sex difference factor, 148–9; and social class factor, 139
Bengali, children speaking, 153
Bennett, N., 2, 7, 81
Berliner, D. C., 259
Black Report (1980), 130, 139
Blackstone, T., 21, 117
Bland, R., 130
Blatchford, P., 96
Boydell, D., 6, 83
boys, *see* sex difference
Broader Perspectives course, 45
Brookover, W. B., 1, 256, 259, 261
Brophy, J., 163, 166, 170, 258
Brunel University, 280
buildings, school, 9–10, 249: disruption from work on, 38; and LEAs, 275; shared, 30
Bunch, C., 101, 145, 154

Burstall, C., 169
Burt, Sir Cyril, 264

California State Department of
    Education, 256, 257, 258, 260
Canada, 263, 265, 272, 276, 279
Cane, B., 15, 42, 67
career development, deputy
    headteachers', 50–1
Caribbean children: attainment, 152–62;
    differences in school effectiveness,
    211–13; intake, 92, 177–8; and teacher
    expectations, 168–9
change, in junior schools, 32–9; see also
    management structure; teachers
Chartered Institute of Public Finance and
    Accountancy (CIPFA), 92
Chatfield, C., 7
Chazan, M., 149
Checkpoints scheme, 18, 76
"Child at School" behaviour schedule, 97,
    102, 169
children young in their years, support for,
    and LEAs, 278
Chinese children, attainment, 152
Church of England schools, 12
class; see also classroom; social class
class interactions, and school
    effectiveness, 228
class organisation and policies, 5–6
class size, 13–14: implications for
    headteachers, 281; and LEAs, 274–5;
    and school effectiveness, 226–7, 242
class teachers, see teachers
classes: criteria for allocation to, 14–15;
    number of, 13–14; single or mixed-age,
    14
classroom: appearance of, 267;
    atmosphere, 5, 60–4: and school
    effectiveness, 241; layout, 55–7;
    planning, 55–60; relationships, 63–4;
    teachers in, 52–77
classroom groupings, and the curriculum,
    80–3
classroom policies, and school
    effectiveness, 227–31
climate: see classroom atmosphere; school
    climate
code of practice for parental involvement,
    proposed, 279
cognitive development, 98–102, 111–16:
    by age, 119–25, 128–9; by race, 151–8;
    by sex, 142–8, 151; by social class,
    130–8; impact of schools on, 185–92,
    200–2; schools good at fostering, 192–4,
    202–4
Coleman, J. S., 1, 186
communication, teacher-pupil, 83–5:
    implications for teachers, 288; and

school effectiveness, 227, 238–9, 254:-
    studies, 259–60; and teacher-training,
    270; see also class interactions
community, parents and the, 30
competence, intellectual, 54
computers, in schools, 10
consistency, and school effectiveness, 224
control, classroom, 67–9, 241; see also
    discipline
Cook, A., 41
Coulson, A., 47, 257
county schools, 12: and LEAs, 273
course attendance, teachers', 71: and
    school effectiveness, 224
Cox, M., 47, 257
craft, teaching of, 89–90
criticism, and school effectiveness, 230–1,
    241
Croll, P., 164
cultural aims, 53
curriculum, 78–91: deputies' role re, 50;
    dividing the, 78–80; guidelines, 17; and
    the headteacher, 42; "hidden", see sex
    stereotyping; limited focus:-
    implications for teachers, 287; and
    school effectiveness, 253:- studies, 259;
    and teacher-training, 269–70; mix of
    activities, and school effectiveness,
    90–1, 228–9; planning, and school
    effectiveness, 224; proposed national,
    266
curriculum policies, 17–20: change in, 37–8
Cuttance, P. F., 176, 183, 213, 256

dance, 18
Davie, R., 21
day, school, see school day
Dean, J., 260
decoration, school, disruption from, 38
Delafield, A., 170, 172
denominational schools, and LEAs, 273;
    see also voluntary schools
Department of Education and Science, 5,
    265–6
deputy headteachers, 46–51:
    administrative responsibilities, 48;
    advisory role, curriculum, 50; career
    development, 50–1; change of, 36–7:-
    and school effectiveness, 245; class
    teaching by, 47–8; desire for change in
    responsibility, 50; headteachers' view of
    role, 51; involvement in policy, 48–9:-
    implications for headteachers, 281–2;
    and school effectiveness, 247–8, 251:-
    studies, 257; job satisfaction, 50;
    pastoral care – of pupils, 49, of staff, 49;
    role, 47, 51; views on contacts with
    parents, 24
development, 53: at entry, of sample
    pupils, 96–8; during junior years,

cognitive and non-cognitive, 98–116; *see also* cognitive developments; non-cognitive development
directions, from teachers to pupils, 64; work, 82–3
disadvantage: changes over time, in school intake, 180–1; overcoming, 214–17
discipline, deputy headteachers and, 49
discussion, informal, among teachers, 72
display, classroom, 60
disruption, in lives of sample schools, 38–9
divisional offices, local, 31
Douglas, J. W. B., 21
drama, 18
Dusek, J., 164
Dweck, C. W., 170, 175

Ecob, R., 136
Edinburgh Reading Test (ERT), 4
Edmonds, R. R., 1, 258, 260, 261
Education Act (1944), 31, 265
Education Act (1986), 280
Education Act (1987), 281
Educational Priority factors, 181; and school effectiveness, 232
Education Reform Bill, 31, 266
educational outcomes, cognitive and non-cognitive, 4–5
effectiveness, search for, 1–8; *see also* school effectiveness
Eggleston, S. J., 117, 168
England, primary class size, 274
English children, *see* ESWI
English language, fluency in sample pupils, 93, 181; and attainment, 151–62
English as a Second Language (ESL), 19, 30
enthusiasm, teacher, 63
equal opportunities, 28; policies, 117–18
Essen, J., 117, 132, 180
ESWI (English, Scottish, Welsh or Irish) children, 152, 156, 158, 159, 160, 161; intake, 177–8; and teacher expectations, 168
ethnic background: of sample pupils, 92–3; in school intakes, 177–8; and teacher expectations, 168–9
expectations, see teachers

families: influence on child development, 1; one-parent, 179, 181
family size; and cognitive attainment, 117; of sample pupils, 94; in school intakes, 180
feedback on work, 85
Fennessey, J., 183
Fifteen Thousand Hours (Rutter et al.), 1–2, 272

Findlayson, D. S., 60
Fisher, C. W., 259
"Fletcher" maths series, 88
forecasts, work, by teachers, 59; and school effectiveness, 224
Frederiksen, J. R., 261
Freyman, R., 118

Galton, M., 2, 6, 64, 81, 170, 172, 173, 228, 249, 258, 259–60
GAP test, 75
gender, *see* sex differences
Ghodsian, M., 117
gifted children, 20
girls, *see* sex differences
Glenn, B. C., 257, 258, 259
Goldstein, H., 2, 7, 183
Good, T., 1, 163, 166
Goodacre, E., 164
Goodlad, J. I., 1
Gorman, T., 5, 102, 146, 190
governing bodies, 30–1
government implications of school effectiveness study for, 265–7; policies, 31
governors, school, implications of school effectiveness study for, 280
Graham, N. C., 21
grant-maintained schools, outside jurisdiction of LEAs, 274
grants: central government support, 266; rate support, 266
Gray, J., 2, 3, 181, 183, 185, 186
Greek children: attainment, 152, 153; intake, 177
Green, A., 164
Grosin, L., 256
groups, classroom, 80–3: criteria for membership, 81; and school effectiveness, 230
groups, within sample pupils, 117–62
guidelines, use of curriculum, 17
Gujerati, children speaking, 152–5

handicaps: of sample pupils, 95; in school intakes, 180
Hannon, V., 183
Hargreaves, D., 5, 190, 260-261
Hargreaves, M., 5, 102, 190
headteachers, 40–51; aims for their pupils, 41; change of, 36–7; and LEAs, 275–6; contact with children, 43–4; contact with parents and outside agencies, 22, 46; contacts with staff, 45–6; and the curriculum, 42; decision-making, 43; emphasis on basic skills, and school effectiveness, 224, 235; implications of school effectiveness study for, 281–5; influence on teaching strategies, 42;

involvement with staff, 44–5;
leadership, and school effectiveness,
234, 246, 250–1;- studies, 256–7;
pastoral care of pupils, 44; role of, 41;
staff appraisal and development, 45;
support to new, and LEAs, 276–8;
teaching, 43; time in present post, and
school effectiveness, 222, 244–5;- and
policies, 237–8; view of their role, 41–2
headteachers' centres, proposed, 277
health problems: of sample pupils, 95; in
school intakes, 180
Her Majesty's Inspectorate (HMI), 2, 31,
39, 78, 183, 266, 267
Hewison, J., 260
"higher-order" communication, 84; and
school effectiveness, 229
Hilsum, S., 15, 42, 67
HMI, *see* Her Majesty's Inspectorate
home background, *see* families; parents;
race; social class
homework, 20
Hunter, J., 94, 117, 180
Hutchison, D., 21, 181, 186

ILEA, 14: Education Welfare Service
(EWS), 32; funding of education
service, 264; Schools' Psychological
Service (SPS), 32; Secondary Transfer
Bulletins, 30, 264, 301
in-service training courses, 37, 45, 50;-
attendance at, 71; and school
effectiveness, 224
income, levels, in school intakes, 179–80
infant departments, schools with and
without, 11–12; *see* also *junior-only; JMI*
infant school experience, age factor and,
128–9
Infant School Project, 96
influences on schools, outside, 29–32
information, from teachers to pupils, 64
Inner London Education Authority, *see*
ILEA
inspections, school, disruption from, 39
inspectorate support, 31
institutions, influence on schools, 29–30
intelligence, views of, 264
investment, in education, 264
Irish children, *see* ESWI

Jacklin, C., 117
Jackson, S., 149
Jacobson, L., 169
Jencks, C. S., 1, 185, 186
JM, schools without infant departments;
see junior-only schools
JMI, schools with infant departments, 9;
and school effectiveness, 231
job satisfaction, teacher, 72

Jones, B., 3, 183, 186
Joseph, G., 164
junior school: 9; change in the, 32–9;
effectiveness studies, 1–8; *see school
effectiveness*
junior-only schools, and school
effectiveness, 221–2, 231, 244;- policies
and, 237

Kellmer Pringle, M., 138, 163, 164, 258
Kendall, A. J., 258
Key factors for effectiveness, 248-56
Kounin, J. S., 269
Kysel, F., 97

language: of sample pupils, 92–3; in school
intakes, 177–8; teaching of, 87; use of
textbooks, 230
leadership: implications for headteachers,
281; studies, and school effectiveness,
234, 246, 250–1, 256–7
learning difficulties, 19–20
Leicester University, 6, 249
Leverhulme Trust, 263
Levine, D. U., 257, 258, 260
Lezotte, L. W., 259
library, 10
Little, A., 176
local education authorities (LEAs), 30;
implications of school effectiveness
study for, 272–9, 289; policies, 31;
relationship with central government,
265, 266–7
London Reading Test (LRT), 5, 99, 119,
132, 143
LRT, *see* London Reading Test
Luzio, J., 13, 221

Mabey, C., 117, 152, 176
Maccoby, E., 117
Mack, H., 41
Madge, N., 117, 180
management, of children's activities in
school, 64–9
management courses for deputies, 47
management structure, change in, and
school effectiveness, 222
Marjoribanks, K., 117
Marks, J., 3, 183
Marland, M., 269
materials, teaching, use of, 85–6
mathematics, 4, 18, 19: age factors in
attainment, 120–1; attainment at entry,
96; attainment during junior years, 99,
101; impact of school on progress and
attainment, 187–8, 215–16; race factor
in, 153–4; relationship with reading
performance, 112; sex difference in,
144; social class factor in, 133–4;
teaching of, 88; use of textbooks, 230

mathematics, practical: age factors in attainment, 122–3; impact of school on progress and attainment, 191–2; race factor in, 154; sex difference in, 146; social class factor in, 136

"Maths Adventure" series, 88

Maughan, B., 186

"Me at School' self-concept assessment, 109

meals, free school, 92, 181

meetings: for parents, 22–3, 289:- attendance at, 26–7; staff, 28–9

Meyer, W. U., 163

mobility, pupil, 33–4

mobility in classroom: pupil, 65; teacher, 65–6

monitoring of pupils, 67

Moos, R. H., 60, 261

moral aims, 53

Mortimore, J., 21, 117, 260

Mortimore, P., 7, 21, 114, 117, 130, 186, 218, 220, 260

movement, classroom, and school effectiveness, 227, 240; *see also* mobility in classroom

Murgatroyd, S., 196

Murphy, J., 164, 172

Murray Barker, D., 272

music, 18

Nash, R., 163, 164

National Child Development Study, 180

National Children's Bureau, 132

National Foundation for Educational Research, Basic Mathematics Test (BMT), 4, 19, 76

Neale Analysis, 75

Newton, 160

NFER, *see* National Foundation for Educational Research

noise, classrooom, 65; and school effectiveness, 227, 240

non-cognitive development, 102–11, 113–16: by age, 125–7, 128–9; by race, 158–62; by sex, 148–51; by social class, 138–41; during junior years, 102–11, 113–16; impact of schools on, 194–9, 200–2; schools good at fostering, 199–200, 202–4

non-teaching time, 71; and school effectiveness, 225

nursery experience: of sample pupils, 94; in school intakes, 180

occupations, parental, of sample pupils, 93–4

Oracle survey, 6, 64; see also Galton

oracy: age factors in attainment, 123; attainment during junior years, 101–2; impact of school on progress and attainment, 190–1; race factor in, 155; relationship with reading performance, 112; sex difference in, 146; social class factor in 136–7

oral skills, 5; *see also* oracy

O'Shea, A. T., 41

Palardy, J., 166

Parent-Teachers' Associations (PTAs), 21–2, 26:- and school effectiveness, 226, 255; implications for headteachers, 284

parental choice, implications, 288–9

parental income levels, of sample pupils, 93–4

parents: attendance at school meetings, 26–7; and the community, 30; contact with headteachers, 22, 46; contacts with staff, 26; help from, 23–4, 27; implications of school effectiveness study for, 288–9; informing about children's progress, 25; involvement, 21–8, 289:- implications for headteachers, 283–4; and LEAs, 278–9; proposed code of practice for, 279; and school effectiveness, 226, 234–5, 255: studies, 260–1, 283–4; and teacher-training, 271; meetings for, 22–3, 26–7, 289; occupation:- and cognitive attainment, 130–42; of sample pupils, 93–4; in school intakes, 178–9; policies for increased power of, 266; role in school effectiveness, 289; views of children's schools, 6, 25–8:- satisfaction, 25–6

part-time teachers, 72–3

pastoral care: by deputy headteachers, of pupils and staff, 49; by headteachers, 44

personal development, 53

physical education, teaching of, 90

Pidgeon, D., 164

Pilling, D., 138, 163, 164, 258

planning, classroom, 55–60

Plewis, I., 186

Plowden Report (1967), 13, 41, 47, 176, 233, 257

postholders, 70–1

Powell, J., 6

Prais, S. J., 7

praise: and school effectiveness, 230–1; and teacher-training, 271–2

preparation time, teachers, 59–60

primary education, school effectiveness study, aims 3; data, 3–6; methods of analysis, 7–8; *see also* school effectiveness

Primary Management Studies Report (1978), 47

Primary Yearly Record Summary, 166, 254

probationary teachers, 72
progress, pupils', 92–116: impact of school on, 185–92
project work, teaching of, 88–9
Proshansky, H., 160
PTA, *see* Parent-Teachers' Associations
punishments, and school effectiveness, 225
Punjabi, children speaking, 152
pupil groupings, and school effectiveness, 223, 230
pupil intakes, 3–4, 176–83
pupil mobility, 33–4
pupil sample, characteristics of, 92–8
pupil-teacher ratio (PTR), 13–14: average for primary schools in England (1986), 274–5
pupils: individual assessment, *see* teachers, assessment of pupils' ability; responsibility for managing work, and school effectiveness, 229–30; teachers' involvement with, 62; work contacts, 83–5; work involvement, and school effectiveness, 239
pupils' progress, 92–116: impact of school on, 185–92
Purkey, S. C., 2, 183, 203, 256, 261

race: differences in cognitive and non-cognitive attainment, 117, 151–62; differences in school effectiveness, 211–13; *see also* ethnic background
Radical Statistics Education Group, 7
Ralph, J. H., 183
Rampton Report (1981), 117, 152, 168
rate-capping, 266, 267
Rathbone, M., 21
reading, 4: age factors in attainment, 119–20; attainment at entry, 96; attainment during junior years, 98–9; impact of school on progress and attainment, 185–7; race factor in, 151–3; relationship with writing performance, 111; sex difference in, 142–3; social class factor in, 131–3; teaching of, 86–7
record-keeping, by teachers, 75–7: implications for headteachers, 284; and school effectiveness, 223, 254:- studies, 260; and teacher-training, 270–1
Registrar's General classification of social class; see social class
relationships, in the classroom, 63–4
religious aims, 54
Repucci, N. D., 170, 175
resources: availability of, 10; central government control of educational, 266; use of, 85–6
rewards, and school effectiveness, 225
Reynolds, D., 1, 140, 185, 196, 256
rolls: first year, 12–13; junior pupil, 13

Roman Catholic schools, 12
rooms, use of, 10
Rosenshine, B., 258, 259
Rosenthal, R., 169
Rowan, B., 237, 256
rules, school, attitudes of sample pupils towards, 107
Russell, R., 128, 129
Rutter, M., 1, 7, 60, 117, 180, 185, 196, 209, 237, 242, 249, 256, 257, 258, 259, 261, 272

Sammons, P., 33, 99, 101, 104, 109, 117, 118, 130, 136, 176, 180
sample schools, difference in size, 12–13
Schonell Graded Word Test, 75
school, importance of individual, 176–205, 265
school buildings, 9–10, 249: disruption from work on, 38; and LEAs, 275; shared, 30
school climate: implications for headteachers, 284–5; and school effectiveness, 235, 247, 255–6:- studies, 261
school day, 15–17: end to, 62–3; start to, 60–1; structuring of, and school effectiveness, 241, 252:- studies, 258
school effectiveness, 176–205: class level – "given" factors, 226–7, 241–5, policies, 227–31, 238–42; differences in, 206–62; and disadvantage, 214–17; factors tested, 218–20; identifying the mechanisms of, 231–48; key factors, 248–56; key question, 248; links with other studies, 256–62; methods, 220; parents' role in, 289; relationship between school and class level "given" factors, 242–5; relationship between school and class level policies, 245–8; school level – "given" factors, 220–3, 231–5, policies, 223–6, 235–8; search for, 1–8; towards improving, 263–90; understanding, 218–62
school effects: how to study, 183–5; on pupils' progress and attainment, 185–92
school environment, 5: and school effectiveness, 222
school governors, implications of school effectiveness study for, 280
school intakes, 176–83
school life, 6
School Mathematics project, 76
school organisation, 5, 11–13: change in, 37–8
school policies, 5, 13–17
school size, *see* size of school
school status, and LEAs, 273–4
schooling, length of, 128–9

schools, 9–39; voluntary, *see* voluntary schools
Schools Council, 52: abolished (1983), 266, 279
SCOTS schedule, 6
Scottish children, 152, 155; *see also* ESWI
Scottish Primary Mathematics series, 88
Scrimgeour, M., 6
secondary school, school effects study, 213
Secondary Transfer Project, 30, 264, 301
Secretary of State, 31, 265–6
self-concept: age factor in, 127; development during junior years, 109–11; impact of schools on, 196–7; and race factor, 160; sex difference factor, 150; and social class factor, 140; see also "Me at School" self-concept assessment
Serbin, L. A., 166
setting, 19
sex balance, in school intakes, 177
sex differences: in cognitive and non-cognitive attainment, 117, 142–51; in school effectiveness, 209–11; and teacher expectations, 166–7
sex stereotyping, 28, 145, 166–7; *see also* curriculum, "hidden"
Sharp, R., 164
Short, G., 168
Simon, B., 2, 228, 258, 259–60
Simpson, S. N., 226
size of class, *see* class size
size of school: difference in sample, 12–13; and LEAs, 274–5; and school effectiveness, 221, 236–7, 244, 266:- and type, 231–2
skills, basic: aims, 53–4; headteachers' emphasis on, and school effectiveness, 224, 235
"Smiley" attitude assessment, 104
Smith, M. S., 2, 183, 203, 224, 256, 261
social aims, 53
social class: in cognitive and non-cognitive attainment, 117, 130–42; in school effectiveness, 207–9; in school intakes, 178–9; and teacher expectations, 164–6
Solomon, D., 258
"Sound Sense" series, 87
speaking skills, *see* oracy
special needs: headteachers' training for, 277–8; provision, 19–20; teachers, 73–5
specialist teachers, 72–3
spiritual aims, 54
SRA (Science Research Associates) workcards, 87
staff: headteachers' involvement with, 44–6:- appraisal, 45; *see also* teachers
staff meetings, 28–9
staffing, stability of, and LEAs, 275–6

Stallings, J. A., 258
Stark, J., 257, 258, 260
Startup, M., 128, 129
Stevens, R., 258
Stoll, L., 104
Stone, M., 160
Strivens, J., 60
Strachan, V., 101
subject areas, aims re, 53–4
Summers, A. A., 1
Swann Report (1985), 117, 168

talk, small, 62, 64
Taylor, W., 256
teacher continuity, and school effectiveness, 241–2
teacher strategies, 6: and curriculum, 80–3; headteachers' influence on, 42; and school effectivenes, 224
teacher-trainers, implications of school effectiveness study, 268–72
teacher-training, central government control over, 266
teachers: aims, 52–5, 285; allocation to classes, 15; assessments of pupils' ability, 75–7:- age factor, 123–5; race factor, 156–8; sex differences, 147–8; and social class, 138; beyond the classroom, 69–75; changes of, 34–6; and school effectiveness, 226, 275–6: between years, 35–6; characteristics, 52; in the classroom, 52–77; consistency of policy:- implications for headteachers, 282–3; and school effectiveness, 246–7, 251:- studies, 258; enthusiasm, 63, and school effectiveness, 256; expectations, 163–75, 285–6; involvement decision – making and school effectiveness 225, 233-4, 251: Studies, 256:- and teacher-training, 271; implications of school effectiveness study for, 285–8; involvement, 62:- implications for headteachers, 281–2; and school effectiveness, 225, 247–8, 251:- studies, 257; job satisfaction, 72; part-time, 72–3; policies, class size, and school effectiveness, 241–2; preparation time, 59–60; probationary, 72; special needs, 73–5; specialist, 72–3; use of other adults in the classroom, 67; use of voice, 67; views on contacts with parents, 24–5; work contacts, 83–5
teachers' dispute (1985–87), 264, 279
Teachers' Federation, Canada and USA, 279
teachers' professional associations, implications of school effectiveness study, 279–80
teaching: by deputy heads, 47–8; by headteachers, 43; stimulating:-

implications for teachers, 286–7; and school effectiveness, 229, 252:- studies, 258; and teacher-training, 269

teaching time, 15–17

tests: for seven and eleven year olds, 266; use of, 18–19, 75–6

textbooks, use of, 17: and school effectiveness, 230

Thomas, N., see Thomas Report

Thomas Coram Unit, 96

Thomas Report (1985), 14, 257, 260

Thompson, D., 118

time: non-teaching, 71–2; spent on individuals, classes or groups, 81–2

timetables, 59

Tizard, J., 7, 21, 260, 283

Toews, J., 272

Tomlinson, T. M., 257, 258, 259

Tower Hamlets String Project, 18

Traub, R., 258

travelling distance to school, and school effectiveness, 221, 244

Trisman, D. A., 256, 258, 261

Turkish children, attainment, 152, 153, 154

UK, school effectiveness and home influence studies, 1–8

underachievement, in ethnic minority children, 117

unemployment, parental, 181

universities, departments of education, 266

US, Department of Education, 256

USA, 1, 2, 263, 269, 272, 276, 279

Varlaam, A., 25, 118, 149

Verbal Reasoning (VR), 124–5, 156–7

visitors, view of schools, 11

voice, teachers' use of, 67

voluntary schools, 12: and effectiveness, 221, 235–6, 243–4; and LEAs, 273

VR, *see* Verbal Reasoning

Wales, primary class size, 274

Weber, G., 1, 256, 259, 260

Wedge, P., 117, 132, 180

Welsh children, *see* ESWI

Welsh secondary schools study, 1

Whyte, J., 166

Widlake, P., 183

Williams, P., 118

Willms, J. D., 213

Wolfe, B. L., 1

women: deputy headteachers, 46; headteachers, 40

work: direction of, 82–3; organization, in classroom, 61–2; structuring of:- implications for teachers, 286; and

school effectiveness, 224, 240; and teacher-training, 268

work contacts, teachers' and pupils', 83–5; and school effectiveness, 227

work-centred environment: implications for teachers, 287; and school effectiveness, 252–3:- studies, 259; and teacher-training, 269

writing: age factors in attainment, 121–2; attainment at entry, 96–7; attainment during junior years, 5, 99–101; impact of school on progress and attainment, 188–90; race factor in, 154; relationship with reading performance, 111; sex difference in, 145–6; social class factor in, 134–6

Wylie, R. C., 160